COOKING
from
QUILT
COUNTRY

COOKING
from
QUILT
COUNTRY

Hearty Recipes from
Amish and Mennonite Kitchens

by MARCIA ADAMS

PHOTOGRAPHS BY ALEXANDRA AVAKIAN

DESIGNED BY LAURENCE VÉTU-KANE

Clarkson N. Potter, Inc. / Publishers

ACKNOWLEDGMENTS

◆

I gratefully acknowledge the many people who helped create this book, and I am especially indebted to David Pottinger for supplying the photos and information about Indiana Amish quilts, as well as introductions to Amish families. His generosity and guidance made the idea a reality. My editor, Pam Krauss, and my agent, Chris Tomasino, led me through the new experience of publishing with patience, skill, and laughter. I have loved it all, because of them.

Photojournalist Alexandra Avakian shared my vision and because of her sensitivity and hard work, she has helped create a very beautiful book. Working with Alex was a joy and I will always be grateful for our association.

My very special thanks and appreciation go to WBGU TV 27 in Bowling Green, Ohio. Their skill and enthusiasm helped produce a cooking series that I hope will give pleasure to thousands of viewers for many years; to the late Bert Greene, mentor and friend, who insisted this book be written, my gratitude for his encouragement; and to *Cooking from Quilt Country*'s sponsors—Maple Leaf Farms, and the Ball Corporation—I especially wish to acknowledge my deep gratitude for their ongoing support.

Lena Lehman at the Mennonite Historical Library and Dr. Sam Yoder of Goshen College helped with research and answered many questions. I deeply appreciate their cooperation.

And most of all, I want to thank the people of the Amish and Mennonite communities in northern Indiana who so graciously supported this book and freely gave their time and their recipes.

Filling Recipe for "Whoopie Pies," from *Maida Heatter's Chocolate Desserts* by Maida Heatter. Copyright © 1980 by Maida Heatter. Used by permission of Alfred A. Knopf, Inc.

Some recipes contained in this book have previously appeared in Marcia Adams's *Good Food* column in Indiana newspapers.

Text copyright © 1989 by Marcia Adams
Photographs copyright © 1989 by Alexandra Avakian

Published by Clarkson N. Potter, Inc., 201 East 50th Street, New York, New York 10022, and distributed by Crown Publishers, Inc.

CLARKSON N. POTTER, POTTER, and colophon are trademarks of Clarkson N. Potter, Inc.

Manufactured in Japan

Library of Congress Cataloging-in-Publication Data
Adams, Marcia.
    Cooking from quilt country.
    Bibliography: p.
    Includes index.
    1. Cookery, Amish.   2. Cookery, Mennonite.
3. Cookery—Indiana.   I. Title.
TX715.A2243   1988   641.5'088287   87–25741
ISBN 0-517-56813-6

10 9 8 7 6

To my husband, Dick Adams, for his confident support,
with gratitude and love;
to my mother, Esther Grabill, whose fine cooking was always
an inspiration, with admiration and appreciation;
and to my friend, Yvonne Diamond, whose recipe
for Chicken Reuben started me on a whole new career,
with heartfelt thanks.

◆

Contents

THE GREENING OF INDIANA

SUMMER DAYS

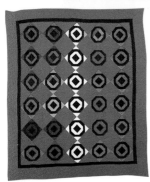

SHADES OF AUTUMN

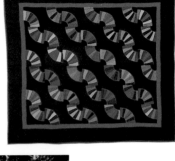

WINTER'S REST

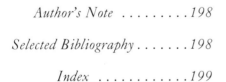

INTRODUCTION

◆

I grew up on a farm in northern Indiana near a large Amish and Mennonite settlement in Elkhart and LaGrange counties. Though aware that the Amish and Mennonites' way of life was unlike my own family's, nonetheless I knew these plain and hardworking people as good neighbors and outstanding farmers. They have always been a part of my life.

Recently, I came back to the community as a food and travel writer and saw afresh the specialness of this distinctive country life-style, which has survived unchanged for nearly two hundred years. The food here is simple, naturally wholesome, and without pretension; it is the heart of regional American cookery, with historical ties to three cultures: Europe, the Pennsylvania Dutch, and the rural Midwest. It has come together in one unique folk cuisine, linked to the land and the rhythm of the seasons.

My mother is a superb cook, and during my childhood on the farm she prepared satisfying and creative meals for her husband, children, and hired men. Many of the family recipes she used (and most of my favorites) were those of my Dunkard great-grandmother. (Dunkards, a very conservative sect of the Brethren, share a common European history and religious doctrine with both the Amish and Mennonites.) As I explored the cuisine of the Amish and Mennonite communities which are flourishing in Indiana, I became increasingly aware that my own family's cooking was deeply rooted in the Amish-Mennonite tradition. Living among these people, eating with them, made me long for those uniquely satisfying foods that appear so rarely on contemporary tables and that I enjoyed as a child. Asparagus pie, maple mousse, rhubarb sherbet, creamed new potatoes and peas, tomato fritters, pineapple upside-down cake, sauer-kraut soup, church-supper ham loaf—these wonderful dishes are memories for most of us, but not for natives of this part of the country.

These "attic receipts"—my name for recipes that are a bit out of fashion and are recorded in fading handwritten ledgers or tattered cards in Aunt Sarah's trunk—are a special enthusiasm of mine. These nearly forgotten and unique recipes are reflections of our culinary heritage, and I prize them all. They deserve to be recorded so they will not be lost, for they give us a culinary glimpse of our past.

Equally important are those recipes that are part of the oral tradition, passed from mother to daughter for generations. As I moved among the Amish and Mennonites, I soon realized that many of the traditional dishes, such as the homemade noodles, soups, breads, and cakes, are no longer prepared as frequently because these women, too, are buying commercial noodles, canned soups, cake mixes, and other convenience foods. They are also integrating more and more recipes devised by the "English," as they call those outside their faith, into their repertoire. Many of these unwritten recipes are on their way to extinction. I knew I had to write this book.

Traditionally, the "Plain People," as the Amish call themselves, are a very private group and do not go out of their way to become involved with the "English." But for the book to be authentic, I wanted to interview Amish women personally and observe them in their kitchens. So I went to my friend David Pottinger. A noted authority on Amish quilts,

he is deeply respected by his Amish neighbors; with his introductions, many doors opened to me. I was able to meet with the Amish women, watch them cook, and record their recipes. They were all open, friendly, helpful, and very interested in my project. Working with them has been both a learning experience and a joy.

◆ ◆ ◆

It would be impossible to write a book about the food of the Amish (pronounced "AH-mish") and Mennonites in northern Indiana without reviewing their history, for their history has written their recipes.

Both groups, as well as the Dunkards, were part of the Church of the Brethren, originating in Germany in the 1700s, and all have roots in the Swiss Anabaptist movement that began in 1525 during the Protestant Reformation. Their acknowledged leader was an ordained Dutch priest, Menno Simons, and his followers were known as Mennonites. They believed in separation of church and state and in adult baptism, and they were against taking political oaths and going to war. They dressed simply and rejected worldly trappings.

In 1693, Joseph Ammann, a Swiss Mennonite elder who thought the church was losing the purity of its original aims, broke from the Mennonites and formed his own group, later called the Amish. Ammann migrated to Alsace-Lorraine in France and was a spokesman for the Anabaptists who lived there. He gathered about him people who shared his views, and the Amish movement grew. To this day, the Amish are more conservative than the Mennonites, and are noted for their unadorned dress, their use of horse and buggy transportation, and their withdrawal from most of society. Ammann believed that by their plain dress and life-style the Amish could best fulfill the Scripture that teaches true believers should be separate from the world.

Because of widespread religious persecution in Europe, the Amish and Mennonites accepted William Penn's invitation to come to Pennsylvania. The first migration was in the eighteenth century and another large one followed in the nineteenth century. The Amish, Mennonites, and other immigrants, including the Dunkards and the Brethren, lived side by side in Pennsylvania and inevitably there was intermingling. The coming together of the German Brethren, the Dunkards, the German and Swiss Mennonites, and the Amish, some of whom had lived in Alsace-Lorraine, yielded a richly diverse society connected by religious beliefs.

Ultimately, some of these Protestant sects moved on to Ontario, Canada, as well as Ohio, Virginia, Kansas, and Indiana. The first Mennonites arrived in Indiana in 1838; the Amish followed in 1841. Today, northern Indiana has the third largest Amish-Mennonite population in the United States.

The Amish and Mennonite communities continue to grow. An Amish family has, on average, 8 children, and infant mortality is low. Should an Amish person decide to leave the church, he or she is likely to become a Mennonite, another reason the two groups live side by side. There is a great deal of communication between them; they share relatives, have common historical roots, and adhere to the same doctrines, differing only in outward practices. The Mennonites are more urban, while the Amish are totally rural.

Over the months I spent with them, observing their way of life and recording their recipes, it became obvious that the Amish and Mennonites are a varied group of people, with many shades of difference in both their religious practices and life-styles. Each community has its own customs and quirks. For every generalization I can make about this society, someone else will point out the exception.

I had many discussions about Amish and Mennonite society with Dr. Sam Yoder, who teaches educational psychology at Goshen College in Goshen, Indiana. He knows of what he speaks; he was raised Amish and is now an active Mennonite.

Yoder is a witty and urbane man, and our conversations were always far-ranging and candid. He immediately debunked several myths about the Amish. A blue gate in front of an Amish house does not mean there is a marriageable daughter living there—it means the owner of the farm likes blue gates. Many people incorrectly assume that all Amish dolls today must be faceless. The original Amish dolls had no faces embroidered on them in accordance with the biblical law that forbids the making of a graven image, but now many Amish children do play with dolls that have faces. It all depends on the rules of their particular church. The Amish women make the faceless dolls for tourists (called *lumba babba*, meaning "rag baby") because they take much less time to sew.

He told me that shunning, a practice that has been around since the

Household auctions are social meeting spots.

seventeenth century, still exists, but how it is practiced varies from community to community. "The extreme form is when the Amish congregation withholds themselves from the guilty party in both social and business dealings. The intent of shunning is not to punish, but to bring the offender back into the church. Shunning practices in Indiana are not as strict as in some places in Ohio and Missouri," he added.

◆ ◆ ◆

Because of the Amish and Mennonites' choice to remain separate from the rest of society (this is more pronounced in the Amish), their folkways, language, and eating habits have changed very little in hundreds of years. Many cooks today are still preparing the same provincial dishes their ancestors prepared in Germany, Switzerland, or Alsace-Lorraine in the seventeen and eighteen hundreds. It is not uncommon to find the most classic European country dishes in this Indiana farming community. For instance, hot cabbage salad, sometimes called fried cabbage, is served at rural tables the year-round. It is identical to a dish I was served in France, where it is called *éminčé de choux verts au lardons chauds*. The Mennonite onion pie, a cousin to quiche, is called *tourte*, or onion tart, in Alsace. The examples go on and on, and when I came across these recipes, I pounced on them with pleasure.

In addition to the recipes shared with me by the Amish women, the stacks of Goshen College's Mennonite Historical Library in Goshen, Indiana, yielded community cookbooks collected from Amish settlements all over the United States. The recipes reflected not only these people's his-

The **Ausbund** *is a German hymnal used by the Amish.*

toric wanderings in Europe, but their assimilation in the New World. It was obvious that these immigrant women began exchanging recipes with their American neighbors the minute they set foot in Pennsylvania.

As they moved to other communities to the north and west, their cooking continued to evolve, reflecting their new location and the availability of different ingredients. In Indiana, for instance, maple syrup was used as a sweetener as frequently as was molasses, and because this is a wheat-growing area, foods using wheat flour became predominant on the tables: noodles, dumplings, and endless variations of breads, rolls, cookies, and cakes. But many components of their European dishes remained intact.

In Indiana there are three distinct regional food communities, and the cuisine is quite unlike the Pennsylvania Dutch cookery in Lancaster County, Pennsylvania. Elkhart and LaGrange counties' Amish prepare foods reflecting their Palatinate, or West German, heritage. There is some Pennsylvania Dutch influence, but less than I expected. Among themselves, the Indiana Amish speak a German dialect, as do the Amish in Pennsylvania.

In Adams County, in the little town of Berne, the food has a Swiss flavor and the dialect is Swiss. When leaving Europe, this group landed in New Orleans and traveled immediately to Indiana, bypassing Pennsylvania, so their cookery shows no Pennsylvania Dutch influence. The Fort Wayne community is an offshoot of the Berne community, so their recipes, too, reflect their Swiss heritage. But they found themselves living in the middle of an area heavily populated with Germans and their dishes are a combination of German, Swiss, and Alsatian. And so is their dialect.

I have developed a real appreciation for the cuisine of the Indiana Amish and Mennonites, as well as an admiration for their life-style. We "English" live in a world of mobile nuclear families amidst a frequently bewildering and hectic industrialized society. But the Amish and Mennonites have retained an extended family system that has given them an enviable stability. Their commonwealth society provides a strong sense of belonging, a firm support system rooted in the Judeo-Christian ethic, and a wholeness within their personal universe that touches the intellect and the heart of the most sophisticated observer.

A NOTE ABOUT THE QUILT ILLUSTRATIONS IN THIS BOOK

The Indiana Amish and Mennonites are known for their fine quilts. They are made for personal use, to give as gifts, or to sell; quilt making is an important cottage industry in northern Indiana. Originally created as bed covers, they are highly prized by collectors and are considered serious folk art. Since the quilts of this community are as distinctive as the food, using pictures of them in the cookbook was a natural step, for the two complement each other historically. Those illustrated are from the David Pottinger collection, a broad cultural collection which includes 270 Amish quilts, as well as toys, clothing, and furniture. It can be viewed at the Indiana State Museum, 202 North Alabama Street, Indianapolis, Indiana.

NOTES ON RECIPES, INGREDIENTS, AND EQUIPMENT

◆

One of my primary aims in assembling this book was to provide authentic recipes with clear instructions; I offer them without a qualm. All of the recipes have been tested and retested in my rather modestly equipped kitchen, and that took longer than I ever anticipated it would. Many of the original older recipes were sketchy indeed, consisting of a list of ingredients without specific quantities, not necessarily in order, and at best, a few notations on how to put the dish together. Instructions for breads, cakes, and cookies were generally, "mix, add enough flour to make a dough, and bake." Those made me sigh a bit. I tested one roll recipe six times before it was right—but it was worth it.

Some of these original recipes called for ingredients that are not widely available to most cooks or are no longer used with much frequency in modern kitchens. Where necessary I have adapted these recipes for today's use and have also adjusted some to better please modern palates (for instance, reducing the amount of salt or sugar). Wherever possible, though, I have preserved these recipes as nearly verbatim as possible, and the results of each one can truly be considered authentic.

As a food writer, I hear frequent complaints from my readers about the recipes that appear in newspapers and food magazines. Many, they complain, are too complex, too costly, take too much time to prepare, and require hard-to-find ingredients. I did try to keep all that in mind when selecting these recipes. But at the same time there were some more time-consuming dishes, such as mincemeat and Christmas pudding, that had to be included because they are favorites in the Amish-Mennonite communities. I think you'll find them well worth the extra effort.

Each recipe is the best of its kind, and I hope you find this book is as much fun to use as it was for me to research and write it.

INGREDIENTS

• Eggs: All recipes use jumbo eggs.
• Flour: I am very specific about the types of flour to use in each recipe. The flour our great-grandmothers used is quite unlike what is available today. (Unbleached all-purpose flour comes the closest.) In the process of updating these old recipes, I experimented with different flours and how they are combined with other ingredients. It is important that you use the kind of flour suggested in each recipe.
• All fruit juices called for should be fresh if possible, especially lemon juice.
• Shortenings: Lard is used frequently in many of the pie, cake, and cookie recipes. In some cases, it gives a richness of flavor and a tenderness to the baked goods that cannot be achieved with any other shortening. You will have quite edible results if you substitute another shortening or butter, but it won't be—I am sorry to say—"right" or nearly as good in texture or moistness. If the recipe says "lard," that means use lard, please!

I never use margarine. If I am going to consume the calories, let them be butter calories. Unsalted (sweet) butter gives the best results, but lightly salted butter can be substituted.

Vegetable oil is used for deep-frying and in some of the rolls and pastries. I personally like sunflower oil, though many of the cooks in this region prefer corn oil.

For "greasing" the baking pans, I use a vegetable spray, just because it is so convenient, which is why I use the term "oiling the pan" in the recipes.
• Sour cream: Unless otherwise stated, this means dairy sour cream.

• Brown sugar: This should be packed so firmly into the measuring cup that it will keep its shape when you shake it out. Unless otherwise specified, the brown sugar used in these recipes is light brown sugar.

• Nuts: Use pecans or English walnuts interchangeably, unless otherwise specified.

• Pork: This meat has been badly maligned in our diet-conscious society, and that's a pity. There is certainly no reason to avoid it completely, other than for religious reasons. You are not going to leave this world prematurely because you eat an occasional pork chop. Because of genetic improvements, pork is 15 percent less fatty than it was thirty years ago, and its cholesterol content compares favorably with beef, dark turkey meat, and chicken. In the Midwest, as in the South, pork is a popular staple and bacon an important seasoning.

• Herbs: Unlike the Shakers, the Amish and Mennonites use most herbs sparingly. However, they do use liberal amounts of parsley, bay leaf, sage, dill, and garlic. Occasionally, I found newer recipes that called for oregano and basil, but in the authentic recipes, never. To heighten flavors, these cooks make do with liberal use of Worcestershire sauce, Tabasco, seasoned salt, and powdered meat extracts. I have added herbs to some recipes when I felt the addition truly enhanced the end result, yet kept the integrity of the dish. In these cases, I have indicated that the ingredient is optional.

• Garnishes: Perhaps garnishes were created for and by the leisure class. For the Amish cook, who is responsible for feeding twelve people three times a day in a kitchen without electricity, garnishes don't have a high priority. Parsley is most commonly used because it is widely available. However, I think that the way food is presented is very important, so sometimes I have made alternate garnishing suggestions, such as fresh flowers, mint, grape leaves, and so on. Again, these are optional.

EQUIPMENT

You do not need a lot of expensive equipment to cook well. Many of my pots and pans have come from restaurant and bakery supply stores, and have well earned their keep. You can also find most of these items in a hardware store. Most of these recipes can be made with the equipment you already have in your kitchen. However, I find the utensils and equipment that follow useful, even though the Amish have been creating marvelous dishes for years without them:

• A heavy-duty electric mixer, with dough hook and grinder.

• A heavy-duty food processor or a blender.

• An electric fry pan. This can also be used as a French fryer.

• Deep metal pie pans. A thin, cheap pan will not hold all of the ingredients or conduct heat properly. Never use foil pans—you simply will not get decent results. Deep glass pie dishes are acceptable, but it is necessary to lower the baking temperature by 25° F. when they are used.

• Cake pans: I prefer metal pans and have them in oblong, round, and square sizes. If you do use glass dishes for cakes, again, lower the temperature by 25° F.

• Pastry cloth and stocking for rolling pin: These will make your rolled cookies, pie crusts, and noodles a lot easier to prepare. I can't imagine baking without them.

• A heavy-duty whisk: Indispensable for creating smooth sauces.

• Timer: Mine hangs from a cord that I wear around my neck. I prize it above rubies. Also helpful for timing sauce cookery and the like is a 3-minute egg timer. If you do a lot of baking you may want to have more than one.

• Meat thermometer: This is essential when you are preparing large roasts and poultry. The instant-reading type is easiest.

The GREENING *of* INDIANA

Spring comes to Indiana in quiet ways. The last patches of snow surrender to the sun, and the woods' floor is a matted aromatic carpet of last year's leaves and winter ferns. Violets push up through the sodden leaves and later the woods are white with trillium. Jacob's ladder, with its blue bell-shaped flowers, and white Solomon's seal vie for attention with wild phlox. Cardinals flash through the green budding sassafras, and the spring peepers sing their frog song from the swamp on warmer nights ♦ In the farmyard, the willow trees begin to resemble inverted golden fountains and the dogwoods bloom with layers of white silklike flowers delicately edged with brown. Newly washed clothes dance on the clothesline and eight-paned windows, bare of curtains, shine in the sunlight. Squealing baby pigs eat at the barn trough. Plume-tailed colts run in the pasture, and black-and-white–dappled calves watch with curiosity through the fence as the farmers, plowing behind a team of horses, turn the earth into rich brown furrows ♦ The farm women and their daughters work barefoot in the vegetable gardens, planting seeds in the freshly worked soil, sun warmed and soft underfoot. The male red-winged blackbirds display their bright red shoulders and sing their lusty *konk-la-ree* song, and the killdeers keen as they swoop low over meadows and fields ♦ The earth once again unfolds to nourish its people ♦

In LaGrange, girls' dresses have four buttons in the back and look like an apron pinafore.

BREAKFAST AT DAWN

In rural communities, the days start early, and during the winter months, the days start in the dark. The livestock will be fed, the cows milked, and eggs slipped from under scolding hens before most of the rest of the world is out of bed. By mealtime, the family is ready for a large, hearty breakfast; there is not much concern about calories.

Omelets prepared from the freshly gathered eggs are a favorite dish, and the hams and bacon on the table most days are either home or locally cured. Oatmeal is served year-round, and homemade graham nuts, another regional dish, is regular breakfast fare. Several kinds of pancakes are prepared in this area, all served with the local maple syrup or sorghum molasses. Fried cornmeal mush with tomato gravy is an underground regional specialty. It is served at every Amish breakfast table and in most local restaurants, but is seldom listed on the menu;

you have to ask for it. There are many versions of tomato gravy—some are bland, some are spicy. Some are smooth, and some have a bit of texture if canned tomatoes are used as the base. It is, altogether, a most unusual dish, but could be an acquired taste. I personally think it quite interesting and delicious.

Frosted cinnamon rolls, without nuts or raisins, are favored in this part of the country, and restaurants vie to outdo each other in the size of their rolls. In the summer, fresh fruit, such as strawberries, raspberries, blueberries, and peaches, is also on the table, but in the winter, canned fruits are brought up from the basement and served in side dishes. Coffee and assorted fruit juices are the traditional beverages at breakfast, and creamy hot chocolate is made especially for the children. No matter what your age, though, you will never walk away from an Amish breakfast table hungry.

SAUSAGE GRAVY ON BISCUITS

HOMEMADE GRAHAM NUTS

BAKING POWDER BISCUITS

FRIED CORNMEAL MUSH WITH TOMATO GRAVY

SCRAPPLE

INDIANA FARM SAUSAGE

BAKED HAM SLICES IN MILK AND BROWN SUGAR

SUETTA BECHTEL'S CINNAMON ROLLS

GREEN MEADOWS SIX-WEEK BRAN MUFFINS

SPICED PRUNES

GERMAN APPLE PANCAKES

CORNMEAL PANCAKES

OATMEAL PANCAKES

SAUSAGE GRAVY ON BISCUITS

◆

Serves 4–6

Sausage gravy is a specialty among the country folk in this area, and traditionally is served over hot biscuits. It is also part of an oral tradition. No one bothers to record it in writing, and every cook makes it a slightly different way; I prefer the roux method.

1 pound sage-flavored bulk sausage,
*   as lean as possible*
2 tablespoons finely minced onion
6 tablespoons all-purpose flour
1 quart milk
¼ teaspoon grated nutmeg, rounded

¼ teaspoon poultry seasoning, rounded
*   Dash of Worcestershire sauce*
*   Dash of Tabasco*
18 large hot Baking Powder Biscuits
*   (page 4)*

Crumble the sausage into a large saucepan, and sauté over medium-low heat, breaking the meat into small pieces while it cooks; do not allow it to brown or get crisp. When meat is about three-quarters cooked, add the onion and cook until the onion is transparent.

Drain off all but 2 tablespoons of the meat drippings—you don't have to be too precise about this. Stir in the flour with a whisk, and cook over medium-low heat for 6 to 7 minutes, or until the flour turns golden and bubbles up.

Pour in the milk all at once, and add the seasonings. Cook and whisk until the mixture thickens. Place at least 3 biscuit halves on each plate and top with sausage gravy.

HOMEMADE GRAHAM NUTS

◆

Makes 8 cups

This cereal has a great crunchy texture and is a bit sweeter than the commercial Grape-Nuts® cereal. "Why make your own?" you ask. Because it's addictive.

3½ cups graham (whole wheat) flour
1 cup brown sugar
1 teaspoon salt
1 teaspoon baking soda

1 teaspoon ground cinnamon
2 cups buttermilk
2 teaspoons vanilla extract

Preheat oven to 350° F. In a large bowl, combine flour, brown sugar, salt, baking soda, and cinnamon. Add the buttermilk and vanilla and mix well. Pour out into an oiled 12 x 16-inch flat baking pan and spread evenly with a spatula. Bake for 20 to 25 minutes or until the batter is firm, medium-brown in color, and shrinks slightly from the sides of the pan. With a metal spatula, completely loosen the hot pattie from the pan. Allow to cool on a rack for several hours or overnight.

Preheat oven to 275° F. Break pattie into chunks and put through a meat grinder, using a coarse blade, or pulse in a food processor until coarse crumbs are formed. Divide crumbs between two 12 x 16-inch pans. Bake for 30 minutes, stirring every 10 minutes. Let cool, then store in an airtight container. Serve as a cold cereal, with milk and a bit of brown sugar, if desired.

BAKING POWDER BISCUITS

◆

Makes 30 biscuits

This is one of my favorite biscuit recipes since the rolled-out biscuits can be frozen and then baked just before using. The combination of lard and butter makes them especially tender.

6 cups all-purpose flour
½ cup instant nonfat dry milk powder
¼ cup baking powder
¼ cup sugar
2 teaspoons salt

2 teaspoons cream of tartar
1 cup cold lard, cut into chunks
1 cup (2 sticks) cold butter, cut into chunks
1¾ cups buttermilk, approximately

Preheat oven to 400° F. In a very large bowl, combine all the ingredients except the shortenings and buttermilk. With a pastry blender, cut in shortenings until mixture resembles coarse crumbs. Make a well in the center and pour in the buttermilk. With a fork, quickly and lightly combine the ingredients. Not all of the flour will be incorporated at this point.

Turn the dough out onto a well-floured pastry cloth or board and, with floured hands, knead it 8 to 10 turns until smooth. Roll out to about ¾ inch thick. Use a 2½-inch biscuit cutter to cut the dough, and prick each biscuit 3 times with a fork.

At this point, either bake or freeze the biscuits. If using immediately, place about 2 inches apart on oiled cookie sheets and bake for 13 to 15 minutes or until golden brown. To freeze, place unbaked biscuits on sheets in freezer. When hard, transfer to plastic bags. To serve, remove as many biscuits as needed and bake frozen on oiled cookie sheets in a 400° F. oven for 15 to 18 minutes.

This old wood-burning stove, housed in a separate summer kitchen, can bake 50 loaves of bread at a time.

Every farm raises chickens, and the eggs are gathered daily.

FRIED CORNMEAL MUSH WITH TOMATO GRAVY

◆

Serves 4–6

Some people think of cornmeal mush as a porridge, but in this area it is mostly eaten fried.
Made a day in advance of serving, the mush is put in a loaf pan to
give it shape, chilled, then sliced either thick or thin depending on your preference, and fried.
It can be served with maple syrup poured over the top,
but another way to eat it is with Tomato Gravy (page 6). The addition of
flour to this simple but satisfying dish yields a smoother
loaf that doesn't crumble when fried.

*1¼ cups yellow cornmeal, preferably
    stone ground
1 teaspoon salt
¼ cup all-purpose flour*

*1 cup cold water
3 cups hot water
    Vegetable oil or bacon fat for frying
    Flour for dredging*

In a small bowl, combine the cornmeal, salt, and flour. Gradually whisk the cold water into the mixture. Bring the hot water to a boil in a large saucepan over high heat and gradually whisk in the cornmeal mixture. Stir and whisk until it boils. Cover, lower heat, and simmer for 5 minutes. The mixture will be very thick. Pour into an oiled 9 x 5 x 3-inch loaf pan and refrigerate overnight.

The next day, cut the loaf into ½-inch slices. In a skillet, heat 2 teaspoons of oil or bacon fat. Dredge 3 or 4 slices in the flour and fry them over low heat until golden brown on both sides. Continue to cook remaining mush, adding oil to the skillet as needed. Serve with either maple syrup or Tomato Gravy and plan on 3 to 4 slices per person.

TOMATO GRAVY

◆

Serves 4

Tomato Gravy is a breakfast specialty among the Amish and Mennonites in
this area, and is traditionally served with Fried Cornmeal Mush (page 5),
though some people like it on toast, scrapple, or mashed potatoes. Like Sausage Gravy
(page 3), the recipe is part of an oral tradition and every cook makes
a slightly different version. I like this version *very* much! Using the bacon
drippings in the roux is important for flavor.

2 tablespoons bacon drippings
¼ cup chopped onion
3 tablespoons all-purpose flour
1 bay leaf
1½ cups tomato juice or tomato cocktail

½ cup milk or cream
2 teaspoons brown sugar
⅛ teaspoon celery salt
⅛ teaspoon black pepper

Melt the drippings in a medium saucepan
over medium heat, add the onion, and cook
until the onion begins to turn yellow. Add the
flour and bay leaf, and continue to cook until
the flour is deep gold, about 4 to 5 minutes.
Add tomato juice, and then whisk mix-

ture until smooth. Add the rest of the ingredients, and cook until mixture completely
thickens and is the consistency of thick gravy,
about 4 to 5 minutes longer. Remove bay leaf,
and serve hot over fried slices of cornmeal
mush.

SCRAPPLE

◆

Serves 6–8

Scrapple making used to be part of butchering day, a big job which involved the whole family
and frequently neighbors, too. Traditionally, scrapple used
up the odds and ends left over from butchering the pig, but we can make it in our own
kitchen today with this adapted recipe. Liver sausage and buckwheat
flour are essential for authenticity. This recipe has German origins; the Swiss
Amish and Mennonites do not make it. The loaf can be made
five days in advance and can also be frozen.

2 pounds lean bony pork (I use country-
    style ribs, cut in 5 pieces)
2 quarts water
2 teaspoons salt
16 whole peppercorns
1 bay leaf
½ teaspoon rubbed sage

¼ teaspoon dried marjoram (optional)
⅛ teaspoon ground mace
2 slices liver sausage, 3 inches in
    diameter and ¼ inch thick
1½ cups yellow cornmeal
¼ cup buckwheat flour
Vegetable oil for frying

In a large, deep kettle place pork, water, salt, peppercorns, and bay leaf. Bring to a boil over high heat, reduce heat, and simmer, covered, until meat is very tender, approximately 1¼ hours. Remove meat from broth and cool slightly. Chop it finely (do not grind), discarding all fatty tissue. Cover and reserve. Refrigerate broth overnight.

The next day, skim the hardened fat off the cold broth. Measure 1 quart broth into a deep saucepan. Add reserved meat, sage, marjoram, mace, and liver sausage. Bring to boil. Meanwhile in a small bowl, combine the cornmeal and buckwheat flour. When the broth boils, dribble in the corn mixture very slowly, stirring constantly. The mixture will be very thick. Reduce the heat to the lowest possible setting, and cook, covered, for 30 minutes, stirring now and then.

Oil a 9 x 5 x 3-inch loaf pan, and rinse with cold water. Pack scrapple firmly into pan. Cover and refrigerate until very firm, approximately 6 hours. Unmold, and cut into ⅜- to ½-inch slices.

To serve, fry slices on both sides over low heat in a little bit of hot oil until nicely browned. Serve with warm maple syrup or Tomato Gravy.

INDIANA FARM SAUSAGE

Makes 24 slices or 50 balls

This is a well-seasoned sausage and would enhance any breakfast table. For company brunches, form the sausage into large marble-size balls instead of patties. I have also made this dish with ground turkey, and it is equally delicious.

*2 pounds lean ground pork, at room
    temperature*
⅓ cup finely chopped onion
2 teaspoons finely minced fresh parsley
2 teaspoons salt
1 teaspoon rubbed sage

1 teaspoon dried basil (optional)
1 teaspoon dried marjoram (optional)
1 teaspoon chili powder
1 teaspoon black pepper
½ teaspoon ground red pepper
¼ teaspoon dried thyme (optional)

In a deep bowl, combine all ingredients, using hands if necessary. On wax paper, shape and roll mixture into 2 logs 6 inches long and 2 inches in diameter. Wrap in plastic wrap or foil and refrigerate overnight.

To serve, slice the rolls into rounds about ½ inch thick and fry in a heavy skillet over medium-low heat for 3 to 4 minutes on each side or until done. Drain on paper towels and serve immediately.

An alternate way to prepare sausage is to shape mixture into large marble-size balls. Freeze if desired. To serve, bake frozen on a rack, starting in a cold oven, for 20 minutes at 325° F.

BAKED HAM SLICES IN MILK AND BROWN SUGAR

◆

Serves 8

Baking ham in milk is a novel idea to most of us, but it is done frequently
in farm kitchens. The ham absorbs the milk, and the flavor is faintly sweet and spicy.
There will be a lovely, thin clotted gravy in the bottom of the casserole at the
end of the cooking time, so plan on serving mashed potatoes with this dish.

2 slices center-cut cured ham,
¾ to 1 inch thick
1 teaspoon powdered mustard
4–6 tablespoons brown sugar

1 teaspoon ground allspice
¼ teaspoon black pepper
Milk to cover, about 2 cups

Preheat oven to 325° F. Layer the ham slices in a large casserole. Sprinkle the top of the meat with the mustard and then the brown sugar; add the allspice and pepper. Pour in enough milk to barely cover the ham and bake, covered, for 1 hour, checking now and then to make sure the milk doesn't cook away. Add more milk if necessary.

When the ham is tender and the milk gravy slightly thickened, remove slices and cut into wedges. Serve hot, with milk gravy over mashed potatoes.

RIGHT: *The country woman's garden is her pride and joy.* BELOW: *The Amish prize their beautiful horses and gladly bring them out of the barns for display.*

SUETTA BECHTEL'S CINNAMON ROLLS

◆

Makes 8 very large rolls, or 27 standard rolls

This breakfast treat is a meal in itself. I give you two ways to form the rolls:
the first yields the enormous rolls you find in the local restaurants, and the second yields
more conventional-size ones.

1½ cups warm water
½ cup sugar
½ cup vegetable oil
½ cup mashed potatoes, unseasoned
    and without milk
1 egg
2 teaspoons salt
3 envelopes active dry yeast
3 tablespoons nonfat dry milk powder
3 cups unbleached all-purpose flour

2½–3 cups bread flour
⅓ cup butter, softened
¾ cup brown sugar
1½ tablespoons ground cinnamon

FROSTING

½ cup (1 stick) butter, softened
2 tablespoons all-purpose flour
1 cup confectioners' sugar
Speck salt
1 teaspoon vanilla extract

In a large mixer bowl, place the warm water, sugar, oil, potatoes, egg, salt, and yeast and mix thoroughly. Add the milk powder and the all-purpose flour; beat for 3 minutes. Gradually add the bread flour, and when the dough is workable, transfer to a lightly floured surface (or use the dough hook attachment on your electric mixer) and knead for 10 minutes. Grease a large, deep bowl with either white vegetable shortening or butter; form the dough into smooth ball and place in the bowl. Using your hands, grease the top of the dough. Cover with a tea towel and allow dough to rise in a warm place until it has doubled, approximately 1¾ hours.

Punch dough down very thoroughly to break up any air bubbles. Form again into a smooth ball, place in the regreased bowl, turning it over so the top of the dough is also greased. Cover, and let rise for 1 hour.

Punch dough down again, then transfer to a lightly floured surface. Roll out to a rectangle 15 x 12 inches—it should be about 1¾ inches thick. Spread the dough with the softened butter.

In a small bowl, mix the brown sugar with the cinnamon. Sprinkle it over the butter. Tightly roll dough up from the long side. If the roll has stretched out longer than 16 inches, pat the ends toward the center to make a fat 16-inch roll. With a serrated knife, cut the roll using a sawing motion into eight 2-inch rolls. Place slices cut side up, 1½ inches apart, in 2 greased 10-inch square pans that are at least 2 inches deep. Cover with a tea towel and allow the dough to rise in a warm place for 1 hour.

Preheat the oven to 325° F. Bake the rolls for 10 minutes, then raise the oven temperature to 350° F. and bake 5 minutes longer. Remove from oven, and invert pans onto wax paper-lined wire racks. Allow rolls to cool completely.

To make frosting: In a mixer bowl, place the softened butter, flour, confectioners' sugar, salt, and vanilla. Beat until blended, then use to frost the tops of the cooled rolls.

For smaller rolls, after the second rise, divide the dough into thirds. Roll out one-third at a time to a 12 x 8-inch rectangle. Spread each with about 1½ tablespoons of the butter mixture and sprinkle each with about ⅓ cup brown sugar and ½ tablespoon of cinnamon mixed together. Tightly roll each third up from the short side. Cut into nine 1-inch slices. Place slices cut side up, 1 inch apart, in 3 greased 8- or 9-inch pans. Cover and let rise for 1 hour. Bake as above, then use 1½ times the recipe for frosting these smaller rolls.

GREEN MEADOWS SIX-WEEK BRAN MUFFINS

Makes 42–48 muffins

This is a most practical recipe because the batter stays fresh for six weeks, and you can bake them anytime without further mess. And they are the best bran muffins I've ever eaten, bar none.

5 cups all-purpose flour
5 teaspoons baking soda
2 teaspoons salt
2 teaspoons ground allspice
1 15-ounce box bran flakes with raisins

3 cups sugar
4 eggs
1 cup vegetable oil
1 quart buttermilk
2 teaspoons vanilla

Using the largest bowl you have, combine the first four ingredients. Add the bran flakes and sugar, and mix. In a mixer bowl, beat the eggs. Add the oil, buttermilk, and vanilla to the eggs and blend. Pour the egg mixture over the flour mixture and stir well. Transfer the batter to a large plastic container that has a tight-fitting cover, and store in the refrigerator until ready to use. This batter will keep for 6 weeks. (Date the container the day you make the muffins.)

When ready to bake, do not stir batter when dipping out to fill the muffin pan. To bake, preheat the oven to 375° F. Using about ½ cup batter for each, drop the batter into paper-lined muffin tins. Bake the muffins for 20 minutes, or until the top springs back when touched with your finger.

SPICED PRUNES

Serves 6

Spices and a touch of lemon make these stewed prunes elegant enough for a company brunch. In Berne, Indiana, the Swiss Amish always serve these at weddings.

1 pound dried prunes
3 cups water
1 cinnamon stick
1 teaspoon whole allspice
½ teaspoon whole cloves

2 strips lemon rind, ½ inch wide
and 3 inches long
1 cup brown sugar
¼ cup lemon juice

In a large saucepan, combine prunes and water. Place spices and lemon rind in a piece of cheesecloth and tie tightly. Drop into saucepan. Cover pan, bring to a boil over high heat, then lower heat and simmer for 10 minutes.

Remove pan from heat, and stir in brown sugar and lemon juice. Let cool, then store in a glass jar in refrigerator overnight. Remove spice bag just before serving. These will keep for 5 days, refrigerated.

GERMAN APPLE PANCAKES

◆

Serves 6

German Apple Pancakes are sometimes called puff pancakes and
can be made without the apples. Either way, this is an unbeatable breakfast
or luncheon dish and great for company.

*2 large cooking apples, such as Yellow
Delicious or Granny Smith*
¼ cup (½ stick) butter
1 cup all-purpose flour
1 cup milk
 6 eggs

1 teaspoon vanilla extract
½ teaspoon salt
¼ teaspoon grated nutmeg
Confectioners' sugar

Preheat oven to 475° F. Peel, core, and very thinly slice the apples; you should have approximately 1½ cups. Melt 2 tablespoons of the butter over medium low heat in a small fry pan, and sauté the apples until they are just tender, about 3 minutes. Keep warm while preparing the batter. Place a 9- or 10-inch cast-iron skillet or very heavy ovenproof pan in the oven to heat for at least 5 minutes—the pan has to be very hot for this recipe to really work properly. When it is well heated, add the remaining 2 tablespoons of butter to melt and put skillet back in oven; the butter should be very hot but not brown when you add the apples and the batter.

While the skillet is heating, place the flour, milk, vanilla, salt, and nutmeg in a blender, and whiz until smooth. (This can also be done with a rotary beater.) Remove the skillet from the oven, quickly arrange the warm sautéed apple slices over the melted butter, and pour the batter evenly over all. Bake for 15 minutes, reduce heat to 375° F., and bake 10 minutes longer. The pancake will puff and climb up the sides of the pan. Sprinkle with confectioners' sugar, then cut in wedges and serve with maple syrup and crisp bacon. **NOTE:** If you do not use apples, add ¼ cup (½ stick) of butter to the hot skillet.

CORNMEAL PANCAKES

◆

Makes 18–20 pancakes, approximately 4 servings

This is a thin, crisp sort of pancake with lots of flavor. For company, it is nice
to offer both these and the plump, soft Oatmeal Pancakes.

*1 cup yellow cornmeal, preferably
stone ground*
1 teaspoon salt
1 cup boiling water
2 tablespoons (¼ stick) butter, melted
1 egg

1 cup buttermilk
¾ cup all-purpose flour
½ teaspoon baking powder
¼ teaspoon baking soda
Vegetable oil or bacon fat for frying

In a medium bowl, combine the cornmeal and salt. Slowly stir in the boiling water, then the melted butter. Cover tightly and let stand for 10 minutes. In a small bowl, beat the egg slightly, then add the buttermilk. Stir this into the cornmeal mixture and blend. In another small bowl or on wax paper, combine the flour, baking powder, and soda and stir quickly into the cornmeal mixture.

Using about 2 tablespoons of batter for each pancake, fry over medium heat in a well-oiled skillet. (I use about 2 teaspoons of fat per batch.) When bubbles appear on the top of the pancake, turn and brown the other side. Transfer pancakes to a heated platter and keep in a warm oven while cooking the remaining batter. Serve with maple syrup or sorghum molasses.

OATMEAL PANCAKES

Makes 16 pancakes, or 4–6 servings

Oatmeal pancakes are a hearty dish—they puff up delightfully and resemble English muffins. Because of the oatmeal and whole wheat flour, these pancakes have a wonderful flavor and texture. If you have a plate of these in the morning, you can go all day without stopping. Note: You must start the batter the night before serving.

2 cups old-fashioned rolled oats
2 cups buttermilk, plus a bit more
½ cup unbleached all-purpose flour
½ cup whole wheat flour
2 teaspoons sugar
1½ teaspoons baking powder

1½ teaspoons baking soda
1 teaspoon salt
2 eggs
2 tablespoons (¼ stick) butter, melted and cooled
Vegetable oil for frying

Partially prepare batter the night before. In a small bowl, combine the oatmeal and 2 cups of the buttermilk. Cover and refrigerate overnight. The next morning, sift together the flours, sugar, baking powder, baking soda, and salt; set aside. In a large mixer bowl, beat the eggs until frothy. Add the butter and blend, then add the oatmeal mixture. Quickly blend in the flour mixture. The batter will be very thick, so you might need to add 2 to 4 more tablespoons of buttermilk, but not more than that.

Fry pancakes in an electric skillet at approximately 345° F., using about 1 tablespoon of oil per batch. Use a heaping tablespoon of batter for each cake, and pat it out a bit. The pancake will be about ¾ inch thick, and will puff up when turned over. Serve with warmed maple syrup.

THE EARTH STIRS

When March and April finally arrive, the drab, yellow-brown grass turns green overnight. Clumps of daffodils make a brave showing against white farmhouses. Early gardens are plowed, and along the quiet roadsides, women and children gather dishpans of dandelion greens for salads.

March is also maple syrup season, and at the sugar bush, farmers tap the trees and hang buckets on the rough, gray-brown trunks to collect the sap. Brought to the sugarhouse by horse and wagon, it is boiled down for hours in evaporator pans set over wood fires. The smoke adds its own special flavor to the bubbling syrup. This amber liquid is then filtered, poured into containers, and used all year long as a sweetening agent.

Even though it is a time of companionship for Amish farmers, it is also a time of long hours and hard work. I spent a day in Elkhart County, watching the syrup-making process. "It takes thirty gallons of sap to make one gallon of syrup," Eli Herschberger told me, as he stirred the steaming syrup with a long wooden paddle. "Sometimes you have to stay with it all day and night, 'til it gets to be the right consistency. We've been here cooking this batch down since six this morning." I checked my watch; it was three-thirty in the afternoon, and the weak spring sun was already beginning to lower in the sky.

Several men came in carrying armloads of oak wood from the wagon, and stacked it in the corner. They wore dark work pants with suspenders and dark jackets without buttons. Their wintertime black hats and their beards indicated they were all married. Three girls arrived carrying baskets of sandwiches and cookies. Black capes covered their longish dresses of dark-toned, plain fabrics. Their cap *(kop)* strings were untied.

To get back to my car, I walked down a lane to the road. The winter wheat made narrow green lines in the muddy fields. A flock of glossy bronzed cowbirds landed in the field to feed. Spring had arrived.

ASPARAGUS SOUP

PUMPERNICKEL CROÛTONS

DANDELION GREENS WITH
HOT BACON DRESSING

MAPLE SYRUP DUMPLINGS

MAPLE MOUSSE

MAPLE CREAM PIE

RHUBARB JUICE WITH
PUNCH VARIATIONS

RHUBARB SHERBET

RHUBARB DUMPLINGS

RHUBARB CONSERVE

OATMEAL-CINNAMON
CRISPIES

WHOLE WHEAT BREAD

CURRIED EGG SALAD
SANDWICHES

ASPARAGUS SOUP

◆

Makes 6 small servings

Asparagus is prepared simply in this part of the country;
generally it is quickly boiled and then drenched with butter or Hollandaise.
This soup is one of the few other ways it is presented.

25 medium-thick asparagus spears, about
    6 inches long, or 1 10-ounce
    package, frozen
2 cups Homemade Chicken Broth
    (page 159), or canned broth
2 tablespoons (¼ stick) butter
2 tablespoons minced onion

2 tablespoons all-purpose flour
¼ teaspoon salt
¼ teaspoon grated nutmeg
⅛ teaspoon powdered mustard
⅛ cup half-and-half
Dash of Tabasco
Pumpernickel Croûtons

Cut 1½ inches of the tips off the spears; reserve. Trim off the tough bottom ends of the spears and discard or reserve for stock. Place the stalks and the broth in a medium saucepan, and bring to a boil over high heat. Lower the heat and cook, covered, for 5 minutes. Remove the pan from heat and allow the contents to cool. Transfer the asparagus with a slotted spoon to the bowl of a food processor (or press through a sieve) and puree. Return the puree to the broth and blend.

In another saucepan, melt the butter.

Add the onion and cook over low heat until the onion is transparent. Stir in the flour, salt, nutmeg, and mustard. Cook and whisk until the mixture bubbles up, about 2 minutes. Add the half-and-half all at once, cooking and whisking until the mixture thickens. Add the asparagus puree and broth, reserved tips, and Tabasco. Bring to a simmer and cook over low heat just long enough to cook the tips—about 3 minutes. Pour into serving bowls and sprinkle the croûtons over the top.

PUMPERNICKEL CROÛTONS

Makes 1½ cups croûtons

The deep color of these croûtons adds an attractive touch to many soups, such
as Dutch Pea Soup (page 166) or Homemade Tomato Soup (page 125).

4 slices pumpernickel bread
¼ cup (½ stick) butter
⅛ teaspoon salt

⅛ teaspoon black pepper
2 tablespoons minced fresh parsley

Preheat oven to 375° F. Trim the crusts from the bread and dice slices into ½-inch cubes. Spread in a single layer on a shallow pan or cookie sheet and bake for 10 to 15 minutes, or until dry and lightly browned.

Heat the butter in a small skillet. Add

the croûtons, salt, pepper, and parsley, tossing lightly to mix. Sauté for 1 to 2 minutes over medium heat. Remove the croûtons to paper towels to cool and drain. These can be made in advance and kept in a tightly closed container.

DANDELION GREENS WITH HOT BACON DRESSING

Serves 4

Dandelions are a popular spring green, and this sweet-and-sour dressing, thickened with egg, is a favorite of the Amish. The hot dressing can also be tossed with fresh leaf lettuce, creating a dish we call wilted lettuce.

2–3 *quarts cleaned young dandelion greens*
6 *slices bacon, coarsely chopped*
2 *tablespoons minced onion*
¼ *cup sugar*
1½ *tablespoons all-purpose flour*
½ *teaspoon salt*

½ *teaspoon celery seed*
¼ *teaspoon black pepper*
1 *egg, slightly beaten*
¼ *cup cider vinegar*
1 *cup milk*

Wash greens several times to remove all grit. Place greens in a kettle and set aside.

In a medium saucepan, fry the bacon until crisp over medium heat. Remove to paper toweling with a slotted spoon and reserve. Pour off all but 2 tablespoons of the fat and add the onion. Sauté onion until it is lightly browned; remove skillet from heat.

In a medium bowl, mix sugar, flour, salt, celery seed, and pepper. Add the beaten egg, stirring with a whisk until smooth. Slowly add the vinegar, then blend in the milk.

Return skillet to stove, and place over medium heat. When the fat in the pan is hot, add the egg mixture, whisking and stirring constantly. Cook until thickened and continue to simmer gently for 1 minute. Remove from heat, and add reserved bacon.

Meanwhile, add enough water to the greens to cover them about halfway, cover kettle, and bring to a boil over high heat. Reduce heat to medium, and cook for 3 to 5 minutes, turning once with a long fork. Check for doneness, and cook a bit longer if needed. Drain and place greens in a large bowl (preferably warmed). Pour hot dressing over and toss. Serve immediately.

NOTE: Some cooks pour boiling water over the greens, cover them, and let them stand for 5 minutes instead of boiling them. The leaves will be less wilted using this method; it all depends on how chewy you like your greens.

MAPLE SYRUP DUMPLINGS

◆

Serves 6

This is a most unusual and unforgettable early spring dessert.
Nutmeg and mace scent these light dumplings, which simmer on top of buttered maple syrup. Serve them with a pitcher of thin cream.

SYRUP
2 *cups maple syrup*
1 *cup water*
2 *tablespoons (¼ stick) butter*
DUMPLINGS
1 *cup unbleached all-purpose flour*
2 *teaspoons sugar*
1½ *teaspoons baking powder*

½ *teaspoon salt*
¼ *teaspoon ground mace*
¼ *teaspoon grated nutmeg*
1 *tablespoon cold butter*
1 *egg*
½ *teaspoon vanilla extract*
½ *cup milk, approximately*

In a large saucepan, combine the maple syrup, water, and butter. Bring to a boil over high heat and then lower the heat to a simmer.

In a medium bowl, combine the first 6 dumpling ingredients. Cut in the butter with a pastry blender (or this can be done in a food processor) until mixture resembles crumbs. In a small bowl, beat the egg until frothy. Add the vanilla and milk; blend. Pour over the flour mixture and stir lightly, just until the ingredients are all moistened.

Drop batter by tablespoonfuls on top of the gently bubbling syrup. There should be 6 dumplings. Cover tightly and cook over low heat for 20 minutes, *without* lifting the lid. Serve warm in sauce dishes (sometimes these are called nappy dishes in the Midwest) and pass a pitcher of thin cream.

MAPLE MOUSSE

Serves 10

An old, old recipe, this maple mousse is an utterly beguiling dessert. Macadamia nuts are not Amish, but are an ideal garnish. If you prefer to be authentic, substitute pecans.

1 envelope unflavored gelatin
¼ cup cold water
4 eggs, separated
1 cup maple syrup
⅛ teaspoon cream of tartar

¼ cup sugar
2 cups heavy (whipping) cream
½ teaspoon maple extract
*   Chopped macadamia nuts or pecans*
*   and maple syrup*

In a small bowl, soften the gelatin in the cold water. In a small mixer bowl, beat the egg yolks until light. Continuing to beat, add the maple syrup slowly until the syrup is incorporated into the yolks. Add the gelatin and blend. Transfer the mixture to a large, heavy saucepan and cook over medium heat just until it bubbles up in the center, about 3 or 4 minutes. Watch carefully, stirring with a whisk, because the mixture will burn easily. Set aside to cool, but do not refrigerate. This mixture will set surprisingly fast—in less than an hour —so be vigilant; you don't want it to be firm.

Meanwhile, beat the egg whites and cream of tartar in a large mixer bowl until soft peaks form. Beat in the sugar 1 tablespoon at a time, and continue beating whites until they are stiff and shiny. Gently fold one-third of the egg whites into the not-quite-firm maple syrup mixture to lighten it. Pour over the remaining whites and fold in.

In a large mixer bowl, beat the cream and maple extract together until soft peaks form. Fold into the maple syrup mixture. Spoon mousse into large, stemmed wineglasses, sherbet glasses, or pots de crème. Refrigerate for several hours or overnight. Sprinkle mousse with the macadamia nuts or pecans, and serve with a pitcher of additional maple syrup to pour over the top.

MAPLE CREAM PIE

Serves 6

Sweetened condensed milk is a staple in farm kitchens and is used
to create desserts that are always reliably rich and smooth. The combination of
these simple ingredients makes a fantastic pie.

1 14-ounce can sweetened condensed
milk
⅔ cup maple syrup
Dash of salt
1 baked 8-inch pie shell
(page 170 or 171)

1 cup heavy (whipping) cream
¼ cup confectioners' sugar
1 teaspoon vanilla extract
3 tablespoons toasted chopped pecans
(see note)

In a medium saucepan, combine the condensed milk, maple syrup, and salt. Cook over low heat, stirring constantly until mixture bubbles up, then cook, uncovered, for 4 minutes, watching carefully to prevent scorching. Pour into the baked shell. Let cool completely, about 3 hours.

In a chilled bowl, combine the cream, confectioners' sugar, and vanilla. Beat until stiff peaks form. Spread on the cooled pie, and top with toasted pecans. Chill until ready to serve.

NOTE: To prepare pecans, place chopped nuts in a shallow pan, then dribble with a bit of vegetable oil and a speck of salt. Bake in a preheated 350° F. oven for 5 to 8 minutes, stirring now and then.

RHUBARB JUICE WITH PUNCH VARIATIONS

Makes 7–8 cups

This is a charmingly innocent and nostalgic beverage. Suggested
variations for punch are given that are very pleasant, but it is hard to beat the delicate
and refreshing flavor of the rhubarb, all by itself. The juice can be
canned or frozen for winter use.

8 cups coarsely chopped unpeeled
rhubarb
5 cups water

2⅔ cups sugar, approximately
Red food coloring (optional)
Fresh mint sprigs

In a large saucepan over low heat, simmer the rhubarb and water, covered, until the fruit is completely tender, about 10 minutes. Let cool.

Line a large sieve with a large piece of dampened cheesecloth and place in a large measuring cup or bowl. Pour in the fruit mixture and work the liquid through, using your hands to squeeze out every bit of juice. Measure the liquid and transfer to another deep pan. For each cup of juice, add ⅓ cup sugar. Tint the mixture with food coloring, if desired, to achieve the proper pink, then heat until the sugar is dissolved. Chill. The mixture can be frozen or canned at this point for later use, though you may have to re-tint it at serving time—it depends on how long you keep it.

To serve, pour over ice in a punch bowl or over cubes in crystal glasses. Garnish with fresh mint.

PUNCH VARIATION 1: Add ¼ cup orange juice and 1 teaspoon lemon juice for each cup of the sweetened rhubarb juice. Serve over ice.
PUNCH VARIATION 2: Add one 12-ounce bottle of ginger ale to 4 cups of the rhubarb-orange juice mixture. Serve over ice.

RHUBARB SHERBET
◆
Makes 6 cups, or 8 servings

This is a subtly flavored spring dessert, with an exquisite color.
By freezing the puree base, you can serve it year-round. A tablespoon of raspberry liqueur over the top of each serving is an elegant addition, though the original recipe certainly didn't call for that.

2 pounds fresh rhubarb
2¼ cups sugar
½ cup water
Speck of salt
1 tablespoon light corn syrup
1 cup heavy (whipping) cream

2 egg whites
Red food coloring (optional)
Fresh mint sprigs, or little spring flowers such as violets or sweet woodruff (optional)

Wash rhubarb and cut into 1-inch pieces; you will have approximately 6 cups. In a large saucepan, combine rhubarb, sugar, water, and salt. Bring to a boil, then cover and cook over low heat until fruit is very tender, about 10 minutes. Cool to lukewarm, about 1½ hours.

Puree cooled mixture in a blender or food processor; there should be 4 cups of puree. Stir in the corn syrup and pour into 3 freezer or ice-cube trays. (If you are freezing to store for future use, pour into 1-quart plastic containers.) Freeze the puree until it is hard around the edges, but still soft in the center.

Turn the rhubarb mixture into a large chilled mixer bowl and beat thoroughly and quickly. Whip the cream until stiff. Beat the egg whites until stiff peaks form. Fold the whipped cream, then the beaten egg whites into the rhubarb. Add enough food coloring to tint the mixture an attractive rose shade, then return the mixture to the freezer trays and chill until firm, several hours or overnight. Serve in crystal dishes. Garnish with mint or fresh flowers.
NOTE: The frozen puree can be kept indefinitely; the sherbet can be made only 1 week in advance; it tends to separate after that.

RHUBARB DUMPLINGS

◆

Serves 12

Most people are familiar with apple dumpings and peach dumplings, but rhubarb dumplings
are something just a tad different. Roll the rich,
buttery biscuit dough, lined with chopped rhubarb, like a jelly roll, and then bake the
slices in a sheer pink cinnamon sauce. This absolutely wonderful
recipe is from the Berne Swiss community.

SAUCE
- 1½ cups sugar
- 1 tablespoon all-purpose flour
- ¼ teaspoon ground cinnamon, rounded
- ¼ teaspoon salt
- 1½ cups water
- ⅓ cup butter
- 1 teaspoon vanilla extract
- Red food coloring

DOUGH
- 2 cups all-purpose flour
- 2 tablespoons sugar
- 2 teaspoons baking powder
- ¼ teaspoon salt
- 2½ tablespoons cold butter
- ½ to ¾ cup milk

FILLING
- 2 tablespoons (¼ stick) butter, softened
- 2 cups finely chopped fresh or frozen rhubarb (see note)
- ½ cup sugar
- Ground cinnamon

Preheat oven to 350° F. Prepare sauce first. In a small saucepan, combine sugar, flour, cinnamon, and salt. Gradually mix in the water, and add the butter. Bring to a boil over high heat and cook 1 minute. Add the vanilla and, if desired, enough food coloring to tint the mixture a deep pink. Let cool.

Prepare the dough. In a medium mixing bowl or food processor bowl, combine the flour, sugar, baking powder, and salt. Cut in or process in the butter until the mixture resembles small corn niblets. Add the milk and mix quickly—do not overmix. Gather dough into a ball and roll out on a floured board or cloth to a 12 x 10-inch rectangle.

Spread the dough with the softened butter, and arrange rhubarb on top. Sprinkle sugar over all, and dust liberally with cinnamon. Roll up from the long side, and place on a cutting board, seam side down. With a sharp knife, cut the roll into 12 slices. Arrange cut side up on an oiled 3-quart flat glass baking dish. Pour cooled sauce over top of dumplings. Bake for 35 minutes, until the dumplings are puffy and golden brown. Serve with heavy cream, if desired.

NOTE: Frozen rhubarb can be substituted. Do not thaw before arranging on dough. Cook the same length of time.

RHUBARB CONSERVE

Makes 4½ cups

Conserves are jamlike mixtures that contain a combination of fruits,
frequently including citrus fruits, raisins, and sometimes nuts. The consistency is slightly
jellied, with little or no syrup. This conserve is a flavorsome combination of rhubarb,
orange, and lemon, with a hint of cloves. Try it on hot Baking Powder Biscuits (page 4).

1¼ pounds fresh rhubarb, chopped
1 large orange, sliced as thin as possible
½ large lemon, sliced as thin as possible
4 cups sugar
¼ cup very coarsely chopped pecans

2 tablespoons golden raisins
¼ teaspoon ground cloves
*Few drops of red food coloring
(optional)*

Place rhubarb in a large saucepan. Cut each orange slice into 8 pie-shape wedges, and each lemon slice into 14 pie-shape wedges. Add to the rhubarb along with the sugar, and mix well. Bring to a boil over high heat, then lower heat and simmer, uncovered, for 40 minutes. Add remaining ingredients and cook 5 minutes longer. Ladle into sterilized jars and process in a water-bath canner at a simmering temperature of 180–185° F. for 10 to 15 minutes. This conserve also freezes very well.

OATMEAL-CINNAMON CRISPIES

Makes 100 2½-inch cookies

Oatmeal cookies do not have to be dull. This version is delightfully crisp,
and the molasses gives them an unexpected depth of flavor.
You will want to eat these by the handful.

2½ cups (5 sticks) butter, softened
5 cups sugar
⅓ cup dark molasses
4 eggs
1⅓ tablespoons baking powder
1 teaspoon baking soda
1 teaspoon salt

1 tablespoon ground cinnamon
1 tablespoon vanilla extract
4⅓ cups all-purpose flour
*4¾ cups old-fashioned rolled oats
(not instant)*
2 cups finely chopped pecans

Preheat oven to 375° F. Grease 2 baking sheets. In a large mixing bowl, cream the butter. Add the sugar gradually, then the molasses, and beat until the mixture is light and fluffy. Beat in the eggs, 1 at a time. Shut off the mixer and add the baking powder and soda, salt, cinnamon, and vanilla to the batter. Turn the beater back on and blend.

Add the flour and blend. Last, add the oats and the nuts and blend. Drop by rounded teaspoonfuls onto the baking sheets. Bake for 5 to 9 minutes, or until the cookies are medium brown and a bit crinkly looking. It may be necessary to turn the cookie sheets around in the oven so they will brown evenly. Allow the cookies to set on the sheets for about 3 minutes, then remove to a wire rack and let cool completely. These freeze very well.

WHOLE WHEAT BREAD

Makes 2 small loaves

Suetta Bechtel operates a restaurant called the Oil Lamp, close to Goshen, Indiana, and her cookery reflects her Mennonite background. Her breakfasts are especially popular, and there are two reasons for this: one is her Cinnamon Rolls (page 10) and the other is her Whole Wheat Bread. It is a fragrant, sweet, moist, and fine-textured loaf, and its hearty flavor can be enjoyed best if cut in thick slices. For a totally self-indulgent breakfast, I like to spread St. Andre triple-crème cheese on this hot toasted bread. That's not Amish or Mennonite, but it is absolutely splendid. Note: Because there's whole wheat flour in this recipe, rising time is longer than usual.

2 envelopes active dry yeast
3 tablespoons granulated sugar
3 tablespoons brown sugar or honey
1 tablespoon salt
1½ cups warm water
½ cup vegetable oil

¼ cup mashed potatoes, without milk or seasonings
2½ cups whole wheat flour
2½ cups bread flour
    Melted butter for brushing tops of loaves

In a large mixer bowl, combine all of the ingredients in the order given, but reserve 1¼ cups of the bread flour. Mix well for 5 minutes. Gradually blend in the rest of the bread flour, using as much as needed to make a workable dough. Transfer to a floured surface, or use your electric mixer dough hook, and knead for 10 minutes. Place dough in a greased large bowl (use either white vegetable shortening or butter), cover with a tea towel, and allow to rise in a warm place until dough doubles in size, approximately 2 hours.

Punch dough down very thoroughly (and I do mean thoroughly) to break up any large air holes that might have developed. Form into a smooth ball and place in the regreased bowl. Allow dough to rise until it doubles again in size, approximately 1½ hours.

Punch dough down again, cut in half, and form into 2 loaves. Place loaves in greased (8½ x 4½ x 2¾ inches) loaf pans. With a dinner fork, prick each loaf 8 times, plunging the fork all the way down to the bottom of the pan; this keeps those nasty air bubbles from forming. Cover the loaves with a tea towel and let rise until they are double in size, approximately 1½ hours.

Preheat oven to 325° F. Bake the loaves for 15 minutes, then raise the temperature to 350° F. and bake for 20 to 25 minutes longer.

Remove pans from oven, brush tops of loaves liberally with melted butter, and tip the loaves out of their pans onto a wire rack to cool. This keeps the loaves from getting soggy from their own steam.

CURRIED EGG SALAD SANDWICHES

◆

Makes 1⅔ cups filling, enough for 4 or 5 sandwiches

The secret of perfectly shelled hard-cooked eggs is to peel them while they are warm.
But they should be completely cool before being used in any recipe.

5 hard-cooked eggs
½ cup coarsely chopped celery
2 tablespoons coarsely chopped onion
⅓ cup fresh parsley sprigs
⅓ cup mayonnaise
2 teaspoons stone-ground prepared
    mustard

1 teaspoon curry powder
½ teaspoon celery salt
¼ teaspoon black pepper
2 tablespoons coarsely chopped sweet
    pickles
Whole Wheat Bread

In a deep saucepan, cover the eggs with cold water by at least 2 inches. Bring the water to a full rolling boil, turn off the heat, and allow the eggs to stand for 25 mintues. Rinse in cold water and peel immediately. Allow the eggs to cool before using.

In a food processor bowl, pulse the celery, onion, and parsley 2 times. Quarter the eggs, then add to processor bowl along with the mayonnaise, mustard, curry, celery salt, and pepper. Pulse 2 more times, or until the eggs and vegetables are well combined but not overly chopped. Mix in the pickles by hand—you want to be able to feel and taste the crunch of the individual sweet pickle pieces in the egg salad. Spread on thick slices of buttered bread.

EARLY GARDEN

Indiana in the spring is a lovely place—forsythia and red tulips bloom in dooryards, and many days are sunny and warm. As I drove through the countryside to the Swiss Amish and Mennonite community of Berne, Indiana, I saw many farm women outside working in their early vegetable gardens.

The first cool-weather crops are planted as soon as the ground can be worked—this includes spinach, peas, radishes, onion sets, beets, and carrots. Many kinds of salad greens are put in: deer tongue, oak leaf, salad bowl, bibb, and ruby leaf lettuces, to name a few. Depending on the weather, these tender young lettuces can be harvested in a matter of weeks and eaten with a variety of dressings, all homemade (not only more economical but better tasting).

After the danger of frost is past, the more tender vegetables will be planted: green beans, zucchini, cucumbers, sweet corn, and melons. Old-timers say there is seldom a killing frost after the last full moon in May, so it is safe then to set out tomato plants, as well as green bell pepper plants and annual herbs.

I found Nellie Graber, who is Swiss Amish, hoeing in her garden on an April afternoon. Empty seed packets were skewered on sticks at the ends of many rows, indicating what had been planted. Green onions, radishes, and leaf lettuce greens, planted weeks earlier, were already good sized. We went inside to sit down and share a mug of coffee and soft molasses cookies.

Like all the "English," I was curious to see the inside of an Amish house. She led me into the living room, where I sat on a wooden church pew, bought at a Methodist Church auction, that acts as their sofa. The chairs were bentwood rockers, locally made; there was

---

SWISS MEAT LOAF

GREEN BEAN AND POTATO SALAD

GREEN BEANS WITH ZUCCHINI AND BACON

NEW LETTUCE WITH SOUR CREAM DRESSING

GINGERED MAYONNAISE FOR RAW VEGETABLES

CREAMED NEW PEAS AND POTATOES

NOODLES WITH BUTTERED CRUMBS

POPPY SEED DRESSING

CHILI SAUCE SALAD DRESSING

CELERY SEED DRESSING

SOFT GINGER COOKIES WITH ORANGE GLAZE

no upholstered furniture. As always in Amish homes, the foot-pedaled sewing machine was placed in front of a window to give the stitcher good light. A coal stove, with several scuttles of coal beside it, stood in one corner of the room. A row of kerosene lamps on a shelf were all filled and ready to be lit for the night. Cheerful red geraniums lined the windowsills. The walls were painted white, which is the custom of this area. I asked her about the white curtains at the windows, for in some communities curtains are not permitted.

"Our bishop thinks curtains are all right because they keep out the sun," Nellie told me. "We use dark ones in the bedrooms. Some communities have rugs in their houses, but you can see our floors are bare. Each community or settlement varies in its customs. See my apron? It has two strings, like yours would, but we tie them in front. In another community, the apron might have just one long tie, and it is wrapped around the front and pinned. And our caps are black instead of white. Another way the Berne Swiss Amish community is different is that our buggies are open, and they are open the year-round. Though we do use black umbrellas to stop the wind sometimes. We don't make pieced quilts here either. They are just stitched, but the colors can be different on each side."

I asked her to explain the many differences among the various Amish communities; Berne appeared to be quite a conservative area.

"Well, the bishops in the settlements mostly decide such things such as the buggies being open or closed, or whether we can have bicycles or not. Here, we are mostly Old Order Amish, and sometimes we are called 'House Amish' since we have church in our houses—and that can be up to thirty or forty families—and all the houses are built to hold all the people in that church district for services. The backless church benches go from house to house in what we call the 'bench wagon.' Some Amish build church structures, but not us."

As we chatted, Nellie's hands kept busy with some mending from a basket next to her rocker. "We are moving soon to another community; we need more land so our sons can have farms of their own. My husband is there now, building the new house. We'll only be the second Amish family there, and we will have to drive an hour and a half by buggy to go to church at the nearest neighbor's, for we won't have a preacher of our own until more Amish move in."

"An hour and a half by open buggy?" I inquired incredulously.

"Oh, I don't mind," Nellie assured me cheerfully. "I like riding in the buggy; it gives me a chance to rest." Her eyes twinkled. "We really are like pioneers, opening up this community, only we go by buggy instead of covered wagons."

I asked if an Amish girl from Berne were to marry an Amish fellow from Elkhart and move there, whether she would keep the customs of this community, or change to that community's ways. "She would adopt the customs of her husband's community," Nellie replied. "I think moving is always harder on the woman, don't you?"

From the kitchen I could hear the clattering of dishes and pans. "What are you having for supper tonight?" I inquired.

"Tonight it's meat loaf, and we have added some Swiss cheese to it. And we'll fix some noodles, and today we picked our first lettuce, so the salad will be a real treat. And fresh rhubarb pie for dessert. Doesn't that sound good!"

SWISS MEAT LOAF

Serves 6

Meat loaf can be boring, but the addition of Swiss cheese to this recipe gives it
a distinctive flavor. This is an unusually good meat loaf.

1 egg
½ cup evaporated milk
1 teaspoon rubbed sage
1 teaspoon salt
½ teaspoon black pepper
1½ pounds lean ground beef

1 cup cracker crumbs (round buttery
type, approximately 24)
¾ cup grated Swiss cheese
¼ cup finely chopped onion
2–3 strips bacon, cut in 1-inch pieces

Preheat oven to 350° F. Beat the egg in
a large bowl. Add evaporated milk, sage, salt,
and pepper, and mix. Add beef, crumbs, ½
cup of the cheese, and the onion; blend. Form
into a loaf and place in a 2-quart rectangular

baking dish. Arrange bacon pieces on top of
the loaf.

Bake for 40 minutes. Sprinkle remaining
¼ cup cheese on top and bake 10 minutes
longer.

GREEN BEAN AND POTATO SALAD

Serves 6

Here is a Mennonite adaptation of one of those Alsatian recipes that crop up in
old church cookbooks. The salad has better flavor and texture if not
refrigerated, so prepare it just before you plan to serve it.

2 large potatoes
1¼ pounds fresh green beans
½ cup chopped onion
2 tablespoons fresh herbs of your choice
—savory, basil, or thyme (optional)

½ cup chopped fresh parsley
7 slices bacon, diced
¾ cup cider vinegar
½ teaspoon black pepper

Peel the potatoes, halve them, and cook
for 20 to 30 minutes or until tender. Slice
potatoes while still warm; set aside.

While the potatoes are cooking, wash,
snap, and halve the beans. (If the beans are
very young and slender, leave them whole.)
Steam the beans until barely tender, 3 to 5
minutes. Refresh them in cold water and set
aside to drain.

Heap the beans in the middle of a large
platter. Arrange the potatoes around the beans.

Sprinkle the onion, herbs, and parsley over all.

In a small skillet, cook the bacon until
crisp. Transfer the bacon and drippings to a
small bowl (there should be about ¼ cup). To
the same pan, add the vinegar and reduce it to
½ cup over high heat. Return the bacon and
the drippings to the pan and add the pepper.
Bring to a boil, and pour over the beans and
potatoes. Serve at room temperature. This is
especially good with Oven-Fried Chicken
(page 66).

GREEN BEANS WITH ZUCCHINI AND BACON

Serves 6

My friends with zucchini plants are always dropping their excess crop
off at my door; this is a good recipe for using them. The combination of the zucchini
disks and the slender green beans makes a most attractive vegetable dish.

1¼ pounds fresh green beans (see note)
4 slices bacon, coarsely chopped
1 tablespoon vegetable oil,
  approximately
2 8-inch slender zucchini, sliced
  ¼-inch thick

½ cup finely chopped onion
¼ teaspoon dried savory or thyme,
  rounded (optional)
⅛ teaspoon salt
½ teaspoon black pepper

Wash and snap green beans, then steam for 3 to 4 minutes—they should still be firm. Drain and set aside in a covered bowl.

In a large skillet, sauté the bacon until crisp. Remove with a slotted spoon and set aside. To the skillet, add enough additional oil to make about 3 tablespoons of fat in the pan. Add the onion, zucchini, and savory or thyme.

Cook over medium-high heat until the zucchini is tender-crisp, about 4 minutes. Stir in the beans and bacon, season with salt and pepper, and cook about 1 minute longer or until the beans are heated through.

NOTE: Two 9-ounce boxes of frozen green beans can be used, but cook them only half as long as the package directs.

NEW LETTUCE WITH SOUR CREAM DRESSING

Serves 4

Nothing tastes better in the spring than a tender lettuce salad, with the greens
coming freshly picked from one's own garden. This simple dressing
is tossed with an assortment of delicate new lettuces—bibb, red leaf, and perhaps deer
tongue—and a few chopped green onions for color and crunch.

1 pound assorted young leaf lettuce
½ cup sour cream
2 tablespoons milk
1 teaspoon sugar

1 teaspoon cider vinegar
¼ teaspoon celery seeds
4 green onions, chopped, including
  some of the tops

Soak the lettuce briefly in water to remove all the sand. Place in a colander and shake out excess water, wrap in a tea towel jelly-roll fashion, and place the rolled towel in the refrigerator for 2 hours; the lettuce will become very crisp.

Combine the remaining ingredients except the green onions in a small bowl and blend. Place chopped green onions on the bottom of a large bowl and top with the lettuce. Pour over the cold dressing and toss lightly. Chill until serving time.

GINGERED MAYONNAISE FOR RAW VEGETABLES

Makes 1 cup

Prepare this dressing a day or so in advance of serving so the flavors
can meld. Serve it as a dip with new green onions, red and white
radishes, zucchini strips, broccoli and cauliflower flowerets, and, of course,
carrots and celery.

1 cup mayonnaise
2 tablespoons finely chopped onion, or
*   1 tablespoon dried chopped onion*
2 tablespoons milk

1 teaspoon ground ginger
1 teaspoon cider vinegar
5 teaspoons soy sauce

In a small bowl, combine all the ingredients and blend thoroughly. Refrigerate overnight to allow the flavors to develop. Serve chilled with vegetables.

CREAMED NEW PEAS AND POTATOES

Serves 6

An innocent country dish, the peas and potatoes in this buttery white sauce
are nonetheless a pretty and tasty combination. I like to serve them in a clear glass
bowl with finely snipped mint leaves scattered over the top.

2 pounds small red potatoes
*   (approximately 16 2-inch ones)*
1½ cups shelled fresh peas, or 1 10-ounce
*   package frozen tiny peas*
¼ cup (½ stick) butter
¼ cup all-purpose flour

2 cups milk
¼ teaspoon salt
¼ teaspoon grated nutmeg
⅛ teaspoon white pepper
*   Minced mint leaves or chives*
*   (optional)*

Peel the potatoes and place in a medium saucepan, adding enough water to almost cover them. Cover pan, and cook over medium heat about 20 minutes, or until potatoes are tender when pierced with a knife. Drain well and keep warm.

In another saucepan, steam the fresh peas over hot water about 5 to 6 minutes or until barely done; reserve. (Frozen peas do not need to be precooked; just defrost.)

Meanwhile, in a medium saucepan over medium heat, melt the butter. Add the flour and cook, stirring, until the mixture bubbles up well, but do not allow the roux to brown. Add the milk all at once, and cook and whisk until mixture is smooth. Blend in the salt, nutmeg, and white pepper. Add the peas to the white sauce, turn the heat to low, and cook the mixture 5 minutes.

Place the potatoes in a 6-cup serving dish and pour the creamed peas over them. Sprinkle the mint leaves over the top.

NOODLES WITH BUTTERED CRUMBS

◆

Serves 6

In any part of the United States where a great deal of wheat is raised, you will find excellent breads and noodles. In fact, this part of the country could be called the Noodle Belt without exaggeration. The Amish cook prepares noodles in some form for her family at least once a day. The following recipe is a pleasant variation; I prefer using party crackers for the crumbs—they stay very crisp and add flavor. The method I give you for cooking the noodles is the simplest I've found.

3 quarts water
½ teaspoon salt
1 tablespoon vegetable oil
8 ounces thin or medium-wide noodles (about 5 cups)
⅔ cup butter

2 cups cracker crumbs (see note)
3 tablespoons minced fresh parsley or coriander
¾ teaspoon poppy seeds
¼ tablespoon black pepper
Paprika

In a very deep kettle, bring the water, salt, and oil to a full rolling boil over high heat. Sprinkle in the noodles; return to a boil. Cover tightly, remove from the heat, and allow the noodles to stand for 25 minutes, or until they are tender. Drain in a colander. Add ⅓ cup of the butter to the noodle kettle and melt it over low heat. Return the drained noodles to the kettle and toss lightly.

Meanwhile, in a medium skillet, melt the remaining ⅓ cup of butter over medium heat and add the cracker crumbs. Stir and toast until the crumbs begin to turn golden. Add the parsley or coriander, poppy seeds, and black pepper, and blend. Transfer the buttered noodles to a serving dish, sprinkle the buttered crumbs on the top, and drift a bit of paprika over all.

NOTE: Any type of party crackers can be used in this recipe.

LEFT: *In the summer, the one-room schoolhouse, which serves 8 grades, is quiet.* RIGHT: *In Amish homes, mirrors are partially covered to discourage vanity.*

POPPY SEED DRESSING

Makes 1 quart

Poppy Seed Dressing is good on lettuce salads or fruit salads. This keeps indefinitely in the refrigerator. It remains my favorite sweet dressing, and I've tried them all.

1½ cups sugar
2 teaspoons powdered mustard
2 teaspoons salt

⅔ cup cider vinegar
2 cups vegetable oil
3 tablespoons poppy seed

In a large mixer bowl, combine the first 4 ingredients. Slowly add the oil and beat until thick. Then beat 5 minutes more. Add the poppy seed and blend well.

CHILI SAUCE SALAD DRESSING

Makes ½ cup

A bright red, intensely flavored dressing because of the chili sauce, this is quite unlike other tomato-based dressings. Try it on lettuce, with grapefruit and avocado wedges, and topped with toasted almonds.

½ cup vegetable oil
½ cup good-quality chili sauce
    (homemade, page 123, is the
    very best, of course)
2 tablespoons water

1 teaspoon salt
1 teaspoon sugar
¼ teaspoon coarsely ground black pepper
1 tablespoon lemon juice

Combine ingredients in the order listed in a 2-cup jar, and shake to mix. This will keep 2 weeks if refrigerated and tightly covered. Serve chilled.

CELERY SEED DRESSING

Makes 2 scant cups

This recipe is seldom seen anymore. A clear, sweet-and-sour dressing with lots of celery seed, it is popular at country restaurant salad bars. Serve over tossed mixed greens, with a few chopped radishes and onions added.

⅔ cup sugar
2 teaspoons lemon juice
1 teaspoon powdered mustard
1 teaspoon salt
¼ teaspoon white pepper

1 small onion, very finely minced
⅓ cup cider vinegar
1 cup vegetable oil
1 teaspoon celery seed

Place the first 6 ingredients and half the vinegar in a blender jar. Blend well. With blender still running, add the oil and remaining vinegar and blend thoroughly. This method prevents dressing from separating. Stir in the celery seed.

SOFT GINGER COOKIES WITH ORANGE GLAZE

Makes 3½ to 4 dozen cookies

My mother's recipe notes that these cookies were also called Belsnickel Cookies.
During Christmas week, the Pennsylvania Germans would be visited by
masked revelers called Belsnickels, and these mischievous
callers would be served these cookies and other confections.

1 cup buttermilk
2 teaspoons baking soda
¾ cup vegetable oil
1 cup sugar
1 cup dark molasses
2 eggs
3¾ cups unbleached all-purpose flour
1 teaspoon salt
2 teaspoons ground cinnamon
1 teaspoon ground ginger
1 teaspoon grated nutmeg

½ teaspoon ground allspice
½ teaspoon ground cloves
GLAZE
2 cups plus 1 tablespoon confectioners'
* sugar*
1 tablespoon butter, very soft
¼ cup orange juice
2 teaspoons grated orange rind
½ teaspoon vanilla extract
* Speck of salt*

In a small bowl, combine the buttermilk and baking soda and set aside; it will foam up. In a large mixer bowl, place the vegetable oil, sugar, molasses, and eggs. Beat for 1 minute or until well mixed. Add the buttermilk mixture and blend. Sift together the flour, salt, cinnamon, ginger, nutmeg, allspice, and cloves. Add slowly to the molasses mixture, and beat on medium speed until just blended. Allow the batter to stand for 15 minutes.

Preheat oven to 325° F. Drop batter by heaping tablespoons onto oiled cookie sheets. Bake for 8 to 9 minutes, or until the top of the cookies spring back when touched with your finger. Do not overbake—these cookies should be very soft, almost like little round gingerbreads. While the cookies are baking, combine the glaze ingredients in a medium bowl and beat until well mixed.

Remove the baked cookies to a wax paper-lined wire rack. Frost while warm, spreading ½ teaspoon of glaze over each cookie. Let cool completely, then transfer to trays and place in the freezer to completely set the glaze or to freeze for storing. Pack cookies in tins, using wax paper to separate each layer. These freeze very well.

E A S T E R

On Easter morning, the sun stains the east with layers of strawberry pink and then explodes into a golden rinse of light. Symbolically, this day also signifies the resurrection of the land. Since the Amish religion is so closely tied to agrarian living, this holiday is especially important, though their weekly church services are also looked forward to because of the opportunity they provide for fellowship and a change in routine.

The Old Order Amish have church every two weeks, held at a different family's house each time; the locations rotate on an annual basis. The services are in German, another reminder of their ethnic heritage. Hymns are also sung in German, without accompaniment, for musical instruments are forbidden. Preachers and bishops, who serve for life, are nominated and chosen by each of the congregations.

Easter services for the Amish last the usual three hours, while the Mennonite Easter service resembles most Protestant services and lasts approximately an hour. As congregations increase, new Mennonite churches are being built, and the architecture, though contemporary, reflects the simplicity of their faith.

Since this is a religious holiday, the Mennonite Easter dinner features more elaborate dishes. Lamb is not commonly eaten in this area, but might be served on Easter as a special treat. Pork is often on the menu, reflecting the German and Alsatian affection for this meat, and smoked ham is doubtless the most popular dish of all on this day. Pigs are easy to raise, and the meat can be used for any number of dishes. Nothing is wasted. The scraps go into sausage, scrapple, head cheese, and souse, and lard is an important baking ingredient.

A typical Easter dinner would feature a special salad or two, such as a sweet-and-tart broccoli salad; and on this holiday, when there are lots of leftover decorated hard-cooked eggs, pickled beets and eggs will be on the table. Desserts include the pies and cakes that these cooks are famous for, such as a brown sugar pie or rhubarb pie, plus perhaps a pudding or two.

ASPARAGUS PIE

COLE SLAW WITH PEANUTS

BROCCOLI SALAD

NEW POTATOES WITH
LEMON-BUTTER SAUCE

TOMATO FRITTERS

LEG OF LAMB WITH
MINTED PRUNE STUFFING

MAPLE BAKED HAM

ORANGE-GLAZED PORK
LOIN

OVERNIGHT BUTTER ROLLS

CUSTARD PUDDING WITH
MERINGUE

ORANGE-PINEAPPLE ICE

ASPARAGUS PIE

◆

Serves 6

The first asparagus of the season is a real treat, and asparagus pie is
a way to make those initial few spears go a long way. This is a substantial dish, and a
good entrée for lunch. Cut in wedges, the colorful combination of eggs and
asparagus is very attractive on the plate.

25 fresh asparagus spears, or 1 10-ounce
    package frozen
1/3 cup butter
5 tablespoons all-purpose flour
2 cups milk
2 teaspoons lemon juice
3/4 teaspoon curry powder (optional)

1/2 teaspoon celery salt
1/8 teaspoon black pepper
1 baked 9-inch pie shell
    (page 170 or 171)
4 hard-cooked eggs, peeled and sliced
1/2 cup grated sharp cheddar cheese
    Paprika

Preheat the oven to 350° F. Trim the fresh asparagus spears and cut into 1½-inch lengths. Place in a skillet with enough water to barely cover. Cook, covered, for 2 to 3 minutes or until just done; drain and set aside. If using frozen asparagus, thaw the spears on paper toweling, then cut into 1½-inch lengths. You need 1⅔ to 2 cups of chopped asparagus.

In a medium saucepan, melt the butter and add the flour. Cook over medium-low heat until the mixture bubbles up in the pan, but do not allow the roux to brown. Add the milk all at once, and whisk and cook until the mixture thickens. Add the lemon juice, curry powder, celery salt, and pepper. Cook mixture over low heat for 2 to 3 minutes, then remove from heat.

In the baked pie shell, alternate layers of asparagus and sliced eggs. Pour the sauce over the asparagus (it will be very thick), and spread out evenly. Top the sauce with the grated cheese and sprinkle paprika over all. Bake for 40 to 45 minutes, or until the sauce bubbles up in the middle and the cheese is a deep golden brown. Remove from oven and allow the pie to stand 10 minutes before cutting into wedges.

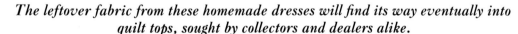

*The leftover fabric from these homemade dresses will find its way eventually into
quilt tops, sought by collectors and dealers alike.*

COLE SLAW WITH PEANUTS

Makes 8 small servings

This version of cole slaw, using an old-fashioned boiled dressing, appears in early Mennonite cookbooks; this is an updated version. Add the dressing to the cabbage mixture just an hour before serving; that way the peanuts stay crunchy.

1/3 cup sugar
1 tablespoon all-purpose flour
1 teaspoon powdered mustard
1/2 teaspoon salt
1/4 teaspoon black pepper
1 egg
1/3 cup cider vinegar
1 tablespoon butter
2 ribs celery, chopped

1/2 cup plus 2 tablespoons coarsely
  chopped roasted peanuts
1/4 cup chopped onion
1/4 cup finely minced green bell pepper
1/4 cup finely minced fresh parsley
4 cups shredded cabbage (approximately
  1 pound)
1/2 cup mayonnaise

In a small bowl, combine the sugar, flour, mustard, salt, and pepper. In a small saucepan, beat the egg well; add the vinegar and mix. Then add the sugar-flour mixture gradually, and blend. Cook over low heat, whisking smooth, until the mixture bubbles and thickens, about 3 minutes. Stir in the butter, then set aside and let cool.

In a large bowl, combine the celery, peanuts, onion, bell pepper, and parsley. Add the shredded cabbage and toss to mix.

In a small bowl, combine 1/2 cup of the boiled dressing and the 1/2 cup of mayonnaise. Toss with cabbage mixture. Serve chilled.

BROCCOLI SALAD

Serves 10–12

This sweet and colorful version of broccoli salad appears on many tables and also in the local grocery delis. The addition of raisins and bacon gives it great texture and flavor.

2 bunches broccoli (approximately
  2 1/4 pounds)
10 thin slices bacon
1 large red onion
1/3 cup dark raisins

1 cup mayonnaise
1/4 cup sugar
2 tablespoons cider vinegar
1/2 teaspoon black pepper
1/2 cup toasted sunflower seeds (optional)

Cut broccoli flowerets into smaller than bite-size pieces. Cut off the tough outer layer of the stalks and chop the tender part into small pieces. You need approximately 8 cups of broccoli. (This can be done the day before and stored in a plastic bag.)

In a small skillet, sauté the bacon until crisp and set aside. Slice the onion lengthwise, then cut into julienne strips. In a large bowl, combine the broccoli, onion strips, raisins, and bacon. In a small bowl, whisk together the mayonnaise, sugar, vinegar, and pepper. Combine dressing with the vegetables, and refrigerate for at least 2 hours before serving, mixing once during this time. Top with the sunflower seeds.

NEW POTATOES WITH LEMON-BUTTER SAUCE

Serves 8

Pour this sprightly lemon-butter sauce, with its touch of green,
over plain boiled potatoes, and a humble root vegetable becomes
unexpectedly "dressed up."

8 medium red-skinned potatoes
½ cup (1 stick) butter
¼ cup vegetable or olive oil
6 tablespoons lemon juice
3 tablespoons finely minced fresh chives
2 tablespoons finely minced fresh parsley

1 tablespoon grated lemon rind
½ teaspoon salt
½ teaspoon black pepper
½ teaspoon grated nutmeg
⅛ teaspoon ground mace

Peel the potatoes, leaving a band of skin about 1½ inches wide around the middle of each. Place in a medium saucepan, cover with cold water, and boil until tender, about 20 to 25 minutes.

Meanwhile, in a small saucepan, combine the remaining ingredients and bring to a boil—but do not allow the butter to brown. Drain the potatoes and transfer to a shallow serving dish. Pour the hot butter sauce over all. Serve immediately.

TOMATO FRITTERS

Makes 26 fritters, or 4–6 servings

This is a most unusual reddish-gold fritter, with a distinctive flavor. It can be served as a breakfast dish with maple syrup, but I prefer it as a vegetable side dish. Tomato fritters are not well known outside the Mennonite-Amish community, and that's regrettable.

1 cup all-purpose flour
1 teaspoon baking powder
1 teaspoon sugar
¾ teaspoon salt
 Rounded ¼ teaspoon dried basil, or
 2 tablespoons fresh minced basil

1 28-ounce can tomatoes, drained
1 tablespoon finely minced onion
1 tablespoon finely minced fresh parsley
½ teaspoon Worcestershire sauce
1 egg
 Vegetable oil for frying

In a large bowl, combine the flour, baking powder, sugar, salt, and basil. Cut the tomatoes into approximately ½-inch pieces and place them on a paper towel to drain further. Add them, along with the onion, parsley, and Worcestershire sauce, to the flour mixture, but do not mix in. In a small bowl, beat the egg and add it to the flour-tomato mixture. Blend lightly with a fork.

To an electric skillet heated to 360° F., add ¼ inch of oil. Drop the batter by tablespoons, patting them down a bit, into the hot oil. Fry until golden brown on one side, then turn and fry the other side. Keep fritters warm in the oven until serving time while frying the remainder.

LEG OF LAMB WITH MINTED PRUNE STUFFING

◆

Serves 8–10

Mint grows wild along the roadsides and is used freely in country recipes; perhaps those fragrant shoots escaped from the fields during the early 1900s, when the distillation of mint extract was an important industry in this area. Mint extract was used in medicines and was considered so valuable that it was kept in local bank vaults until it was shipped to pharmaceutical firms for final processing.

2 cups small dry bread cubes
½ cup chopped celery
2 tablespoons chopped onion
1 tablespoon chopped green bell pepper
1 tablespoon chopped fresh parsley
1 bay leaf, crumbled
2 tablespoons finely minced fresh mint,
*   or 1 tablespoon dried*
¼ teaspoon dried marjoram

¼ teaspoon black pepper
⅓ cup butter
1 tablespoon lemon juice
6 moist pitted prunes, coarsely chopped
1 5–6 pound leg of lamb, boned (reserve
*   bones for soup)*
2 ribs celery
1 carrot, sliced lengthwise
1 onion, quartered

Preheat oven to 325° F. Place the bread cubes in a large bowl. Add the vegetables, along with the bay leaf, mint, marjoram, and black pepper. Melt the butter and add the lemon juice; pour over the bread-cube mixture and blend. Add the prunes and toss lightly.

Spread out the lamb; it will be an irregularly shaped piece of meat. Spread the dressing over the meat and bring 2 opposite sides of the meat up to meet each other; truss with metal skewers and string. Bring up the other 2 sides and repeat. Insert a meat thermometer.

Place the meat, skewer side down, in a shallow roasting pan and place the celery, carrot, and onion around it. Roast at 20 minutes per pound until a meat thermometer registers 145° F. for medium-rare or 160° F. for well-done—approximately 1½ hours for medium.

Transfer the meat to a heated platter and remove vegetables with slotted spoon. Pour the drippings into a bowl so the fat can rise to the top and be skimmed off. Slice the lamb thinly and serve with the pan juices.

The Green Meadows Bed and Breakfast, whose Mennonite owners collect antiques.

The table is ready for company in this Mennonite home.

MAPLE BAKED HAM

Serves 10–12

Most hams available in supermarkets today are fully cooked
and just need to be reheated; this recipe is for that type of ham. If you are
lucky enough to find an old-fashioned uncooked smoked ham, you will need to
cook it longer (see note). This is quite a rich dish, so serve it with a simple
vegetable, such as Brussels sprouts with dill or green lima beans with peas.

*One-half boneless precooked smoked
ham (approximately 5 pounds)
1 cup maple syrup for each 5 pounds
of ham
¼ cup all-purpose flour*

*1 cup water
½ teaspoon powdered mustard
2 teaspoons Worcestershire sauce
Maple extract (optional)*

Preheat oven to 325° F. Place the ham fat side up on a rack in a shallow roasting pan. Do not cover or add water. Insert a meat thermometer and bake the ham. (For a precooked ham, the internal temperature should be 130° F. when finished; if the ham is uncooked, the internal temperature should be at 160° F. when served.) When the ham is about half-baked, approximately 45 minutes, pour the pan juices into a medium saucepan. Skim off excess fat and set the drippings aside. Pour the maple syrup over the ham, and return to the oven. Occasionally baste the ham with the syrup from the pan while it finishes baking; the total cooking time for a 5-pound precooked ham is about 1½ to 1¾ hours.

To make the sauce, remove the ham from the pan and set aside on a carving board. With a whisk, blend the flour into the reserved drippings in the saucepan. Add the water, mustard, Worcestershire sauce, and maple syrup drippings from the roasting pan and combine. Add a bit of maple extract if desired. Bring to boil, stirring constantly, then remove from the heat and keep warm.

Carve the ham into thin slices. Pour the hot maple sauce into gravy boat and pass with the ham.

NOTE: For an uncooked 5-pound half ham, allow 2¼ to 2½ hours.

ORANGE-GLAZED PORK LOIN

Serves 10–12

This is an orange-and spice-flavored roast pork with a beautiful glaze.
Season the meat the day before for best results; you can also do the sauce in advance.
When ordering the roast, have the butcher tie it with string. The webbed
stocking they sometimes use will not work with this glaze.

½ teaspoon salt
½ teaspoon dried thyme, or 1 tablespoon
    fresh (optional)
½ teaspoon ground ginger
½ teaspoon black pepper
1 5-pound boneless pork loin roast, rolled
    and tied
3 large garlic cloves, each sliced into
    4 pieces

1 tablespoon all-purpose flour
2 tablespoons cornstarch
1 cup sugar
1¼ cups orange juice
½ cup water
¼ cup lemon juice
2 tablespoons mustard
1 tablespoon soy sauce
2 teaspoons grated orange rind

Preheat the oven to 325° F. Combine the salt, thyme, ginger, and pepper in a small bowl. With a sharp knife, make 12 slits in the roast, and insert a slice of garlic and some of the spice mixture into each. Rub the roast with any leftover spice mixture. Insert a meat thermometer. Place the roast, uncovered, in a roasting pan and bake for a total of 3 hours.

Meanwhile, in a medium saucepan, combine the flour, cornstarch, and sugar. Add the orange juice gradually, then the remaining ingredients. Cook over medium heat and whisk about 3 to 5 minutes, until smooth and thick. After the pork has roasted for 2 hours, brush the roast frequently with the glaze. Continue roasting and basting for another hour, or until the meat thermometer registers 170° F. Heat remaining glaze and serve as a sauce with the sliced pork.

OVERNIGHT BUTTER ROLLS

Makes 30–32 rolls

This speedy, no-knead dinner roll has a fine-grained texture and a deep buttery
flavor. For a special treat, the unbaked dough can be spread with pesto, a basil,
pine nut, and Parmesan cheese mixture, instead of butter. The dough does
need to rest overnight, so plan accordingly.

2 packages active dry yeast
1¼ cups very warm water
3 eggs
5 cups unsifted unbleached all-purpose
    flour

½ cup sugar
¾ cup (1½ sticks) butter, melted
2 teaspoons salt
    Softened butter (or pesto)

Sprinkle both packages of yeast into ¼ cup of very warm water and stir with a fork. Set aside for 10 minutes.

In a large mixer bowl, beat the eggs and blend in the dissolved yeast. Add 2½ cups of flour, alternating with the remaining 1 cup of very warm water. Mix in the sugar, ½ cup of melted butter, and the salt. Mix until smooth. Beat in the remaining flour to make a soft dough, then cover with a tea towel, put in a warm, draft-free place, and let rise until doubled in bulk, about 1 to 2 hours.

Punch dough down with vigor, cover with plastic wrap, and refrigerate overnight.

Punch the dough down and divide in half. On a floured cloth or board, roll out each half into a rectangle 8 x 15 inches. Spread lavishly with the softened butter (or pesto). Starting with the long edge, roll up dough jelly-roll fashion. With a very sharp knife, cut in 1-inch slices. Place slices in cups of an oiled muffin tin, cut side up. Let rise until doubled in bulk, 40 minutes to 1 hour.

Preheat the oven to 400° F. Bake rolls for 8 to 10 minutes, or until golden brown. Immediately brush with remaining ¼ cup melted butter. Place on a rack to cool.

CUSTARD PUDDING WITH MERINGUE

Serves 12

This dish surely comes under the heading of nursery desserts, but is relished at many an adult table. And this nostalgic version has a graham-cracker crust, which adds a crisp texture. Graham crackers have been popular since 1882, and they appear in many old recipes.

½ pound graham crackers
2 cups sugar
¾ (1½ sticks) butter, melted
1 teaspoon ground cinnamon
¼ cup cornstarch

Speck of salt
6 eggs, separated
1 quart milk
1 teaspoon vanilla extract

Crush the graham crackers with a rolling pin or whiz in a food processor until fine crumbs are formed. Transfer to a medium bowl and combine with ¾ cup of sugar, the melted butter, and the cinnamon. Reserve 2 tablespoons of the mixture for the topping and press the remainder into the bottom and up the sides of a 9 × 13-inch baking pan.

In a large saucepan, combine ¾ cup sugar, the cornstarch, and the salt. Beat the egg yolks slightly, then add the yolks and the milk to the sugar mixture and blend. Cook over medium heat and stir, using a rubber spatula, until the mixture bubbles up in the middle, about 3 to 4 minutes. Add the vanilla, then let cool for 20 minutes. Pour mixture into the crust; let cool 15 minutes longer.

Preheat oven to 325° F. Beat the egg whites until frothy. Gradually add the remaining ½ cup sugar and continue beating until stiff peaks form. Spread the egg whites on top of the custard, spreading it out so it touches the sides of the pan. Sprinkle the reserved crumbs over the top. Bake for 15 minutes, or until the top is nicely browned. Cool, then refrigerate until ready to serve.

ORANGE-PINEAPPLE ICE

◆

Serves 8–10

This is a very old recipe, in which the undisguised fruit flavors are intense.
Its marvelous simplicity makes you wonder why anyone would want to create something
as pretentious as baked Alaska. This does not require stirring during the
freezing period; you want it to be a bit crystallized.
Today we would call this a sorbet.

2 cups sugar
2¼ cups water
  1 envelope unflavored gelatin
  1 8-ounce can crushed pineapple and
    juice

1 cup orange juice
6 tablespoons lemon juice
2 very ripe bananas, mashed very well
  Fresh mint

In a medium saucepan, combine sugar and 2 cups water and bring to a boil over high heat, stirring until dissolved. Soften the gelatin in ¼ cup cold water, then stir into the hot syrup mixture. Let cool completely.

Add fruits and fruit juices to the syrup, then pour into a refrigerator tray and freeze. Let soften slightly before serving, garnished with fresh mint.

OPPOSITE: *During church services, the men leave their hats outside.* BELOW: *Antique Amish quilts, recognizable by their jewel-toned designs, air on a line.*

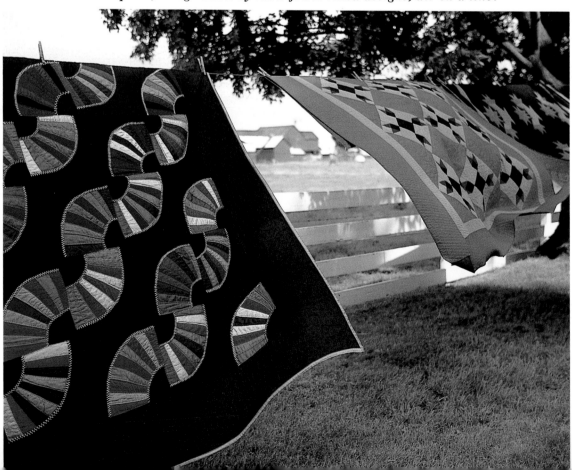

FAMILY MEALS

In this part of the country, the big meal is served at noon and is called dinner. It is quite usual for meat to be served three times a day, and the ubiquitous noodle is always served at dinner and frequently again at supper, the evening meal. Since the women are as busy throughout the day as are the men, many of the dishes are assembled early in the morning and allowed to cook slowly, unattended, on wood or kerosene stoves as the women busy themselves with other tasks.

Noodles are prepared in a variety of ways and served at all large gatherings: weddings, barn raisings, and reunions.

In Sevilla Knepp's kitchen, I watched her roll out and cut noodles. Her hands fairly flew as she deftly sliced the rolled dough into narrow strips.

Sevilla is a pro; she makes noodles for a restaurant in a nearby town. Noodles vary from community to community. Some cooks make pot-pie noodles—the large square ones—while others cut narrow ones like Sevilla's. And then there are rivels, a type of noodle made of flour, beaten egg, and salt, which is mixed with the fingers and dropped a few at a time into a hot, rich broth.

On an earlier occasion Sevilla had prepared rivels for me, and I recalled sitting in another kitchen, in another time and place, at a wooden table in front of a coal stove, watching my grandmother fix the same dish. "*Rivels* is a German name," she explained. "*Reiben* in German means to rub, and you can see how I rub the dough between my fingers right into the soup."

Sevilla's daughters were setting the table, and I counted fifteen place settings, the usual number of people she cooks for at least two times a day. "It's spareribs and sauerkraut tonight," she says. "That's one of our favorite meals, and it's been cooking on the back of the range all afternoon. The girls will fix potato pancakes as a special treat tonight instead of noodles. And we always put out a platter of cheese on the table, too—Swiss and cheddar mostly. We like the young cheddar best; we call it squeaky cheese."

ONION RIVEL SOUP

POT ROAST

SPICY MEAT LOAF

COUNTRY STEW

SPARERIBS AND
SAUERKRAUT

MASHED CARROTS AND
PARSNIPS

HOMEMADE NOODLES

FRIED NOODLES

HASH BROWNED POTATOES

STEAMED BREAD PUDDING

CHOCOLATE FUDGE
PUDDING

ONION RIVEL SOUP

◆

Serves 6

Rivel soup is a terribly old-fashioned recipe, and it is a bit hard to describe.
A rivel is a rather informal dumpling or free-form noodle, dropped
into any broth or soup. Some people even like it in hot milk, which I
personally can skip. What does a cooked rivel look like, you might ask? The
best description I can give is a little, soft, chewy dumpling. Onion Rivel Soup,
with its beef-stock base, is an absolutely first-rate dish.

*¼ cup (½ stick) butter, or rendered
    chicken fat*
2 cups sliced onions
*6 cups Brown Stock (page 163), or
    canned stock*

1 egg
¾–1 cup all-purpose flour
½ teaspoon salt
Liberal dash of black pepper

In a large saucepan, melt the butter or chicken fat and add the onions. Sauté over low heat until the onions are golden brown, about 7 or 8 minutes. Add the broth, and bring to a boil over medium-high heat.

In the meantime, prepare the rivels. In a medium bowl, beat the egg well. Add the flour, salt, and pepper and mix first with a tablespoon, then finish mixing by rubbing the dough between your fingers. The largest pieces should only be pea-size.

Sprinkle the rivels slowly into the boiling broth, stirring constantly but gently. Reduce heat to medium, cover, and simmer about 8 to 10 minutes. Serve immediately.

POT ROAST

◆

Serves 6–8

Farm cooks generally are thrifty and seldom throw anything out, not even
leftover coffee from breakfast. Using coffee with pot roast gives that dish a
real depth of flavor. Slices of this roast are also good served on hard rolls, with
the pan juices in a little bowl on the side as a French dip sandwich.

3 pounds Swiss steak, trimmed of fat
1 tablespoon vegetable oil
¼ cup soy sauce
1 cup coffee, regular or decaffeinated
2 bay leaves, crumbled

1 garlic clove, finely minced
½ teaspoon dried oregano
2 onions, sliced
*Additional coffee and soy sauce, as
    needed*

Preheat oven to 300° F. Do not pound or flour the meat. Heat oil in a heavy skillet over high heat, then sear meat on both sides.

Meanwhile, in a large roasting pan, combine the soy sauce, coffee, bay leaves, garlic, oregano, and one of the sliced onions. Transfer the browned meat to the roasting pan. Top with the second sliced onion. Cover and bake for 3½ to 4 hours, basting every hour with pan juices. If the liquid begins to boil away (this depends on the heaviness of your pan), add another cup of coffee and a liberal splash of soy sauce. You may have to repeat this procedure; there should be quite a bit of liquid.

Cut the meat in thin slices and serve with pan juices.

This wood-burning brick stove, originally designed for cooking meat down for souse and head cheese, is now used to heat water for washing clothes.

Frugal Amish housewives still make soap from rendered animal fat, borax, and ammonia. This is done primarily in Swiss communities.

Hot water is carried from the butchering shed to the outdoor washing machine, where the clothes are run through the wringer by hand.

Freshly washed clothes dance in the wind. The Amish housewife will wash her family's laundry—without the aid of electricity—at least twice a week.

SPICY MEAT LOAF

Serves 6–8

Here is another meat loaf that is nicely flavored—leftovers of this,
sliced cold, make great sandwiches.

2 tablespoons (¼ stick) butter
½ cup chopped onion
½ cup chopped celery
½ cup chopped green or red bell pepper
½ cup finely minced carrot
2 finely minced garlic cloves
2 eggs
½ cup catsup
½ cup evaporated milk

½ teaspoon salt
2 teaspoons chili powder
1 teaspoon ground allspice
½ teaspoon black pepper
¼ cup finely chopped fresh parsley
1½ cups soft fine bread crumbs
1½ pounds lean ground beef
½ pound lean ground pork
2 slices bacon, cut in 1-inch pieces

Preheat oven to 350° F. Melt the butter in a medium saucepan. Add the next 5 ingredients and sauté over medium heat until vegetables begin to brown, about 5 minutes. Set aside.

In a large bowl, beat the eggs well, and then add the next 8 ingredients. Mix. Add the meats and the sautéed vegetables. Combine well, using your hands, if necessary, but do it lightly. Transfer mixture to an oiled 10 x 6-inch casserole and form into an oval loaf. Arrange bacon pieces on top. Bake for 45 minutes. Remove from oven, drain off fat, and allow to stand for 10 minutes.

COUNTRY STEW

Serves 8

Another easy entree for country cooks is stew, for it can be made
early in the morning, put in a slow oven to cook, and forgotten until
dinnertime. A simple green salad would complete the meal.

2 pounds beef stew meat
3–4 potatoes
3–4 carrots
2 ribs celery
3 small onions
1 28-ounce can tomatoes
¼ cup water
5 tablespoons minute tapioca
2 tablespoons Worcestershire sauce

1 tablespoon brown sugar
1 teaspoon salt
½ teaspoon black pepper
½ teaspoon ground allspice
¼ teaspoon dried marjoram
¼ teaspoon dried thyme
1 bay leaf
½ cup chopped fresh parsley

Preheat oven to 300° F. Cut meat into bite-size pieces. Peel and cut the potatoes into pieces a bit larger than the meat. Clean the carrots, celery, and onions, and cut all into 1-inch pieces. In a large, heavy roasting pan, or a ceramic slow-cooker pot, combine all the ingredients except the parsley. Bake, covered, for 5 hours without stirring. Add parsley just before serving.
NOTE: This dish does not freeze well.

SPARERIBS AND SAUERKRAUT

Serves 8

Spareribs and sauerkraut—a perfect combination. Use the meatier pork loin country-style spareribs for this. The kraut is expertly seasoned with apple, onion, and whole cloves. Potato Pancakes (page 191) are good with this dish.

6–7 pounds pork loin country-style
    spareribs
    Salt and pepper
3 1-pound cans sauerkraut, preferably
    mild Bavarian style
1½ cups coarsely chopped cooking apples,
    such as Yellow Delicious or
    Granny Smith

¾ cup coarsely chopped onion
8 whole cloves
2–4 tablespoons brown sugar
¼ teaspoon black pepper
1½ cups Homemade Chicken Broth
    (page 159), or canned broth.
    Chopped fresh parsley

Preheat broiler. Arrange the ribs in a shallow roasting pan, and sprinkle with salt and pepper to taste on all sides. Broil 6 inches from heat, browning all sides; this will take about 30 minutes.

Reduce oven to 325° F. Drain sauerkraut very well. In a deep, heavy Dutch oven, combine kraut and the remaining ingredients except parsley. Arrange ribs on top, pushing them down into the sauerkraut. Cover and bake for 2 hours. Baste twice by spooning pan juices up over the ribs. Make sure the liquid does not cook away; if it gets low, add more stock. (This will not be a problem if you use a heavy pan.) Transfer ribs and sauerkraut to a large platter, and sprinkle with parsley.

MASHED CARROTS AND PARSNIPS

Serves 4

Combining carrots and parsnips is an inspired notion.

4 large carrots (approximately 1 pound)
6 large parsnips (approximately 1
    pound)
3 whole cloves
2 teaspoons granulated sugar

½ teaspoon salt
2 tablespoons (¼ stick) butter
2 tablespoons brown sugar
    Finely minced fresh mint or new green
    onion tops

Scrape the carrots and slice coarsely. Peel the parsnips, and cut in half lengthwise. Cut again and remove the pithy centers. In a deep saucepan, place the carrots, parsnips, cloves, granulated sugar, salt, and water to cover. Cover pan, bring to a boil over high heat, and cook 25 to 30 minutes, or until the vegetables are tender. Drain, removing the cloves, and then add the butter and brown sugar. Mash with a potato masher (or use the food processor) and place in a serving dish. Sprinkle the mint or green onions over the top.

HOMEMADE NOODLES

◆

Makes 4 cups dry noodles, or 6 servings

If you have never made homemade noodles, let me assure you that
they are very easy to do—the recipe is just another version of homemade pasta. How
thin you roll the dough will probably depend on your own memories of how
thick or thin the noodles were at your grandmother's house. I like to
roll the dough not too thick but not paper-thin, either. Using bread flour gives a better
noodle because the flour is higher in gluten and more like
the way flour used to be.

1 cup bread flour
¾ teaspoon salt
1 egg

1 tablespoon vegetable oil
3 tablespoons water
Bread flour for rolling and dusting

Place the flour in a medium mixer bowl. Make a well in the center, and add the rest of the ingredients. With a fork, stir to combine until a ball of dough forms. Turn out onto a lightly floured board or cloth and knead until a smooth dough is achieved—about 5 minutes. You can add more water if you absolutely have to, a teaspoonful at a time, but the noodles will be better if you don't. Cover dough with a tea towel and allow to rest for 45 minutes.

Cut the dough in half. Roll out one-half to an approximate 14 x 8-inch rectangle; it will not be quite paper-thin. Sprinkle dough surface lightly with a bit more flour, flip over, and sprinkle more flour on the other side. Transfer to a tea towel and repeat with remaining dough. Allow the rolled-out dough to stand 20 to 30 minutes.

Roll dough up like a jelly roll, starting from the short side. Using a very sharp knife, cut noodles to the width you prefer. Unroll each slice onto the tea towel, sprinkle with a bit more flour, and allow to stand until noodles are completely dry—this may take several hours, depending on the humidity in the air or the amount of moisture in the flour.

To use, cook noodles in simmering salted water or broth for 5 to 7 minutes or until tender. Allow ½ cup dried noodles per serving. (The cooking time will vary considerably, depending on the flour, humidity, and so on, so taste to check for doneness.) Use for buttered noodles (page 29), Beef and Noodles (page 67), or Fried Noodles (page 50).

OPPOSITE: *It's noodle day in this Amish farm home near Berne.*
Flour from hard spring wheat makes the best noodles. **BELOW:** *The dough rests twice before*
being cut into strips.

FRIED NOODLES

Serves 4

Fried Noodles doubtless came into being as a way to use leftovers. Actually, they are so good that it is too bad the dish has such a humble reputation.

3–3½ cups fine noodles (approximately ½ pound)
3 tablespoons chopped onion

2 tablespoons chopped fresh parsley
¼ teaspoon Tabasco
¼ cup (½ stick) butter

Cook noodles according to package directions (or see page 48). Drain them well in a colander. To the noodles (and you can do this while they are still in the colander—anything to save a dish), add the onion, parsley, and Tabasco and toss.

Melt the butter in a large skillet. Add the noodles and pat them into an even layer. Cook over low heat, uncovered, for about 15 minutes, gently turning with a spatula as they become golden brown.

HASH BROWNED POTATOES

Serves 4

One of the tests of any country cook is the quality of her Hash Browned Potatoes. Crunchy on the outside, creamy on the inside, and with a hint of onion, these hash browns traditionally are sautéed in either bacon or rendered chicken fat. But they are still pretty good cooked in vegetable oil. For perfect results, use an electric skillet.

3 large potatoes, boiled
¼ cup milk
3 tablespoons all-purpose flour
2 tablespoons minced onion
2 tablespoons minced fresh parsley or chervil

½ teaspoon salt
½ teaspoon black pepper
¼ teaspoon dried oregano (optional)
Dash of Tabasco
3 tablespoons bacon drippings, rendered chicken fat, or vegetable oil

Preheat an electric skillet to 300° F. Peel and dice the boiled potatoes and place in a medium bowl; you should have about 3 cups. Add the rest of the ingredients, except the cooking fat, and blend.

Add the cooking fat to the skillet and heat. Pack the potato mixture in firmly, spreading it out in an even layer. Cook 7 to 9 minutes, or until the bottom side is richly brown. Turn the mixture over in segments, and smooth down again into a pattie. Continue cooking until the other side is browned, another 7 to 9 minutes. Cut into wedges and serve.

STEAMED BREAD PUDDING

Serves 8

This elegant dessert has a flanlike caramel topping. Believe me,
this is not your usual bread pudding.

1 cup brown sugar
½ cup seedless raisins
5 thin slices good-quality white bread
¼ cup (½ stick) butter, softened
3 eggs

2 cups milk
1 teaspoon vanilla extract
½ teaspoon ground cinnamon
¼ teaspoon salt

In the top of an oiled double boiler, mix the brown sugar and raisins. Remove crusts from bread, butter the slices on one side, and then cut them into ½-inch cubes; you should have about 2 cups. Place the cubes on top of the brown-sugar mixture.

In a medium bowl, beat the eggs lightly, then add the remaining ingredients—just blend, don't overmix. Pour the egg mixture over the bread cubes, but do not stir in. Cook, covered, over simmering water, for about 1 hour and 20 minutes. A knife inserted in the center should come out fairly clean. (Pudding will continue cooking after taken out of pan, so don't worry if it is still a bit shaky at the end of the cooking time.)

Immediately loosen the edges of the pudding with a rubber spatula and invert onto a 12-inch round platter with a lip. Arrange any stray raisins decoratively around the edge of the platter. Serve warm.

CHOCOLATE FUDGE PUDDING

Serves 8

This pudding has a brownie texture, and also forms its own
chocolate sauce as it bakes. It is quick and easy to prepare and is a perfect family dessert.
Serve it a bit warm.

1 cup sifted all-purpose flour
2 teaspoons baking powder
1 teaspoon salt
⅔ cup granulated sugar
6 tablespoons cocoa powder
½ cup milk

2 tablespoons (¼ stick) butter, melted
1 teaspoon vanilla extract
½ cup chopped pecans
1 cup brown sugar
1½ cups boiling water

Preheat oven to 350° F. Sift together the flour, baking powder, salt, granulated sugar, and 2 tablespoons of the cocoa into a large bowl. Add the milk, butter, and vanilla; mix only until smooth. Stir in the pecans, then transfer to an oiled 1-quart (10 x 6-inch) baking dish.

In a medium bowl, combine the brown sugar and the remaining 4 tablespoons cocoa; sprinkle over the top of the chocolate mixture. Pour the boiling water over all, and do not stir in. Bake for 40 minutes, or until the top appears to be firm. Remove from oven and allow to stand for 10 minutes before cutting into squares. Serve warm, pudding side up. If the dessert is made in advance, it can be covered with foil and reheated in a low oven or in the microwave.

SUMMER
DAYS

Summer in northern Indiana is a mellow, generous time, with hazy soft mornings and limpid nights punctuated by the sound of crickets and the miniature lamps of fireflies darting about in the dusk ◆ The July days are long; the cloudless blue skies cover fields of wheat where Amish farmers stack shocks of grain by hand. Delicate Queen Anne's lace and orange day lilies line the roadsides. The bright blue flower of the chicory weed contrasts smartly with the yellow black-eyed Susans, and blooming elderberry hedges edge the lanes like frothy white embroidery ◆ The newly cut alfalfa hay exudes a sweet musky fragrance, and the sharp cry of the quail can be heard in the meadows. When farmers stop in the fields, they rest in the shade of hedge apple trees lining the fencerows. Their wives send the children with lemonade or rhubarb punch and cookies for refreshment. As the men talk quietly among themselves, the cicadas sing a calm, persistent vibrato ◆ Flower gardens flourish in front of these immaculate white farmhouses, and trumpet vines wind their way along the narrow picket fences. Roadside stands offer a dazzling selection of fruits, vegetables, and occasionally home-made breads, rolls, and cookies ◆ The black raspberries are just about finished, but the red ones are coming on, and already the boughs of the early Green Transparent apple trees are heavy with fruit. Everywhere, the call of the bobwhite is heard; his voice is the sound of summer ◆

Flowers are a happy way for the Amish woman to indulge her delight in color and scent.

THE RIPENING GARDEN

The Amish and Mennonites, as well as their neighbors, eat directly from the land. The women and girls do most of the gardening, which is considered light work, even though some of the vegetable patches encompass a quarter of an acre. Sweet corn and melons take extra space and, consequently, are grown along the edges of cultivated fields, rather than in vegetable gardens.

The bounteous gardens spill plenty from every hill and vine, providing a magnificent assortment of vegetables from spring until frost. From June until September, the farmers' markets and roadside stands are visual delights, with tiny zucchini, slender string beans, dusky beets, satiny eggplants, rosy tomatoes, and bouquets of fresh dill to entice the city shopper. The income from these farmstands is generally kept by the women for their personal use.

What is not eaten at the dinner table or sold, the women preserve by canning. In some areas, there are frozen lockers that can be rented in the neighboring towns, and the surplus produce is prepared for freezing and taken to the locker—by buggy, of course.

Second plantings of some vegetables are made in even the smallest garden, and it is possible to find lettuces, sugar snap peas, spinach, red Swiss chard, and tiny beets long after they have disappeared from other markets. Country Gentleman sweet corn, an old variety with deep, narrow, and irregular rows, is sometimes cooked with a bit of milk and sugar to further enhance its sweetness.

In Indiana, produce is prepared simply, without fancy sauces, and with few herbs; the natural flavors shine through. The recipes reflect the hallmarks of midwestern country cooking at its best.

GREEN BEANS WITH
PEANUT SAUCE

CUCUMBERS WITH SOUR
CREAM

EGGPLANT SLICES IN
TOMATO SAUCE

GREEN LIMA BEANS AND
PEAS

SAUTÉED SUGAR SNAP PEAS

LORRAINE POTATOES

QUICK-COOK SPINACH

SUCCOTASH

FRESH TOMATOES AND
ONIONS WITH DILL

CREAMY SAUTÉED
TOMATOES

ZUCCHINI AND TOMATO
CASSEROLE

ZUCCHINI AND TOMATO
SAUTÉ

GREEN BEANS WITH PEANUT SAUCE

Serves 4

Finely chopped peanuts give an interesting texture to green beans.
Sometimes I substitute English walnuts, and that's good, too.

6 cups water
1/2 teaspoon salt
2 teaspoons sugar
1 1/4 pounds green beans

1/4 cup (1/2 stick) butter
1/4 cup chopped peanuts
1/4 teaspoon grated nutmeg
1/4 teaspoon coarsely ground black pepper

In a large kettle, bring the water, salt, and sugar to a boil over high heat. Snip the ends off the beans and, if they are small and slender, leave them whole. If beans are mature, cut them into 1-inch pieces. Add the trimmed beans to the boiling water, allow the water to come to a boil again, then let them cook, uncovered, until they are just tender, about 3 to 4 minutes.

Drain beans in a colander and place in a warmed serving bowl. Return the pan to the stove and melt the butter. Add the peanuts; cook and stir the mixture over medium-high heat until the peanuts are nicely browned, 2 to 3 minutes. Add the seasonings and blend. Pour over the hot green beans and serve.

CUCUMBERS WITH SOUR CREAM

Serves 4

By August, the cucumber vines are producing thick and fast. Many are pickled
for winter use or served at the table in addition to other salads.
Sour cream is the perfect foil for cucumbers, and the following dressing can be
changed to suit your taste by varying the amount of vinegar or sugar.
But it should not be too sweet.

1 cup sour cream
1 scant tablespoon sugar
2 tablespoons cider vinegar
1/4 cup chopped fresh dill
1/4 teaspoon white pepper
1/2 teaspoon salt

1 teaspoon celery seed
2 long, slender cucumbers
1 small onion, the same diameter as the
    cucumber
Chopped fresh dill

In a medium bowl, combine the sour cream, sugar, vinegar, dill, pepper, salt, and celery seed; blend. Pare the cucumber and slice as thin as possible—an old-fashioned potato slicer is good for this, or use the slicing blade on your food processor.

Clean the onion, but slice it by hand, a bit thicker than the cucumber. Add the vegetables to the sour cream mixture and toss lightly. Refrigerate for at least 2 hours so the cucumbers can absorb the dressing. Sprinkle with additional dill and serve.

EGGPLANT SLICES IN TOMATO SAUCE

Serves 6

Eggplant, that dusky purple globe, is one of the less-appreciated vegetables in
the Midwest, and that's a pity. To remove the bitterness that has contributed to
the eggplant's bad reputation, some cooks will salt the slices and allow them to
"weep" before cooking. It works.

1 large eggplant
Coarse salt
Vegetable or olive oil for sautéing
1 tablespoon vegetable or olive oil
1 garlic clove, finely minced
¾ cup chopped onion
1 8-ounce can tomato sauce
1 tablespoon brown sugar

1 tablespoon fresh thyme, or ⅓ teaspoon
dried (optional)
1 teaspoon ground allspice
¼ teaspoon salt
¼ teaspoon black pepper
1 cup grated Swiss cheese
Chopped fresh chives

Peel the eggplant with a vegetable parer, then cut crosswise in ½-inch slices. Sprinkle both sides with the salt and place slices in a colander to drain for 30 minutes.

Pat each eggplant slice dry with a paper towel. Heat 2 tablespoons of oil in an electric skillet to 325° F. Sauté a few eggplant slices on both sides until golden brown, about 4 to 5 minutes on each side. Transfer to paper towels, add more oil to the skillet (eggplant is notorious for soaking up oil, and each eggplant seems to have its own absorption rate), and continue sautéing the eggplant until all the slices are done.

In the meantime, in a medium saucepan, place the 1 tablespoon of oil, the garlic, and onion, and cook over medium heat until the onion is transparent, about 4 minutes. Add the tomato sauce, brown sugar, thyme, allspice, salt, and pepper; simmer 5 minutes.

Remove all drippings from the skillet and discard. Place a layer of eggplant in the bottom of the skillet, then half the sauce, and half the grated cheese. Repeat. Cover the skillet and turn the temperature to low; cook for 20 minutes. Keep warm until ready to serve; it doesn't reheat very well. Sprinkle with the chives just before serving.

GREEN LIMA BEANS AND PEAS

Serves 4–6

By cooking beans and peas in a large amount of water, it takes less time to cook
them and you have fresher-tasting vegetables.

1½ quarts water
2 teaspoons sugar
1½ cups shelled fresh lima beans
    (approximately 2 pounds in shell)
1½ cups shelled fresh peas
    (approximately 2 pounds in pod)

3 tablespoons butter
3 green onions, finely minced, including
    part of the tops
2 tablespoons fresh savory (optional)
¼ teaspoon salt

In a large, deep kettle, bring the water and sugar to a boil over high heat. Add the lima beans, bring the water back to a boil, and cook 2 minutes. Don't cover the pot during any of the cooking time—that way the vegetables will stay green. Add the peas to the kettle and cook 2 minutes longer, then test for doneness; if they are young and freshly picked, vegetables will cook very quickly.

Drain the vegetables in a colander, and return the pan to the stove. Melt the butter, return the vegetables to the pan, add the green onions, savory, and salt, and toss lightly until beans and peas are coated with the butter.

SAUTÉED SUGAR SNAP PEAS

Serves 4

This novelty pea with an edible pod has developed into a popular vegetable.
It has a distinct sweet flavor, and I like to toss a few raw ones into spring salads.
And these peas are sweeter cooked than when they are raw. You can eat them pod and all,
so you don't have the boring job of having to shell them.

1 pound sugar snap peas
3 tablespoons vegetable oil
    (½ sesame oil is ideal)
1 teaspoon finely minced garlic

1 tablespoon finely shredded fresh ginger
½ teaspoon salt
¼ teaspoon black pepper
⅓ cup julienned red onion

String the peas by beginning at the tip of the pea and pulling it down; if the peas are very young, you can omit this step. Cut off the stem ends and leave the peas whole. Place in a colander and rinse under cold water; shake well and drain.

In a large skillet, heat the oil. Add the garlic and ginger and sauté briefly, about 30 seconds. Add the peas and, over medium-high heat, toss and cook for 2 to 4 minutes, depending on how large they are. Do not overcook. Add the salt, pepper, and red onion just as they are finishing cooking. Serve immediately. **NOTE:** An attractive variation on this dish is to substitute a julienned red bell pepper for the onion. It should be added when the peas are about half cooked.

LORRAINE POTATOES

Serves 6–8

Lorraine Potatoes readily reveal their origin.

5 medium potatoes
¼–⅓ cup bacon drippings or vegetable oil
   Salt and black pepper
2 eggs
½ cup grated Parmesan cheese

1½ cups milk
½ teaspoon grated nutmeg
1 tablespoon chopped fresh parsley
Paprika

Preheat oven to 400° F. Peel potatoes and slice thin. Heat the bacon drippings or oil in a 10-inch cast-iron or ovenproof skillet over medium-high heat. Add the potatoes in layers, sprinkling each layer with salt and pepper. Reduce heat to medium-low, partially cover, and sauté potatoes, turning them now and then carefully with a metal spatula without breaking them up. This takes longer than you might think, for you want as many of them browned as possible and completely cooked—approximately 20 minutes.

In a medium bowl, slightly beat the eggs; blend in the cheese, milk, nutmeg, and parsley. Pour over the potatoes. Sprinkle paprika on top. Bake uncovered for 10 minutes.

QUICK-COOK SPINACH

Serves 4

Spinach is gathered by the dishpanful and brought into Amish kitchens to use in salads, to freeze, and to quick-cook as a vegetable side dish. Spinach is inclined to be sandy, so be sure to rinse it several times until the water is completely clear.

2 pounds fresh spinach
3 tablespoons butter
3 tablespoons vegetable or sesame oil
½ teaspoon sugar

½ teaspoon salt
¼ teaspoon black pepper
⅓ cup julienned red onion
Lemon wedges (optional)

Cut the roots off the spinach and remove the heavier stems. Rinse well. In a large skillet, melt the butter and oil. Add the spinach, and cook over very high heat, tossing constantly with a long-handled fork. Cook only about a minute—the water clinging to the leaves is sufficient moisture. Add the rest of the ingredients and toss. Serve immediately with lemon wedges, if desired.

SUCCOTASH

Serves 8

An attractive dish combining two vegetables, succotash is frequently frozen or canned for winter use and appears on the Thanksgiving Day table. Some cooks even add a few pieces of fresh tomato just before serving. Personally, I frown on that version; the original is fine just the way it is.

4 ears fresh corn, husked and silked
2 cups shelled lima beans
(approximately 2½ pounds, in pod)
2 cups water
½ cup half-and-half

3 tablespoons butter
2 teaspoons finely minced fresh savory,
or ½ teaspoon dried (optional)
¼ teaspoon salt
¼ teaspoon black pepper

Bring a kettle of water to a rolling boil over high heat, add the corn, and after the water again returns to a full boil, cook the corn for 3 minutes. Remove the corn with tongs and refresh under cold water. Cut the kernels off the ear and measure out 2 cups; set aside.

Place the lima beans and water in a deep saucepan over high heat. Cover, bring to a boil, reduce heat, and simmer for 15 minutes. Drain.

In the same saucepan, combine the corn, lima beans, and rest of the ingredients. Simmer, uncovered, over medium heat to reduce the cream a bit; the corn will also absorb some. Serve in individual dishes.

FRESH TOMATOES AND ONIONS WITH DILL

Serves 6–8

Dill reseeds itself and comes up year after year in rural gardens, and because of
its availability, the soft, feathery green leaves are a commonly used
seasoning in many vegetable dishes, including tossed green salads. This simple
country recipe of tomatoes and dill is a perfect accompaniment
to broiled chicken or steak.

6 large tomatoes	*½ teaspoon freshly ground black pepper*
2 large onions	*2¼ teaspoons celery seed*
2 tablespoons fresh lemon juice	*2½ teaspoons sugar*
½ teaspoon salt	*5 tablespoons chopped fresh dill*

Peel tomatoes and onions, and cut into thin slices. Separate the onions into rings. On a large serving platter with a lip, arrange alternate rows of tomatoes and onion rings.

In a small bowl, combine the remaining ingredients. Pour over the tomatoes and onions, tucking the dill under and between the tomatoes. Refrigerate for at least 2 hours. Pour the dressing off the tomatoes into a small bowl and then pour it back over them 2 times during this period.

CREAMY SAUTÉED TOMATOES

Serves 6–10

This is a favorite recipe during tomato season. The creamy pan gravy
poured over the tops of the tomatoes is a fine addition. Use firm tomatoes,
just orange-ripe but without green streaks.

6 medium tomatoes	*1½ teaspoons sugar*
3 tablespoons all-purpose flour	*1 teaspoon Heinz 57 Steak Sauce*
¾ teaspoon salt	*1 teaspoon prepared mustard*
¼ teaspoon black pepper	*1½ cups milk*
¼ cup (½ stick) butter	*Chopped fresh parsley*

Core, but do not peel tomatoes. Halve crosswise and set aside.

Combine 1 tablespoon flour, salt, and pepper in a saucer. Sprinkle over the tomato halves. Melt the butter in a large skillet until bubbling. Add the tomatoes and sauté on both sides over medium-low heat until they are golden brown and just tender, 3 to 4 minutes. Transfer 10 tomato halves to a large hot platter. Mash the remaining 2 tomato halves in the skillet with a wooden spoon. Add remaining 2 tablespoons of flour, and cook, stirring continually until mixture bubbles up. Add the remaining ingredients except the parsley, and cook, over medium-low heat, stirring, until mixture is creamy. Pour over the tomatoes and garnish with parsley.

ZUCCHINI AND TOMATO CASSEROLE

Serves 10–12

It's hard to come up with different ways to use summer vegetables. This old Dunkard recipe is a real winner and is a good buffet dish. Unfortunately, it doesn't freeze.

12 very small zucchini
12 small tomatoes
1 very large onion
  Salt and black pepper
  Brown sugar

Fresh or dried basil (optional)
1½ cups soda cracker crumbs
  ½ cup (1 stick) butter, in pieces
1¼ cups grated sharp cheddar cheese

Preheat oven to 350° F. Wash and thinly slice zucchini. Peel and thinly slice tomatoes and onion; divide onion into rings. In a deep, oiled 3-quart casserole, place a layer of zucchini, tomatoes, and onion rings. Sprinkle a bit of salt, pepper, brown sugar, and basil over the onion. Then add a liberal handful of crumbs, a few bits of butter, and a handful of cheese. Repeat twice; the top layer should be cheese. Bake, covered, for a total of 1¼ hours; remove lid after ½ hour and continue baking for another 45 minutes, or until the center is bubbling hot.

ZUCCHINI AND TOMATO SAUTÉ

Serves 4

The original recipe uses bacon in this hearty vegetable dish, but if you prefer, substitute olive oil and then it becomes a sort of ratatouille. Either way, you use up a lot of zucchini in a very fine fashion.

5 slices bacon, chopped, or
  3 tablespoons olive oil
1 medium onion, coarsely chopped
1 medium zucchini, thinly sliced
1 large tomato, peeled, seeded, and
  chopped

Pinch of sugar
Salt and black pepper
2 tablespoons chopped fresh basil
  (optional)

Sauté the bacon in a large skillet over medium heat until it is half-cooked or substitute the olive oil and heat. Then add the onion and zucchini and cook together, covered, until the zucchini is done, about 2 to 3 minutes. Add the tomato along with remaining ingredients; toss just to mix. Cover, and allow the mixture to stand for 2 minutes. You don't want the tomato to cook; it should just be heated through. Serve immediately.

THE BARN RAISING

The Amish are not only a spiritual community, they are a "community people" and they sustain each other. This is never more aptly demonstrated than during a barn raising. It takes at least 100 to 150 men to put up the framework of a barn in one day, and the activity is lively. The barn's design is similar to a Dutch gambrel roof barn, featuring an upper storage level with trapdoors in the floor so hay can be pitched down to the animals below.

On the day of the barn raising, the men arrive at dawn with their nail aprons and hammers; the women come soon after, bringing food for both the noon meal and an afternoon snack. Tables are set up under the trees, and church benches are brought to the site for seating. By noon the framework of the barn is up, and the women have finished the final preparation of the food and have arranged it on long tables. It is a bountiful display of crisp fried chicken, huge whole baked hams, mashed potatoes and gravy, fresh noodles, many kinds of salads, fresh fruit bowls, relishes, puddings, apple butter, bread and rolls, and, of course, pies and cakes. Coffee and a fruit drink are served. After eating, the men return to work, the women clear the dishes and then can sit down and talk until it is time for them to prepare an afternoon snack of cold drinks and desserts for the carpenters. By nightfall, the barn will be under roof.

A list of food needed for an 1850s barn-raising meal for 175 men was recently reprinted in Emma Showalter's *Mennonite Community Cookbook*. When I showed this list to Esther Hochstetler, an Amish woman, she said with some humor, "Well, it hasn't changed much, though we don't make doughnuts for barn raisings anymore. We do things a bit easier these days."

When I considered that these meals for a hundred men are still prepared in kitchens without electricity, dishwashers, food processors, or air-conditioning and then transported many miles, I had to admire her spirit and interpretation of "ease."

ROASTED BEEF BRISKET

OVEN-FRIED CHICKEN

AMISH DRESSING

BEEF AND NOODLES

CHURCH-SUPPER HAM
LOAF

DRIED LIMA BEAN
CASSEROLE

BAKED GERMAN POTATO
SALAD

PEA SALAD

LEMONADE MADE IN A
CROCK

BUTTERSCOTCH TAPIOCA

Here's the list:

115 lemon pies	300 light rolls
500 fat cakes (doughnuts)	16 loaves bread
3 gallons applesauce	red beets and pickled eggs
3 gallons rice pudding	cucumber pickle
3 gallons cornstarch pudding	6 pounds dried prunes, stewed
16 chickens	1 large crock stewed raisins
3 hams	5-gallon stone jar white potatoes and
50 pounds roast beef	the same amount of sweet potatoes

ROASTED BEEF BRISKET

Makes 12–16 hearty servings

The beef cookery in this area is relatively plain. Roasts, simply seasoned,
are most popular. The cattle here are range-fed, which is reflected in the meat's deep,
distinctive flavor. When you start with a good fresh product,
lots of extras aren't necessary to enhance the dish.
On barn-raising days, several kinds of meats are served.
This recipe is especially good, since the preparation starts the day before, then
the roast is presliced and easily transportable.

5 pounds fresh brisket (not rolled),
well trimmed
4 garlic cloves, peeled
2 teaspoons salt
1½ teaspoons paprika

1 teaspoon black pepper
3 tablespoons lemon juice
½ cup water
1 large onion
3 small bay leaves

The night before serving, place the brisket in a 13 x 8-inch glass baking dish. In a saucer, mash the garlic with the salt. Add the paprika, pepper, and lemon juice and combine. Spread on both sides of the meat. Cover and refrigerate overnight.

To roast, preheat oven to 425° F. Coat a heavy roasting pan with vegetable spray and place the meat in it, fat side up. Add ½ cup water and bake, uncovered, for about 45 minutes, or until the roast is nicely browned. Add more water if necessary—you don't want the drippings in the bottom of the pan to scorch.

Slice the onion and place it on top of the roast. Add an additional cup of water and the bay leaves. Cover, reduce oven temperature to

325° F., and bake it a total of 3 hours longer. Add more water from time to time—you want plenty of pan juices, but the roast shouldn't be swimming in liquid, either.

After it has cooked for 1½ hours, remove the meat from the oven, place on a carving board, and slice thinly. Return meat to pan, putting it back in its original shape as neatly as you can. Spoon some pan juices over it and bake 1½ hours longer, watching it carefully so it doesn't bake dry. Serve with pan juices.
NOTE: By slicing the roast when it is partially done, you'll have neater slices that hold together when served, and you save last-minute preparation time.

OVEN-FRIED CHICKEN

◆

Serves 4–5

This is the best fried chicken recipe I've tried, bar none. It is quick to prepare and doesn't require watching. The outside is crusty, and the inside moist. The flour mixture can be made up in large amounts and stored to use as needed.

⅓ cup vegetable oil
⅓ cup (⅔ stick) butter
1 cup all-purpose flour
1 teaspoon salt
2 teaspoons black pepper

2 teaspoons paprika
1 teaspoon garlic salt
1 teaspoon dried marjoram (optional)
8–9 chicken pieces—legs, thighs, breasts

Place the oil and butter in a shallow cooking pan (a jelly-roll pan is perfect) and put in a preheated 375° F. oven to melt. Set aside.

In a large paper sack, combine the flour and seasonings. Roll the chicken pieces, 3 at a time, in the melted oil-butter mixture, then drop them in the sack and shake to cover. Place on a dish or wax paper.

Place chicken in the pan, skin side down.

Bake for 45 minutes. With a spatula, turn over and bake 5 to 10 minutes longer, or until the top crust begins to bubble. Serve hot or cold, but the crust texture is better if chicken is not refrigerated before eating. If you can afford the calories, the pan drippings make an absolutely divine gravy for either mashed potatoes or Baking Powder Biscuits (page 4).

AMISH DRESSING

Serves 16–20

I especially like this bread dressing—it is so colorful with its flecks of carrot, celery, and parsley. And the texture is heartier too, with tiny bits of diced potato and chicken. Serve it with fried chicken and lots of chicken gravy to ladle over the top.

2 1-pound loaves good-quality bread, cut
    in ½-inch cubes (about 4 quarts)
2 pounds poached chicken thighs
½ cup minced fresh parsley
¾ cup chopped onion
1 cup chopped celery
1 cup shredded carrot
1¼ cups finely chopped boiled potatoes
1 tablespoon rubbed sage

1 tablespoon celery seed
1 teaspoon dried thyme
½ teaspoon black pepper
½ tablespoon turmeric
5 eggs
1 12-ounce can evaporated milk
2½ cups Homemade Chicken Broth
    (page 159), or canned broth

Preheat oven to 350° F. On 2 cookie sheets, toast the bread cubes for 15 minutes, or until the bread is golden brown. Transfer to a very large mixer bowl.

Bone the chicken and very finely chop the meat, discarding the skin. (I do this in the food processor while chicken is still warm.) Add the chopped vegetables and chicken meat to the bread, along with the seasonings. Toss.

In a medium bowl, beat the eggs; add the evaporated milk and broth. Pour over the bread mixture and blend. The mixture will be quite moist. Allow to stand 1 hour.

Preheat oven to 350° F. Transfer the dressing to an oiled 3-quart glass casserole that is 10 inches in diameter and 3 inches deep (at this point, dressing can be frozen for future use; thaw before baking). Bake dressing for 2 hours, or until the center of the dressing puffs up and is golden brown on top.

BEEF AND NOODLES

Serves 12

Beef and noodles is a staple at large Amish gatherings. And dieters will be horrified to find that the best way to eat this dish is on top of mashed potatoes. If having them on potatoes is too much for you, serve the mixture in shallow bowls, for it is a bit soupy.

A country cook makes her own noodles, but since most of you probably won't, this recipe uses commercial ones—they will be able to absorb the broth during the long, gentle cooking. For an even richer flavor, instant beef bouillon granules can be added, but they do contain MSG, so that is an optional ingredient.

3 pounds beef chuck roast, well trimmed
1 large onion, quartered
8 whole cloves
1 small green bell pepper, quartered,
    with seeds and ribs removed
2 large carrots, cleaned and cut
    in thirds
3 ribs celery, cut in thirds
1 cup fresh parsley sprigs

2 bay leaves
¼ cup instant beef bouillon granules
    (optional)
½ teaspoon black pepper
3 quarts hot water
1 1-pound package medium or thin
    good-quality noodles
½ cup chopped fresh parsley

Preheat the oven to 325° F. Place the meat in a large Dutch oven or heavy roasting pan with the rest of the ingredients, except the noodles and parsley garnish. Cover and bake for 3 hours.

Remove the pan from the oven and transfer the meat to a chopping board. Scoop all the vegetables from the broth with a slotted spoon and discard them, reserving 1 or 2 pieces of carrot. With a knife, shred the meat into bite-size pieces, and chop the carrots very finely. Return the meat and carrots to the broth. Stir in the uncooked noodles. Cover the pan and return it to the oven. Bake 1 hour and 15 minutes longer, or until the noodles are tender. Stir once during this time, being careful not to break up the noodles. Also check now and then to see that the broth has not been absorbed by the cooking noodles—if your pan is a heavy one, that won't happen. If it does, add some additional broth as needed. Sprinkle with the chopped parsley just before serving. **NOTE:** This dish freezes very well.

CHURCH-SUPPER HAM LOAF

◆

Serves 8–10

This is not just another ho-hum ham loaf. It is a *superb* ham loaf. The sour cream and seasonings make the difference. Do not fail to make the sweet-and-sour basting sauce.

1 pound ground ham
1 pound lean sausage,
   at room temperature
2 cups soft bread crumbs
2 eggs
1 cup sour cream
1/3 cup chopped onion
2 tablespoons lemon juice
1 teaspoon curry powder

1 teaspoon ground ginger
1 teaspoon powdered mustard
1/8 tablespoon grated nutmeg
1/8 teaspoon paprika
BASTING SAUCE
   1 cup brown sugar
1/2 cup water
1/2 cup cider vinegar
1/4 teaspoon black pepper

Preheat oven to 350° F. In a large mixer bowl, lightly but thoroughly combine the meats and crumbs; use your hands if necessary. In a medium bowl, beat the eggs and add the sour cream, onion, lemon juice, and spices. Mix well, pour over the meat mixture, and blend. Form mixture into a loaf and place in an oiled 9 x 13-inch baking dish. Bake uncovered for 1 hour.

Meanwhile, prepare the basting sauce. In a small saucepan, combine the brown sugar with the remaining ingredients and bring to a boil. When the ham loaf has baked for 45 minutes, remove from oven and drain off the excess fat. Pour the sauce over the loaf and continue baking another 15 minutes, basting now and then with the pan juices.
NOTE: The unbaked loaf freezes very well.

DRIED LIMA BEAN CASSEROLE

Serves 6–8

Boston-type Baked Beans (page 90) are served often at Amish and Mennonite carry-in dinners, and every cook has her own favorite recipe for that good dish. However, this lima bean casserole is just as hearty, and the creamy sweet sauce has its own distinctive flavor. The dried beans must soak overnight, so plan accordingly.

1 pound large dried lima beans
2 quarts cold water
   Pinch of baking soda
1/2 cup (1 stick) butter
1 cup brown sugar
1/4 cup molasses
1 cup sour cream

1/2 cup chopped onion
1 tablespoon powdered mustard
1/2 teaspoon salt
1/4 teaspoon black pepper
4 slices bacon, cut into 1-inch pieces
   Chopped fresh parsley

In a large kettle, soak beans overnight in the cold water.

The next day, add a pinch of baking soda and bring to a boil. Skim off foam. Lower heat, cover partially, and cook over low heat for 30 to 45 minutes or until beans are tender. Preheat oven to 250° F. Cooking time will vary, and you don't want the beans mushy, so watch them. Drain, and transfer beans to an oiled 2-quart flat glass baking dish.

In the same kettle (save yourself a dish), melt the butter. Add the brown sugar and mo-lasses and cook over low heat about 2 minutes, until the sugar is dissolved. Remove from heat and let cool slightly. Stir in the sour cream, onion, mustard, salt, and pepper. Pour the butter-sugar sauce over the beans and mix lightly. Arrange bacon pieces over the top. Cover and bake for 1¼ to 1½ hours, removing the cover after 30 minutes. Do not allow the beans to cook too long; the dish should have a bit of a sauce, but not be too runny. Garnish with the chopped parsley.

BAKED GERMAN POTATO SALAD
◆
Serves 10–12

German potato salad is a hearty side dish and often served at large gatherings,
since it keeps well without refrigeration and is served at room temperature.
Bits of bacon and parsley fleck this well-seasoned salad,
which is baked in the oven.

1 cup diced bacon (scant 5 ounces)
1 cup chopped celery
1 cup chopped onion
3 tablespoons all-purpose flour
1 teaspoon salt
½ teaspoon black pepper
⅔ cup sugar

⅔ cup cider vinegar
1½ cups water
⅓ cup chopped fresh parsley
2 teaspoons celery seed
2 quarts potatoes, boiled, peeled, sliced
⅛ inch thick (red ones are ideal)

Fry the bacon until crisp in a medium skillet. Remove with a slotted spoon and reserve. If there is not approximately ¼ cup of fat left in skillet, add additional bacon fat or vegetable oil to make that amount. Add the celery and onion and cook over medium heat for 3 minutes. Add flour, salt, and pepper and cook 2 minutes longer. Then add the sugar, vinegar, and water all at once and, stirring with a whisk, bring to a boil and cook 1 minute. Add the parsley, celery seed, and reserved bacon and combine; remove from heat.

Preheat the oven to 375° F. Place potatoes in an oiled 13 x 8 x 2-inch casserole and pour the dressing over all. Mix very gently so potatoes aren't broken up. Bake for 45 minutes or until the middle of the casserole bubbles.

PEA SALAD

Serves 6

A beloved salad of Midwesterners that dates back to Depression days, this
combination of canned peas, cubes of natural cheese, and peanuts is special—really.
You still find this dish at church socials and at an occasional country restaurant.

*1 14-ounce can good-quality canned
peas, drained*
*1 cup cubed, mild longhorn or cheddar
cheese*
1 cup salted peanuts (6-ounce bag)
⅓ cup chopped celery
¼ cup chopped onion
*¼ cup chopped sweet pickle pieces
(not relish)*
¼ cup chopped fresh parsley

2 tablespoons chopped green bell pepper
*1 tablespoon chopped red bell pepper, or
canned red pimiento*
1 hard-cooked egg, coarsely chopped
*4 heaping tablespoons creamy salad
dressing*
1 teaspoon lemon juice
1 teaspoon prepared mustard
1 teaspoon celery seed

Combine all the ingredients in the order
given in a large bowl and mix lightly. Chill
for several hours in a tightly covered container
to allow the flavors to meld.

LEMONADE MADE IN A CROCK

Serves 6–8

Though this lemonade is traditionally made in a crock, it is just as delicious
when made in a bowl. Pressing the sliced lemons releases the oils in the
rind and gives this lemonade a superior flavor. Serve it with
cookies on a hot afternoon.

4 large lemons
¾ cup sugar
1 quart water

Ice cubes—enough to fill 8 glasses
Fresh mint

Wash fruit well and cut into thin slices;
remove seeds. Place the lemon slices in a small
crock or heavy pitcher. Cover the fruit with
sugar and mix. Let stand for 10 minutes.
Press lemons firmly with a potato masher
to extract the juice and oil from the rinds. Add
the water, and continue to mash the fruit until
the liquid is well flavored. Just before serving,
add ice cubes. Garnish with mint.

BUTTERSCOTCH TAPIOCA

◆

Makes 2½ quarts, or 12–16 servings

Every Amish and Mennonite restaurant has this buttery, rich pudding on its menu, and it is always served at Amish gatherings. The addition of the browned butter is a definite regional touch, and certainly enhances this dessert. Using dark brown sugar instead of light brown makes it, well, more butterscotchy. The recipe can be halved.

10 cups water
¾ teaspoon salt
1¼ cups small pearl tapioca (see note)
2 cups dark brown sugar, no substitutes
2 eggs

1 cup milk
½ cup granulated sugar
½ cup plus 2 tablespoons (1¼ sticks) butter (not margarine)
2 teaspoons vanilla extract

Bring the water and salt to a boil in a large, deep saucepan. Sprinkle in the tapioca and cook, uncovered, over medium heat for 15 minutes, stirring often. Add the dark brown sugar, lower the heat a little, and cook 5 minutes longer, or until tapioca is clear.

In a small bowl, beat the eggs. Add the milk and granulated sugar and blend. Stir 1 cup of the hot tapioca mixture into the egg-milk mixture, then combine it with the rest of the tapioca. Continue cooking over low heat, stirring often, for about 10 minutes or until mixture bubbles up.

In the meantime, heat the butter in a small saucepan over medium heat until it is light brown. Add to the bubbling pudding, along with the vanilla, and mix well. Pour into a 3-quart serving bowl and allow to cool to room temperature. This pudding will set up without refrigeration (approximately 6 hours), and I think it is really better if it can be eaten right away. If you do refrigerate it, allow pudding to come to room temperature before serving, and stir it up a bit to further soften it.

NOTE: Small pearl tapioca does not have to be soaked before cooking.

THE FRUITS RIPEN

In Indiana berry patches and orchards, there is a mouth-watering progression of sweet, lush fruit all summer long, beginning with strawberries, followed by black and red raspberries, pale jade gooseberries, and a specialty of the area, enormous juicy blueberries. Montmorency cherry trees that were a breathtaking sight with their white blooms in May are now heavy with fruit. For the picker and pie maker, it is a race with the birds to see who gets the cherries first.

Tart blackberries are plentiful, and elderberry bushes line the country roads and lanes. The elder blossoms can be made into lacy fritters with a fragrant, delicate taste. Concord grape arbors are in many backyards and provide a shady spot to sit and snap beans for dinner. The Duchess pear, as well as the juicy Bartlett, are eaten out of hand for a quick snack between meals.

Peaches will begin to ripen in late August, and soon after, the apples come into season, though the early Green Transparents, prized for applesauce, will already have come and gone. Apples appear on every table in many guises: sauce, apple butter, compotes, baked, and in astonishing variations of pies, cobblers, and dumplings. Here you can find an occasional orchard that specializes in the old, nearly forgotten varieties that have such lovely names that I just like to say them to feel the words on my tongue: Black Gillyflower, Sops of Wine, Chenango, Spitzenberg. . . . Since many apples are stored in cool cellars all winter, the varieties that keep well have priority when the orchards are planted. Old Amish and Mennonite cookbooks suggest that apple desserts have always been favorites in Indiana. This is Johnny Appleseed country, and the people have taken him and his orchards to their hearts. And kitchens.

FRIED APPLES

BAKED APPLES WITH
BROWN-SUGAR GLAZE

OLD-FASHIONED APPLE
DUMPLINGS

BLACKBERRY ROLL

APPLE CAKE WITH
HOT CARAMEL SAUCE

BLUEBERRY CAKE WITH
STREUSEL TOPPING

BLUEBERRY UPSIDE-DOWN
CAKE

PEACH COBBLER

DEEP-DISH CHERRY PIE

PEACH DUMPLINGS WITH
CUSTARD SAUCE

ELDERBERRY PIE

STRAWBERRY SHORTCAKE

FRIED APPLES

Serves 4–6

What a perfect accompaniment to roast pork!

¼ cup (½ stick) butter
6 cups sliced, unpeeled Jonathan apples
2 tablespoons granulated sugar

2 tablespoons brown sugar
½ teaspoon lemon rind
¼ teaspoon salt

Melt the butter in a large, heavy skillet. Add the remaining ingredients and cook over medium-low heat, uncovered, for 10 minutes. As they cook, turn the apples carefully with a spatula without breaking them.

NOTE: Use only Jonathan apples; they keep their shape, but still become tender.

BAKED APPLES WITH BROWN-SUGAR GLAZE

Serves 4

This is a different sort of baked apple, and once you have tasted it you'll be spoiled. The rich brown-sugar sauce is a perfect counterpoint to the tart apple, and it's easy to prepare. If you can find Northern Spys for this dish, you are in for a *real* treat. This is a good family dessert, and ideal for a brunch buffet table.

4 very large cooking apples, preferably
    Northern Spy
1¾ cups brown sugar
    Scant ¼ cup all-purpose flour
    Speck of salt

2 tablespoons lemon juice
¾ cup water
2 tablespoons (¼ stick) butter
    Ground cinnamon
    Ice cream or half-and-half

Preheat oven to 375° F. Core and quarter the apples; do not peel. Place the apples in a 3-quart buttered baking dish.

Combine the brown sugar, flour, and salt in a small bowl. Stir in the lemon juice and water and pour this mixture over the apples. Dot with butter, and sprinkle cinnamon over all to taste. Bake, uncovered, for 1 hour, basting twice. Serve warm. The apples are nice with a dollop of ice cream on top, or pass a pitcher of cream.

NOTE: In the beginning, the apples may crowd one another, but they shrink during baking. If you can't find Northern Spys, try Cortlands or Granny Smith apples.

OLD-FASHIONED APPLE DUMPLINGS

Serves 6

This is still one of the best apple desserts ever created. Whole apples are wrapped in pastry, and then baked in a clear vanilla sauce. It is served regularly on Hoosier tables.

Pastry for 2 10-inch pie shells
   (page 170)
6 medium-firm cooking apples
2 tablespoons lemon juice
½ cup granulated sugar
1 teaspoon ground cinnamon
⅔ cup brown sugar
2 tablespoons (¼ stick) butter

SAUCE
2 cups water
¾ cup granulated sugar
2 tablespoons (¼ stick) butter
1 teaspoon vanilla extract
⅛ teaspoon ground mace
⅛ teaspoon grated nutmeg
   Cream

Preheat oven to 375° F. Roll out pie dough to form a rectangle 14 x 21 inches. Cut into 6 uniform squares.

Peel and core the apples, but leave them whole. Pour the lemon juice into a small bowl. In another small bowl, combine the granulated sugar and cinnamon. Roll each apple first in the lemon juice, and then in the sugar and place each on top of a dough square. Fill each apple cavity with approximately 2 tablespoons brown sugar and a teaspoon of butter. Pull the pastry squares up over the apples and crimp the edges tightly; you will have pretty round pastry balls. Place in an oiled 9 x 13 x 2-inch pan. Bake for 1 hour or until apples are tender.

While the apples are baking, combine all the sauce ingredients in a medium saucepan set over high heat. Bring to a boil and cook rapidly for 1 minute. After the dumplings have baked for 30 minutes, pour the sauce over the top of the dumplings and bake 30 minutes longer, basting occasionally. Serve hot with cream.

NOTE: Unbaked dumplings, without the sauce, can be frozen before baking. Bake, unthawed, at 400° F for 30 minutes, then cover with the sauce and proceed as above.

BLACKBERRY ROLL

Serves 10

This is a different summer dessert—not too sweet but very satisfying. Blackberries are rolled into a cheese pastry dough, and the jelly roll is baked unsliced. Serve warm in bowls and pass the cream. It is also good cold.

2 cups all-purpose flour
4 teaspoons baking powder
½ teaspoon salt
¼ cup (½ stick) cold butter
1 cup grated sharp cheddar cheese (not
   processed)
¾ cup milk

2½ cups fresh blackberries, or 1
   12-ounce package frozen berries
½ cup plus 2 tablespoons granulated
   sugar
¼ cup brown sugar
½ teaspoon grated nutmeg
   Heavy (whipping) cream

Preheat oven to 350° F. In a mixer bowl or food processor bowl, combine the first 4 ingredients until butter is worked into fine crumbs. Blend in the cheese and then the milk; do not overmix. Roll the dough out lightly into a 10 x 12-inch rectangle, about ⅓ inch thick. Sprinkle the blackberries on top, then add ½ cup of the granulated sugar, the brown sugar, and the nutmeg.

Starting from the long edge, roll up dough like a jelly roll, and transfer to a greased baking sheet, placing it seam side down. Pinch the ends together and fold under. Pat the roll into a tidy bundle and sprinkle the 2 remaining tablespoons sugar on top. Bake for 45 minutes, or until roll is golden brown. Slice and serve warm in bowls with cream.

APPLE CAKE WITH HOT CARAMEL SAUCE

Serves 8

Apple cakes appear in many guises in Amish and Mennonite cookery and date back to the early 1800s. This version, with a hot caramel sauce, is my favorite. The cake gets better as it ages, keeps for a week in the refrigerator, and also freezes well.

½ cup shelled pecans
2 large cooking apples, such as Granny Smiths or Northern Spys
½ cup (1 stick) butter, softened
1 cup granulated sugar
1 egg
1 teaspoon baking soda
¼ teaspoon salt
1 teaspoon ground cinnamon
1 scant teaspoon grated nutmeg

1 cup all-purpose flour
Whipped cream
Fresh apple slices

CARAMEL SAUCE
½ cup (1 stick) butter
1 cup brown sugar
½ teaspoon salt
1 teaspoon vanilla extract
½ cup evaporated milk

Preheat the oven to 350° F. Chop pecans finely, then set aside. Peel, core, and chop apples to equal 2½ cups. Use a food processor for this and chop apples medium-coarse; pieces should be about the size of your thumbnail. Set aside.

In a large mixer bowl, cream the butter. Add the sugar and beat until fluffy. Add egg and beat until blended, then mix in the baking soda, salt, cinnamon, and nutmeg. Add the flour and stir just until blended. Stir in the apples and nuts. Pour into an oiled 9-inch-round cake pan and bake for 30 minutes or until the top springs back when touched lightly

in the center with your finger.

Prepare sauce. In a saucepan, melt the butter, brown sugar, and salt. Bring to a boil, stirring with a whisk, then remove from heat and whisk in the vanilla and milk. (The sauce can be made ahead of time, but then reheat it over hot water.)

To serve, ladle 2 to 3 tablespoons hot caramel sauce onto 8 serving plates. Cut cake in 8 wedges and place on top of sauce. Garnish with a dollop of whipped cream and 2 thinly sliced apple wedges, peel left on. The cake should be served warm (it can be reheated in the microwave) or at least at room temperature.

BLUEBERRY CAKE WITH STREUSEL TOPPING

Serves 12

This velvety blueberry cake is hard to beat.

STREUSEL
- ¼ cup granulated sugar
- ¼ cup brown sugar
- ⅓ cup all-purpose flour
- ½ teaspoon ground cinnamon
- ¼ teaspoon ground mace
- ¼ cup (½ stick) butter, cold

- 6 tablespoons (¾ stick) butter, softened
- ¾ cup granulated sugar

- 1 large egg
- 2 cups all-purpose flour
- 3 tablespoons cornstarch
- 2 teaspoons baking powder
- ¼ teaspoon salt
- 1 teaspoon vanilla extract
- ½ cup milk
- 2 cups fresh blueberries or free-flowing frozen ones

Place the dry streusel ingredients in a food processor bowl. Drop in the butter and pulse until small crumbs form. (This can also be done in a medium mixer bowl with a pastry blender.) Set aside.

Preheat oven to 375° F. In a large mixer bowl, cream the softened butter. Add the sugar a little at a time and beat until mixture is light and fluffy. Add the egg, and beat well. Sift together the flour, cornstarch, baking powder, and salt. Add to the butter mixture, alternating with the combined milk and vanilla, with the mixer on low speed. Stir in the blueberries by hand. Spread the batter evenly in an oiled 8-inch-square cake pan. Spoon the streusel topping evenly over the batter, and bake for 40 to 45 minutes, or until a toothpick comes out clean from the center of the cake. Let cake cool for 15 minutes, then cut into squares and serve warm.

Below: *On a Saturday afternoon, Amish fishermen enjoy throwing out a line on a quiet lake.* **Opposite:** *The children find the fruit at their father's market irresistible.*

BLUEBERRY UPSIDE-DOWN CAKE

Makes 9 small servings

Blueberry Upside-Down Cake is a different way to use this popular fruit. The cake part is soft and tender, with an undertone of orange flavor.

BLUEBERRY TOPPING
1 tablespoon butter
½ cup plus 2 tablespoons brown sugar
2½ cups fresh or frozen blueberries
Speck of salt
½ tablespoon plus 1 teaspoon cornstarch
1 tablespoon water

1 cup sifted cake flour

¼ teaspoon salt
1 teaspoon baking powder
¼ cup plus 1 tablespoon butter, softened
½ cup granulated sugar
1 teaspoon grated orange rind
1 teaspoon vanilla extract
1 egg, beaten
¼ cup orange juice
Sweetened whipped cream (optional)

Make the topping first. In a medium saucepan combine the first 4 topping ingredients, bring to a boil, then simmer over low heat for 10 minutes. Combine the cornstarch and water in a small cup; add to the blueberries and bring to a boil. Set aside, but keep warm while preparing the cake.

Preheat oven to 350° F. Sift the flour, salt, and baking powder together; set aside. In a large mixer bowl, cream the butter, then add the sugar, orange rind, and vanilla. Cream well. Blend in the egg until the mixture is smooth. Add the sifted dry ingredients alternating with the orange juice and beginning and ending with the flour mixture.

Pour the warm berry topping into an oiled round 9-inch pan and then drop the batter (it is too thick to pour) by even tablespoons on top. Using a knife, gently pat the dollops of batter evenly over the fruit, so an even layer of cake batter is formed. This becomes easier as the warm berries soften the batter. You will have some purple streaks in the batter, but that's all right. Bake for 25 minutes, or until the center of the cake springs back when touched with your finger. Invert immediately onto a platter. This can be eaten warm, if you prefer. Top with sweetened whipped cream.

PEACH COBBLER

Serves 6

This dessert is put together in a rather odd fashion: Fresh peaches and soft, unbaked cake crumbs are layered in a pan; additional sugar is sprinkled over the top; and then boiling water is poured over all. During the baking, the cake and peaches marry, and the sugar forms a crackling brown crust on top.

1 cup all-purpose flour
1¼ teaspoons baking powder
1 teaspoon grated nutmeg
½ teaspoon salt
2 tablespoons (¼ stick) butter, softened
1 cup granulated sugar

6–8 peaches, depending on size, peeled and sliced
½ cup brown sugar
1 teaspoon almond extract
1 cup boiling water
Grated nutmeg

Preheat the oven to 350° F. In a small bowl, combine the flour, baking powder, nutmeg, and salt; set aside. In a large mixer bowl, cream the butter, add ½ cup of the granulated sugar, and blend well. Beat in the flour mixture. (Recipe can be prepared to this point up to a day ahead and refrigerated.)

Oil a 9-inch-square cake pan (using a metal pan gives a better texture to this dessert) and place half the peaches on the bottom.

Sprinkle half the flour mixture over the fruit. Add the rest of the peaches and then the rest of the flour mixture. In a small bowl, combine the remaining ½ cup of granulated sugar and the brown sugar; sprinkle over all. Put the almond extract in a 1-cup measure and fill with the boiling water. Pour over the top of the cobbler, but do *not* mix. Sprinkle with additional nutmeg and bake for 1 hour. Serve warm.

DEEP-DISH CHERRY PIE

Serves 6

Traditionally, deep-dish pies have only a top crust, but lots and lots of fruit underneath. I like this crispy, slightly sweet pastry, and the cherry filling is rich with brown sugar. This pie can be made with either fresh or frozen fruit.

4 cups pitted cherries (1½ pounds
*   fresh), or 1 20-ounce frozen bag*
½ cup granulated sugar
½ cup brown sugar
3 tablespoons cornstarch
1 teaspoon almond extract
*   Few drops red food coloring (optional)*
*   Speck of salt*
⅓ cup (⅔ stick) butter, in pieces

CRUST
*   ½ cup plus 2 tablespoons lard*
*   1 tablespoon granulated sugar*
*   ½ teaspoon salt*
*   ½ teaspoon grated nutmeg*
*   1½ cups all-purpose flour*
*   ⅓ cup ice water*
*   Granulated sugar*

Preheat oven to 325° F. In a large bowl, combine the cherries, sugars, cornstarch, extract, food coloring, and salt. If using frozen cherries, add 2 tablespoons of water so the cornstarch will blend smoothly with the rest of the ingredients. Transfer to an oiled 1½-quart casserole. Dot with butter pieces. Set aside while preparing the pastry.

In a large mixer bowl, cream together the lard, sugar, salt, and nutmeg. Add ½ cup of the flour, and stir in lightly by hand. Add 2 tablespoons of ice water and mix lightly. Repeat, adding flour and ice water alternately,

until all the flour and water are used and a soft dough is formed.

Transfer the dough to a floured surface and roll out to fit the top of the casserole. (This will be thicker than a conventional pie crust.) Place the pastry on top of the cherries, patting it firmly against the sides of the dish. Cut slits in the top of the dough and sprinkle liberally with sugar. Bake 1 hour, or until the juices are bubbling up through the slits in the center of the pie and the crust is golden brown. Cool 15 minutes before serving.

PEACH DUMPLINGS WITH CUSTARD SAUCE

Serves 6

A plump pastry bundle of peaches flavored with nutmeg and mace,
sitting in a splodge of of delicate custard sauce, gives the beloved
Apple Dumpling (page 74) stiff competition.

CUSTARD SAUCE
  1 egg
  ¾ cup granulated sugar
  2 tablespoons all-purpose flour
  2 cups milk
  1 teaspoon vanilla extract
  ½ teaspoon almond extract
  ¼ teaspoon salt
SPICED SYRUP
  ½ cup granulated sugar
  1½ cups water
  2 tablespoons (¼ stick) butter
  1 teaspoon vanilla extract

  ¼ teaspoon grated nutmeg
  ¼ teaspoon ground mace
    Speck of salt

  12 small peaches
    Pastry for 2 10-inch pie shells
      (page 170)
  1½ teaspoons minute tapioca
  6 tablespoons brown sugar
  6 tablespoons granulated sugar
    Ground mace
    Grated nutmeg

First prepare the sauce. In the top of a double boiler, slightly beat the egg. Mix in the sugar and flour, then gradually stir in the milk. Cook over simmering water until the mixture is slightly thickened, about 10 to 15 minutes. Let cool to room temperature, then add the remaining ingredients. Chill in refrigerator. (Makes 2½ cups.)

Next prepare the dumplings. Wash and peel the peaches, remove pits, and cut fruit into ⅜-inch slices. Set aside. On a floured cloth or board, roll out the pastry to a 14 x 21-inch rectangle. Cut into 6 uniform squares. In the center of each square, place the following: ⅙ of the peaches, a scant ¼ teaspoon minute tapioca, 1 tablespoon each of brown and granulated sugar, and a sprinkling of mace and nutmeg. Fold corners of each pastry toward

the center, forming a square package. Pinch edges well to seal. (Dumplings can be frozen at this point.)

Preheat oven to 400° F. to prepare the syrup. In a medium saucepan, combine the syrup ingredients and bring to a boil over medium heat. Cook for 1 minute; set aside.

With a metal spatula, transfer the dumplings to an oiled 13 x 8 x 2-inch baking dish. Bake for 10 minutes, then reduce heat to 350° F. and pour the spiced syrup over the top. Bake for 35 minutes more. Let cool slightly. Spoon chilled custard sauce into serving plates or shallow dessert bowls. Top with the warm dumplings and serve.

NOTE: Frozen dumplings should be placed *unthawed* in the oiled baking dish and baked as above.

ELDERBERRY PIE

◆

Serves 8

Elderberries grow along country roadsides on graceful bushes, which in early summer are covered with panicles of white, fragrant, lacy blooms. Later, tiny purple berries appear, and the branches bend down from the weight of the fruit, which begs to be picked. One way of removing the minuscule fruit from its stems is to use a wide-toothed comb, but, mind you, do it gently. This pie is generally served warm with a scoop of ice cream on top.

*Pastry for a 9-inch 2-crust pie
  (page 170)
1 quart elderberries, stems removed
1 cup granulated sugar
¾ cup brown sugar*

*2 tablespoons lemon juice or vinegar
2 tablespoons minute tapioca
½ teaspoon grated nutmeg
¼ teaspoon salt
2 tablespoons (¼ stick) butter, in pieces*

In a large bowl, combine the elderberries, sugars, lemon juice, tapioca, nutmeg, and salt. Stir gently and allow mixture to stand for 10 minutes.

Preheat oven to 425° F. Roll out the crusts and line pie pan with the bottom crust. Pour the fruit mixture into the pie shell, dot with butter, and top with the second crust. Slash the top crust to allow steam to escape. Bake for 15 minutes, reduce heat to 350° F., and continue baking for 25 to 30 minutes longer, or until the juices bubble up in the middle of the pie. Serve warm.

STRAWBERRY SHORTCAKE

◆

Makes 8 generous servings

In this part of the country, a biscuit is the base for strawberry shortcake. This version has cornstarch among its ingredients, which gives it a very smooth texture. The minute the big biscuit is taken from the oven, it is slathered with butter, and partially crushed berries are ladled over the hot wedges.

*1¾ cups all-purpose flour
¼ cup cornstarch
2 tablespoons sugar
4 teaspoons baking powder
1 teaspoon salt
6 tablespoons (¾ stick) butter, very cold*

*¾ cup milk (or more)
Softened butter
6–8 cups cleaned, sweetened, partially
  crushed strawberries
Cream
Grated nutmeg*

Preheat oven to 375° F. In a large bowl, sift together the first 5 ingredients. Cut in the butter until large crumbs form. Add the milk and stir to make a stiff batter, adding a bit more milk if needed. Mix well, but don't overmix. Pour into an oiled 9-inch pie pan, and spread it evenly. Bake 20 to 25 minutes until golden brown on top. It will be quite high in the middle.

Remove shortcake from oven and spread lavishly with softened butter. Cut in 8 wedges, place wedges in large bowls, and cover the hot biscuit with fresh strawberries. Pass the cream and nutmeg.

THE WEDDING DAY

Weddings are both a joyous and a serious occasion in the Amish and Mennonite communities, for the family is the foundation of their society. Marriages are not arranged in either group.

The Mennonite couple may have met at church or in college, but most commonly they will have known each other all their lives because they have lived in the same community. If they decide to marry, they might have a small wedding in their home, but more frequently weddings are held in the church. There are the usual accoutrements: white gown, flowers, and special music. The service is a short Protestant one, and the reception is held in the church parlor. Ordinarily, just cake and punch are served, but recently a trend has developed for serving a light supper of ham salad or tongue sandwiches and assorted salads in addition to the cake and punch.

The Amish couple most likely will have met at church and courted at Sunday-night singings and suppers held after church services at the host family's house. They have had further opportunity to meet at "frolics," social events that are work-oriented, but fun to do in a group, such as nut crackings and corn huskings. After a frolic, a young man drives his girl home in his buggy. Engagement rings are not exchanged between Amish couples, and they are quite secretive about their plans to marry until they are announced in church by the bishop just a few weeks before the service. The wedding is held at a neighbor's house, but the meal, for 200 to 400 guests, is traditionally held at the home of the bride's parents. The invitations are extended by word of mouth or postcard.

The Amish ceremony, performed by the bishop, starts in the morning and lasts several hours. The bride wears a white organdy cap, apron, and cape (which resembles a lightly fitted triangular overblouse) pinned down in the back; she does not carry a bouquet. The groom wears his dark Sunday church clothes. Two other couples are their attendants. Once the ceremony concludes, the wedding feast begins.

MINTED WHITE GRAPE JUICE

JELLIED CHICKEN

OLD-FASHIONED ESCALLOPED POTATOES

BAKED BEANS "FROM SCRATCH"

PICKLED BEETS WITH EGGS

FRESH PEA AND SPINACH SALAD

FRESH FRUIT BOWL

MARINATED VEGETABLE SALAD

BURNT SUGAR CAKE WITH TWO FROSTINGS

HOMEMADE ICE CREAM

CHOCOLATE FUDGE SAUCE

BLACK RASPBERRY COBBLER

CHERRY COBBLER

PINEAPPLE UPSIDE-DOWN CAKE

The meal is a most generous one, including ham, chicken, turkey, meat loaf, mashed potatoes and gravy, dressing, noodles, cole slaw, vegetables, relishes, and, always at weddings, pickled beets with eggs. For dessert there are fresh fruit bowls, cream and custard pies (the fruit pies are reserved for the evening meal), puddings, cakes, strawberry shortcake in season, and ice cream.

In the Berne community, the Amish wedding table is always set with tall containers of celery marching down the center, like flower arrangements. No one knows when or why this tradition started, but it is unthinkable to have a wedding there without this embellishment. Also traditional at Berne Amish weddings are stewed prunes and raisin pies.

The dinner guests are seated at long tables, but the bridal party has its own table called an *eck*, which always has the best position in the room. Wedding gifts, wrapped in brown paper, are practical items for the house or sometimes hand tools for the groom.

Many of the young people stay through the evening, during which a light meal is served. It includes dishes that have been prepared in advance, such as ham and escalloped potatoes, Baked Beans "from scratch," as the Hoosiers say), fruit and pecan pies, and more cakes. An Amish wedding day is a memorable occasion and a day-long feast.

During my visit to Sarah Schwartz's house in the Fort Wayne area, the kitchen was a busy place; her daughter's wedding was only two days away. Sarah was rolling out pie crusts, apparently by the dozen.

I asked to see the wedding dress, and Sarah went back to her bedroom to get it. "Actually this was my wedding dress," she told me. "I have kept it all these years." It was a deep blue, meticulously made. There were no buttons, no trim of any kind. Straight pins closed the front placket.

Sarah described the wedding cake. "Around Fort Wayne, we make a large five-layer one, using a different flavor for each layer. My daughter wanted white, chocolate, carrot, banana, and black walnut. The frosting is a fluffy white seven-minute kind. The flavors just depend on what the family wants." In most communities, the layered cake is white.

Sarah stroked the dress with her tanned, competent hands. "My daughter is marrying an Ohio fellow and will be moving there. I am really going to miss her."

MINTED WHITE GRAPE JUICE

Serves 4

This is a pleasant drink on a hot summer day. Its pale golden color in a frosty glass garnished with lime slices and mint is enticing. It is essential, though, that you have fresh mint and that the juice is very cold. Bottled white grape juice, widely available in supermarkets, is generally very good, and buying it is much easier than making your own.

4 cups white grape juice
8 4-inch sprigs fresh mint
4 thin lime slices

Ice cubes
Additional mint

Two hours before serving, place the grape juice, mint, and lime slices in a deep pitcher or bowl. Using a potato masher, bruise the leaves and lime slices to release their oils. Refrigerate, stirring now and then. To serve, add ice cubes, and then pour over more ice cubes in 1-cup glasses. Garnish with additional mint.

JELLIED CHICKEN

◆

Serves 12

Jellied Chicken is a very old recipe, and was a favorite dish at midwestern church suppers. It was also called pressed chicken, for some cooks would put weights, such as a flatiron or brick, on top of the loaf so it would set up firmly and with the proper density. The original recipes were all very specific about using an "old hen," and no gelatin was added, for the tough old bones of the chicken provided the gelatin. But when did you last see an old hen? Or hear a rooster crow? Today we can make do with young broiler-fryers and commercial gelatin. This recipe happens to be low in calories, and is an ideal buffet dish. It is also a good sandwich filling, especially on Whole Wheat Bread (page 22).

6 pounds meaty chicken pieces
   (legs, thighs, and breasts)
2 quarts water
2 ribs celery, halved
2 carrots, halved
1 medium onion, studded with
   6 whole cloves
2 bay leaves
   Handful of fresh parsley sprigs
1/2 teaspoon white pepper
2 envelopes unflavored gelatin

1/4 cup cold water
   Cider vinegar or lemon juice
   (optional)
   Additional parsley for garnish
   Sliced hard-cooked eggs
HERB MAYONNAISE
   1 cup mayonnaise
   2 tablespoons finely chopped fresh
   parsley
   2 tablespoons finely chopped fresh chives
   2 teaspoons capers (optional)

In a large stockpot, place the chicken, water, vegetables, and seasonings. Cover and bring to a boil over high heat. Reduce heat and simmer for 1 hour. Remove chicken from broth and let cool slightly. Remove meat from bones while still warm—it's easier that way. Discard skin and place chicken in a lightly oiled 9- or 10-inch loaf pan. Cover and refrigerate overnight. Strain the broth into a large saucepan and also refrigerate overnight.

The next day, skim fat off the broth. (Save this fat for another use; it freezes very well.) Place broth in a large saucepan over high heat and boil until about 2½ cups remain. Soften the gelatin in cold water, add to the hot broth, and bring to a boil again. Add a bit of vinegar or lemon juice, if desired. Pour broth over chicken to cover completely, then refrigerate overnight. This can be made 3 days ahead of time.

Combine ingredients for mayonnaise in a small bowl. Chill until serving. (You should have about 1¼ cups.)

Unmold chicken loaf, garnish with parsley and sliced eggs, and serve with the mayonnaise.

ABOVE AND BELOW: *Preparing fresh peaches is a pleasure when they are to be eaten with homemade ice cream.*

OPPOSITE: *The commercial dough whip in this bakery, used to make pies, cakes, and noodles, has been converted from electric to manual use.*

OLD-FASHIONED ESCALLOPED POTATOES

Serves 4–6

I remember my mother making escalloped potatoes simply by layering
the potatoes with a bit of flour and some seasonings. There was no recipe for this;
it was just something her mother had taught her. I hadn't had this dish for
years, and when I did finally prepare it, it was so delicious I wondered why
it had gone out of favor. This is very easy to fix, especially with a food
processor, and perfect with roasted or grilled meats.

4 large potatoes
2 tablespoons all-purpose flour,
approximately
Salt and black pepper
Grated nutmeg

2 tablespoons finely minced fresh parsley
¼ cup (½ stick) butter
1¼ cups milk
⅛ teaspoon paprika

Preheat oven to 325° F. Peel the potatoes and slice (there will be about 4 cups). Oil a rectangular baking dish (the one I use is 11 x 8 x 3 inches) and arrange some of the potato slices on the bottom. Sprinkle very lightly with a bit of the flour. Add salt, pepper, and nutmeg to taste, then sprinkle on some of the parsley. Repeat, making 2 or 3 more layers.

Meanwhile, heat the butter and milk together in a small saucepan over low heat; pour over the potatoes. Top with paprika. Bake, covered, for 1½ hours, or until a nice golden-brown crust forms on top and the potatoes are tender.

BAKED BEANS "FROM SCRATCH"

Serves 6

This recipe may have originated in Boston, but it appears all over the Midwest
at carry-in dinners. Our version is just a little bit sweeter than the New
England one. The salt pork gives the dish an almost unctuous smoothness,
like a good cassoulet. Once you've eaten these beans, you'll never buy canned
baked beans again. This dish freezes well, so consider making a double recipe.

1 pound pea or navy beans
Pinch of baking soda
¼ pound salt pork, cut in 2 pieces
1 onion, chopped
2 tablespoons brown sugar

½ teaspoon powdered mustard
½ teaspoon salt
¼ teaspoon black pepper
½ cup dark molasses

In a deep kettle, soak the beans overnight in water to cover. Do not drain. The next day, bring to a boil and add the baking soda. Lower the heat, skim the foam, and simmer, partially covered, for about 20 minutes, or until the skins peel back when blown on. Drain, reserving cooking liquid in a separate container.

Preheat over to 300° F. Place one piece of salt pork in the bottom of a bean pot or deep 2-quart ceramic casserole. To the drained beans add the onion, brown sugar, mustard, salt, pepper, and molasses; mix well. Pour the beans over the salt pork and add enough of the cooking water to cover. Place the remaining pieces of salt pork on top.

Bake, covered, for 8 hours. Keep checking the pot, making sure the liquid does not cook away. Add reserved bean cooking water when necessary so liquid remains on top of the beans all the time. Do not stir; beans will break up and get mushy.

PICKLED BEETS WITH EGGS

◆

Makes 2 quarts

Pickled Beets with Eggs appear at all holiday and special meals. The sweet-and-sour piquancy makes this an especially popular relish. And at Eastertime, when hard-cooked eggs are used for decoration, this is a good way to use up the extras.

4 pounds fresh young small beets
1 cup granulated sugar
1 cup brown sugar
2 cups water
2 cups cider vinegar
3 bay leaves
2 teaspoons mustard seed
1½ teaspoons salt

1 teaspoon ground cinnamon
1 teaspoon whole allspice
½ teaspoon ground cloves
½ teaspoon ground allspice
½ teaspoon celery seed
1 dozen small peeled and cooled hard-cooked eggs

Wash the beets; place in a large saucepan with water to cover and bring to a boil; reduce heat and simmer for 45 minutes to 1 hour, or until tender. Drain and cover with cold water; trim off the tops and roots and slip off the skins. Divide between 2 widemouthed quart jars.

In a large saucepan, combine the rest of the ingredients except the eggs. Simmer, covered, for 10 minutes. Divide liquid between the 2 jars and allow to cool completely. Add the eggs to the cold beet mixture and refrigerate for 2 days.

NOTE: If you add eggs to the hot liquid, you get a very rubbery, practically inedible egg.

FRESH PEA AND SPINACH SALAD

◆

Serves 6

In the local cookbooks, I found lots of salads that could be made in advance and then carried to family dinners, quilting bees, and church socials. They were called daisy salads and this one is a favorite: a combination of peas, spinach, and lettuce covered with a mayonnaise dressing, then tossed just before serving. It sounds strange, but it works—the ingredients stay crisp.

1½ cups shelled fresh peas (approximately 2 pounds in the pod)
½ pound fresh spinach leaves
½ head iceberg lettuce and a bit of ruby leaf lettuce if you have it
1 cup alfalfa sprouts
½ cup minced fresh parsley or chervil
8 green onions, chopped

3 hard-cooked eggs, chopped
1 cup mayonnaise
1 garlic clove, mashed
½ teaspoon salt
½ teaspoon coarsely ground black pepper
1 tablespoon chopped fresh tarragon, or ⅓ teaspoon dried (optional)

In a medium saucepan, cook the peas in about 1½ inches of water for 2 to 3 minutes, until they are barely done. Refresh in cold water and set aside to drain and cool.

Wash spinach and lettuce well. Tear the spinach and lettuce into bite-size pieces and place in a large salad bowl. Add the sprouts and parsley; toss to blend. Over the top of the lettuce mixture sprinkle the peas, green onions, and eggs, in that order.

In a small bowl, combine the remaining ingredients. Spread the dressing on the top of the salad, completely covering the ingredients. Chill for several hours. Toss before serving.

FRESH FRUIT BOWL

◆

Serves 12

Fresh Fruit bowls appear at almost every large Amish and Mennonite gathering. This version has a sheer lemony sauce that makes it quite special.

SAUCE
1 egg
1 tablespoon lime juice
¼ cup lemon juice
½ cup orange juice
1 cup sugar

1 large cantaloupe
1 large pineapple
2 grapefruits
2 oranges
1 red apple
1 banana
2 cups blueberries

Make the sauce first. Beat the egg in a small saucepan. Add the rest of the sauce ingredients and blend. Bring to a boil over medium-high heat and cook 1 minute. Set aside and let cool.

Remove the rind from the cantaloupe and pineapple and peel the grapefruit and oranges; do not peel the apple. Cut all the fruit into bite-size pieces. Place in a large bowl, pour sauce over all, and allow to stand for at least 2 hours. Stir once. Just before serving, sprinkle blueberries over the top.

MARINATED VEGETABLE SALAD

Serves 10–12

An ideal salad to make ahead of time, this is an interesting and colorful mélange of cauliflower, green beans, carrots, and zucchini with a zippy vinaigrette dressing.

1 small head cauliflower
⅓ pound small whole green beans, or
*   1 9-ounce package frozen beans*
3 carrots
2 small zucchini
1 cup chopped fresh parsley
VINAIGRETTE DRESSING
½ cup vegetable oil

¼ cup cider or red wine vinegar
3 tablespoons lemon juice
1 teaspoon Worcestershire sauce
1 teaspoon salt
½ teaspoon powdered mustard
½ teaspoon coarsely ground black pepper

Wash and break cauliflower into small bite-size flowerets. Wash and snip fresh beans, or thaw and drain frozen ones. Peel and thinly slice carrots. Wash and thinly slice zucchini. The zucchini, parsley, and frozen beans do not need to be cooked; blanch the following vegetables separately: cauliflower—6 minutes; fresh green beans—4 minutes; carrots—3 minutes. Transfer the vegetables immediately to ice water to stop the cooking. Drain well in a colander and set aside.

Prepare the vinaigrette. In a 2-cup jar, combine the ingredients for the dressing and shake to blend. In a deep 3-quart glass bowl, layer vegetables in the following order: one-third of the cauliflower, beans, carrots, zucchini, and fresh parsley. Add vinaigrette as you layer and repeat 2 times. Do not mix together. Cover tightly and refrigerate overnight. Occasionally pour the dressing off into a bowl, then pour it back over the vegetables. The salad can be served from the bowl just as is, or individually on salad plates on top of Boston lettuce leaves.

BURNT SUGAR CAKE WITH TWO FROSTINGS

◆

Serves 10–12

To get the rich, dark flavor that gives this cake its special distinction, a burnt sugar syrup is used as part of the sweetener. Most frequently it is served with a soft Seven-Minute Frosting, but in hot weather that doesn't keep too well, so a recipe for a Buttercream Frosting is also included.

BURNT SUGAR SYRUP
- ¾ cup sugar
- ¾ cup boiling water
- ⅔ cup (1⅓ stick) butter, softened
- 1 cup sugar
- 1 teaspoon vanilla extract
- 2 eggs, separated
- 3 cups sifted cake flour
- 1 tablespoon baking powder
- ½ teaspoon salt
- ¾ cup milk

BURNT SUGAR SEVEN-MINUTE FROSTING
- 2 egg whites, at room temperature
- 1¼ cups sugar
- ¼ cup cold water
- ¼ teaspoon cream of tartar
- ¼ teaspoon salt
- 1 teaspoon vanilla extract

BURNT SUGAR BUTTERCREAM FROSTING
- ⅓ cup butter, softened
- 1 16-ounce box confectioners' sugar
- Speck of salt
- 1 teaspoon vanilla extract
- 1–2 tablespoons light cream, or evaporated milk
- ¼ cup finely chopped pecans

In a small, heavy skillet or saucepan, heat the sugar over medium heat. Lower the heat to medium-low as a syrup forms, and stir frequently, breaking up the sugar lumps with the back of the spoon. Cook and stir for about 30 minutes, or until a brown syrup forms and the mixture begins to smoke. Very gradually stir in the boiling water and remove from heat. Cool thoroughly. Reserve ½ cup for the cake.

Preheat oven to 375° F. In a mixer bowl, cream the butter and sugar together until light, about 3 minutes. Gradually beat in ½ cup of the burnt sugar syrup. Add the vanilla and the egg yolks, 1 at a time, beating after each addition. Sift together the cake flour, baking powder, and salt. Add the flour mixture alternately with the milk, beating until smooth.

Beat the egg whites until stiff. Gently fold in whites by hand, then pour batter into two 8-inch oiled layer pans, smoothing the batter. Bake for 20 to 25 minutes, or until the top of the cake springs back when touched with your finger, and the sides shrink from the sides of the pan. Take cake from the oven, allow to stand 10 minutes, then remove the cake from the pans. Cover the layers with a terry-cloth towel and allow the cake to cool completely. Fill and frost with either the Seven-Minute Frosting or the Buttercream Frosting.

To make the Seven-Minute Frosting, place all ingredients except vanilla in the top of a double boiler (but don't place over boiling water yet). Add ¼ cup reserved burnt sugar syrup. With a small electric hand mixer, beat ½ minute at low speed. Place pot over boiling water, but don't allow the pan to touch the water. Cook, beating constantly, until the frosting forms stiff peaks, about 7 minutes. Do not cook longer than this. Add vanilla. Remove from heat and beat 2 minutes longer. Fill and frost the cake immediately.

To make the Buttercream Frosting, cream the butter in a large mixer bowl. Beat in the confectioners' sugar, salt, vanilla, and remaining burnt sugar syrup. Add cream to make the frosting a good consistency for spreading. Fill and frost cake, then top with chopped pecans.

HOMEMADE ICE CREAM

◆

Makes 1 gallon, or 16 servings

Lots of cream and lots of eggs make this homemade ice cream, well,
simply fabulous. The secret of the smooth texture is in the proportion of
salt to ice. Serve with chopped, sweetened fresh fruit poured over the top,
or with Chocolate Fudge Sauce.

10 egg yolks
2 cups sugar
¼ cup vanilla extract
Dash of salt

1 quart half-and-half
2 quarts heavy (whipping) cream
Rock salt

In a very large bowl, beat the egg yolks until well blended. Then add the sugar and beat until it is fully incorporated. Add remaining ingredients and blend. (If you do this the day before and store in the refrigerator, you will have an even smoother texture and more volume.)

Pour mixture into the freezer can of an ice-cream maker and pack freezer with 5 parts crushed ice to 1 part rock salt. Freeze until mixture is thick and frozen. Ice cream will still be soft. You can tell if it is done by the grinding sound of the electric motor or the ache in your arm, in case you are doing this by hand.

Drain off water, and repack the freezer, using 8 parts ice to 2 parts rock salt. Cover with a thick terry-cloth towel. Allow to stand and mellow for at least an hour.

CHOCOLATE FUDGE SAUCE

◆

Makes 3½ cups

Thick and with an intense chocolate flavor, this is a sauce that brings back
memories of soda shop days. It is the perfect topping for ice cream.

4 ounces bittersweet chocolate
½ cup (1 stick) butter
1 1-pound package confectioners' sugar

1 12-ounce can evaporated milk
1 teaspoon vanilla extract
Speck of salt

In the top of a double boiler, melt chocolate and butter together over simmering water. Add the confectioners' sugar and milk alternately, ½ cup at a time, blending with a whisk. Cook, uncovered, for 30 minutes, whisking often. Remove from heat, transfer to a mixer bowl, and beat for 5 minutes. *Do not omit this step*. Stir in the vanilla and salt. Serve immediately or transfer to a heat-proof wide-mouthed jar and refrigerate.

To reheat, place jar in a pan of simmering water and heat until the chocolate is soft enough to dip out. You can also transfer to the top of a double boiler and reheat over simmering water.

BLACK RASPBERRY COBBLER

Serves 6

Raspberry enthusiasts argue whether the blacks are better than the reds.
Certainly the black raspberries have more seeds, but I lean toward them when
it comes to cooking; their flavor is a bit more pronounced. Save red raspberries
to eat by themselves with cream or, even better, over homemade ice cream.

4–5 cups black raspberries
½ cup granulated sugar
½ cup brown sugar
2 tablespoons all-purpose flour
¼ cup (½ stick) butter, in small pieces
2 tablespoons lemon juice
½ teaspoon grated nutmeg
    Granulated sugar
    Grated nutmeg

DOUGH
1½ cups all-purpose flour
3 tablespoons granulated sugar
1½ teaspoons baking powder
1 teaspoon salt
½ cup (1 stick) butter, cold
½ cup milk, approximately
½ teaspoon vanilla extract

Preheat oven to 350° F. Place the raspberries in a 1½-quart oiled casserole with medium-high sides. Add the sugars and flour; toss. Dot with butter; sprinkle with lemon juice and nutmeg. Bake for 15 minutes.

Meanwhile, make the dough. Place the first four ingredients in a medium-sized bowl. Cut in the chilled butter with a pastry blender. Combine milk and vanilla, and add to the flour mixture. Stir with a fork until a stiff ball forms, then turn out onto a well-floured pastry cloth or board and roll out approximately ¼-inch thick. Shape the dough to fit the dish you are using. Roll dough back onto the rolling pin, and unroll on top of warm fruit. Slash the middle of the dough, then sprinkle a bit of sugar and nutmeg on top. Continue baking for 30 to 40 minutes, or until the juices bubble up through the slit and the crust is lightly golden. Serve warm, preferably with cream.

CHERRY COBBLER

Serves 6

Tart cherries are ready to pick soon after the Fourth of July, and are a favorite
fruit for canning and freezing. The cobbler can be made with either
fresh or frozen fruit. It is quite juicy, so serve it in shallow dessert dishes.
Garnish with a sprig of mint.

1 quart tart red cherries, washed and
    pitted
1 cup plus 2 tablespoons granulated
    sugar
¼ cup brown sugar
2 tablespoons minute tapioca
½ teaspoon almond extract

1½ cups sifted all-purpose flour
2 teaspoons baking powder
½ teaspoon salt
6 tablespoons (¾ stick) butter, cold
1 egg
⅓ cup milk
½ teaspoon grated nutmeg

Preheat oven to 400° F. In a shallow 2-quart casserole or 12 x 7-inch baking dish, combine the cherries, 1 cup of the granulated sugar, the brown sugar, tapioca, and almond extract. Allow this to stand while you prepare the batter.

In a large mixer bowl, mix together the flour, baking powder, and salt. Cut in ¼ cup of the butter until fine crumbs are formed. In a small bowl, beat the egg and add the milk. Combine egg mixture with the flour mixture and stir just until blended. Dot the cherries

with the 2 remaining tablespoons of butter. Drop the batter on top of the cherries—you should have 6 mounds.

In a small bowl, combine the 2 remaining tablespoons of granulated sugar with the nutmeg. Sprinkle on top of the batter. Bake for 25 or 30 minutes, or until the fruit is bubbling up in the middle of the pan and the dumplings are golden brown. The baking time can vary quite a bit, depending on the pan you use and how big the cherries are. Serve warm or at room temperature.

PINEAPPLE UPSIDE-DOWN CAKE

Serves 6

Pineapple Upside-Down Cake used to be a favorite dessert at midwestern church suppers and Sunday dinners. Then boxed cakes came along, and this cake almost disappeared. It is rare to find a recipe for it anymore; this one yields a thin, buttery, moist cake with a goodly amount of pineapple on top.

TOPPING
*1 20-ounce can sweetened, crushed
    pineapple*
¼ cup (½ stick) butter
1 cup brown sugar

*1¼ cups sifted unbleached all-purpose
    flour*

⅔ cup granulated sugar
2 teaspoons baking powder
½ teaspoon salt
¼ teaspoon ground mace
⅓ cup (⅔ stick) butter, softened
½ cup milk
1 teaspoon vanilla extract
1 egg

Preheat oven to 350° F. Drain the pineapple well in a sieve; discard liquid. Spray the sides and bottom of a 9-inch square pan with vegetable spray, and melt the butter in the pan in the preheated oven.

Add the brown sugar to the butter and blend. Spread the drained pineapple evenly over the sugar mixture, but do not mix. Set aside.

Into a mixer bowl, resift the flour, sugar, baking powder, salt, and mace. Add the soft-

ened butter, milk, and vanilla. Beat on low speed for 1½ minutes, then add the egg and beat 1½ minutes longer. Spread the batter evenly over the pineapple with a rubber spatula—the batter is quite thick. Bake for 35 to 40 minutes, or until a skewer inserted into the middle of the cake comes out clean. Remove from oven, loosen edges with knife, and invert immediately onto a platter. Let cool before serving.

THE AUCTION

Auctions in Amish land serve multiple purposes. They function as social events, as fund raisers, as successful commercial businesses within the community, and as places to find genuine bargains—even an unexpected collector's item now and then. Antiques buyers attend the auctions with serious intent. To the interested observer, it is country theater. The Amish attach a great deal of importance to auctions—they are a permitted social activity and the Amish appreciate bargains. Because of their lack of transportation to the cities for shopping, the household auctions and flea markets provide them with a larger selection of merchandise than they ordinarily would find in their own small towns. And wherever there is an auction, there is food to buy and eat.

Shipshewana, with a population of 500, is ordinarily a quiet town where a dog can doze in the street undisturbed. But on auction day, the population swells to 30,000. The Shipshewana Auction and Flea Market, called the Trading Place of America, is nationally known, draw-ing antiques buffs from all over the United States. The outdoor flea market, covering a forty-acre field, runs weekly on Tuesdays and Wednesdays from May until November, when bad weather forces it to close. But the indoor antiques, livestock, and horse auctions are held year-round. The buggies stream into town by six A.M., for the Amish families enjoy and patronize this auction and flea market as much as the "English."

The men and boys go to the auction barns to note the prices of the livestock and horses and perhaps buy or sell. The women and their daughters browse through the flea market, buying an occasional gaily flowered dish to go on their tables. This trip also enables the women to shop for the few groceries they might need and to purchase sewing materials.

Another well-known auction, held annually, is the Michiana Mennonite Relief Sale held the last Saturday in September at the Elkhart County Fairgrounds. Quilt enthusiasts come from afar for this one. Mennonite churches

PORK AND BEANS

COUNTY FAIR BARBECUE SANDWICHES

JELLIED MEAT

BARBECUED CHICKEN

THICK BEEF VEGETABLE SOUP

OVERNIGHT COLE SLAW

UNCONVENTIONAL CORNBREAD

INDIANA AMISH DATE PUDDING

WHOOPIE PIES

APPLE FRITTERS

KNEE PATCHES

COCONUT CHOCOLATE CANDY

CRACKER JACK

throughout the Midwest send not only breath-takingly beautiful quilts, but crafts and antiques as well. Many of the participating churches have food stands where you can buy Apple Fritters, Knee Patches (fried pastry squares), Barbecued Chicken, Pork and Beans, chicken noodle soup, fried pies, funnel cakes, and on and on. The 400 or so quilts up for auction go for high prices—one recently for $10,500. The sale raises money to support the worldwide relief program of the Mennonite Central Committee, which distributes food and clothing to disaster victims.

Another kind of auction popular in this community—indeed, in the whole Midwest—is the household auction. The Amish, and other thrifty individuals, buy much of their household and farm equipment at such sales.

Since Amish houses are furnished very simply, their purchases are practical ones. When an older farmer retires, one of his sons takes over the family farm, and the parents move into the *grossdaadi Haus* (grandfather's house). This is a smaller residence, either attached to or a few feet from the bigger house, where the son and his family will now live. This move generally takes place in the winter, since the Amish are not then busy in the fields. During this season, there are many Saturday household auctions to which neighbors may also contribute consignment items. These sales start in the morning, run through the afternoon, and if the sale is a large one, food will be available to buy too, so it becomes a social affair; it's an opportunity for the farmers and their families to socialize and break bread together.

PORK AND BEANS

Serves 6

Since there are lots of people to serve at auctions and the food stands are open
for a long period of time, it is important to have food that keeps well.
Pork and Beans fits the bill. With a slice of cornbread, this combination
makes a good, hearty meal.

1 pound Great Northern or navy beans
8 cups water
  Pinch of baking soda
2 pounds country-style spareribs, cut in
    serving-size pieces
1 cup chopped onion
1 carrot, finely chopped
8 whole cloves

2 bay leaves
1 teaspoon salt
¼ teaspoon black pepper
⅛ teaspoon red pepper flakes
¼ cup chopped fresh parsley
  Chopped onions for garnish
  Cider vinegar

Place the beans and water in a very large kettle. Soak overnight.

Add the baking soda to the beans, bring to a boil over high heat, and skim off the foam. Add the remaining ingredients except the parsley, chopped onions, and cider vinegar and bring again to a boil. Reduce heat to low, partially cover, and cook for 1 hour. Remove the lid and continue cooking for 45 minutes longer, or until the beans are tender and the mixture is very thick. (Cooking time will vary since the beans vary in moisture content and age.) Add the parsley to the beans. Ladle into soup bowls, and serve with chopped onions and a little pitcher of vinegar.

COUNTY FAIR BARBECUE SANDWICHES

Makes 10–12 sandwiches

This is not a thin sloppy Joe-type sandwich; it is old-fashioned County Fair Barbecue, like you haven't eaten in years. Flavorful cuts of beef and pork are simmered until tender, then cooked with a robust tomato sauce and seasoned with cumin, paprika, and chili powder.

2½ pounds boneless chuck roast, trimmed
2½ pounds boneless pork shoulder, trimmed
2 quarts water
2 ribs celery, cut in large pieces
1 large onion, cut in large pieces
2 carrots, cut in large pieces
2 small bay leaves
8 whole cloves
1 teaspoon salt
¼ teaspoon black pepper
12 buns
BARBECUE SAUCE
2 tablespoons (¼ stick) butter

1 cup chopped onion
1½ cups water
1 cup catsup
½ cup cider vinegar
⅓ cup granulated sugar
1 tablespoon plus 1 teaspoon Worcestershire sauce
1 tablespoon brown sugar
2 teaspoons celery salt
2 teaspoons paprika
½ teaspoon chili powder
½ teaspoon ground cumin
½ teaspoon black pepper
½ teaspoon salt

Preheat oven to 325° F. Place meats, vegetables, and seasonings in a large roaster. Cover and bake for 3 hours. Remove pork, and continue baking the beef for another hour, or until very tender. Shred and cut the meats into bite-size pieces while still warm. (Reserve broth for another use. It freezes very well.)

In a large, heavy saucepan, sauté butter and onion for sauce until the onion is transparent. Add the remaining ingredients, and mix well. Then add shredded meats. Simmer over low heat until mixture is quite thick but still juicy. This will take about 15 minutes. Don't stir too often; you want the meat to stay in good-size pieces. Serve on hot buns.

JELLIED MEAT

◆

Serves 10

Jellied meat shouldn't be confused with souse, but it is a hearty
first cousin. I like to serve it in the summer, cut in thick slices, and use it like a pâté
on a cold meat platter. It is an attractive loaf, flecked with tiny bits of carrot
and parsley. *Sültze*, as it was called, is an old German recipe. The loaf was kept in
small crocks in the cool basement and brought up for Sunday night suppers.

3 pounds pork loin roast, bone in
3 quarts plus ¼ cup water
1 carrot, quartered
1 onion, quartered
2 celery ribs, quartered
  Handful of parsley sprigs
6 4-inch sprigs fresh thyme, or 1
  teaspoon dried (optional)
1 tablespoon finely minced fresh parsley

1½ teaspoons fresh thyme leaves, or ½
  teaspoon dried
1 envelope unflavored gelatin
2 tablespoons cider vinegar
½ teaspoon black pepper
½ teaspoon salt
  Grape leaves
  Black-eyed Susans (optional)

In a large kettle, place the pork roast, 3 quarts of the water, carrot, onion, celery, parsley sprigs, and thyme sprigs. Cover, bring to a simmer, and cook over low heat for 3 hours, or until the meat is very tender. Remove the meat and carrot, and cool the broth slightly.

Strain the broth, cool it in refrigerator, then skim off the fat. Chop the meat and carrot finely, or pulse just 1½ times in a food processor—there should be some irregular pieces for texture—and transfer to an oiled 8 x 5-inch loaf pan. Mix in the minced parsley and the thyme leaves.

In a medium saucepan, bring 4 cups of the broth (freeze the rest for soup stock) to a boil over high heat and reduce it to 2 cups. Combine the remaining ¼ cup water and the gelatin in a small bowl. Whip with a fork and allow to stand until the gelatin is dissolved. Add it to the broth, along with the vinegar, pepper, and salt and simmer over low heat for 2 minutes. Pour the liquid over the meat and, using a fork, make sure that the broth is evenly distributed around all of the meat in the pan. Refrigerate until firm, at least 6 hours.

To serve, slice the meat and arrange on a platter lined with grape leaves. Add clusters of black-eyed Susans.

BARBECUED CHICKEN

Makes 8 small servings

What I like about this barbecue sauce is that there is no tomato in it so it doesn't char. This is the favorite way to barbecue chicken in this area, and you'll see why. The chicken remains especially moist if you marinate it overnight before broiling. This dish is equally good in small quantities and for a crowd, and both versions are given.

BARBECUE SAUCE

½ cup water
½ cup cider vinegar
2 tablespoons vegetable oil
1 small bay leaf
1½ teaspoons garlic powder, or 3 garlic cloves, crushed
1½ tablespoons Worcestershire sauce

1 teaspoon sugar
1¼ teaspoons salt
¾ teaspoon black pepper
¼ teaspoon celery salt

4 chicken breasts, boned and halved, skin on

In a small saucepan, combine the sauce ingredients and bring to a boil over high heat. Remove from heat. Place the 8 chicken pieces in a shallow glass dish. Pour the sauce over the chicken, cover, and marinate overnight.

The next day, grill chicken about 4 inches above well-heated coals for about 6 minutes on each side, brushing frequently on each side with the sauce. Spoon a bit more sauce over the chicken just before serving.

NOTE: For 16 servings, halve 8 young broiler chickens, and use the following proportions for the marinade: 2 cups water; 2 cups cider vinegar; ½ cup vegetable oil; 4 small bay leaves; 5 tablespoons Worcestershire sauce; 1 tablespoon garlic powder, or 6 garlic cloves, crushed; 1 tablespoon sugar; 1 tablespoon plus 1 teaspoon salt; 1 tablespoon black pepper; 1 teaspoon celery salt. Prepare as above. Broil chicken halves approximately 1 hour, or until a thigh joint moves easily.

THICK BEEF VEGETABLE SOUP

Makes 10 cups

Parsnips give this substantial soup a sweet flavor, and you will have most of the other vegetables on hand. Add any others you might like—cabbage, turnips, and so on. Since the soup is made in the oven, it requires no watching. You could drop dumplings on top of the soup, but do that portion on top of the stove.

2 pounds chuck roast, trimmed of every
    bit of fat
BROTH SEASONINGS
  1 large onion, quartered
  2 carrots, halved
  2 ribs celery, halved
  ½ green bell pepper, halved
  2 bay leaves
  8 whole cloves
  12 peppercorns
  1 teaspoon salt
  ½ teaspoon black pepper
  3 quarts hot water

1 cup chopped raw potatoes, in ½-inch
    dice

1 cup sliced carrots, in ¼-inch pieces
1 cup fresh or frozen lima beans
1 cup chopped parsnips, in ½-inch dice,
    woody core discarded
¼ cup quick-cooking pearled barley
1 28-ounce can tomatoes, drained and
    very coarsely chopped
1 cup fresh or frozen peas
1 cup fresh or frozen green beans
1 cup fresh or frozen corn
½ cup chopped fresh basil, or 1 teaspoon
    dried (optional)
1 tablespoon brown sugar
1 teaspoon Kitchen Bouquet (a dark
    vegetable extract; optional)
Chopped fresh basil

Preheat oven to 450° F. Combine meat with ingredients for broth seasonings in a very large roaster or soup kettle and bake for 30 minutes. Lower the heat to 300° F. and continue baking about 3 hours, until the meat is fork-tender. Remove the meat and let cool slightly. Shred into generous bite-size pieces; set aside. Remove seasonings with a slotted spoon and discard.

Increase the oven temperature to 350° F. Add the potatoes, carrots, lima beans, parsnips, barley, and tomatoes to the broth and bake for 45 minutes. Remove casserole from oven and add the remaining ingredients. Return casserole to the oven and bake 30 minutes longer, or until the potatoes and parsnips are tender. Garnish with additional fresh basil.

OVERNIGHT COLE SLAW

Serves 10–12

Sweet and sour, with a clear vinegar-sugar dressing and a touch of tarragon,
this slaw can be made two days in advance.

DRESSING

2 cups sugar
½ cup cider vinegar
2 teaspoons mustard seed
2 teaspoons salt
1 teaspoon celery seed
½ teaspoon powdered mustard
*½ teaspoon dried salad herbs, or 1
    tablespoon fresh minced tarragon
    (optional)*

¼ teaspoon black pepper

1 3-pound head green cabbage
5 ribs celery
1 medium onion
*1 medium green bell pepper, or ½ red
    pepper, ½ green pepper*
¾ cup fresh parsley sprigs

An hour before you are going to prepare the slaw, combine the dressing ingredients in a very large bowl and set aside. Stir once in awhile to help dissolve the sugar.

Shred the cabbage in a food processor, and add to the dressing. In the processor, chop the celery, onion, bell pepper, and parsley. Add to the cabbage and mix well; you may have to use your hands, but be quick about it. Cover tightly and chill overnight. Serve chilled.

UNCONVENTIONAL CORNBREAD

Serves 8

This is not the usual old cornbread. It is rich with cheese and bacon, and
flavored with onion and green pepper. A bit of cream-style corn gives
it moistness. Even with all of this, the bread has a velvety texture, and no holes!

3 strips bacon
1½ cups yellow cornmeal
½ cup all-purpose flour
1 tablespoon baking powder
1 teaspoon salt
2 eggs
1¼ cups milk

¾ cup shredded sharp cheddar cheese
½ cup vegetable oil
½ cup canned cream-style corn
1 small onion, finely minced
*2 tablespoons finely minced green bell
    pepper*

Preheat oven to 350° F. Lightly oil a 10-inch-round cake pan and place in oven to heat. Fry the bacon until very crisp; drain on absorbent paper, then crumble finely. Meanwhile, prepare the batter. In a medium bowl, combine the cornmeal, flour, baking powder, and salt. In another mixer bowl, beat the eggs slightly, and add the remaining ingredients and mix. By hand, stir in the dry ingredients just until blended. Pour the batter into the hot pan. Bake 30 minutes. Cut into 8 wedges and serve immediately with butter.

INDIANA AMISH DATE PUDDING

◆

Serves 12–15

Date pudding is almost a signature dessert in Indiana Amish country, and there are several versions—some are steamed, some are baked with syrup on the bottom, and some are moist heavy cakes served with whipped cream on top. One version that I have not had anywhere but in this community is almost like a date trifle—the date cake is layered with whipping cream in a deep bowl. The black walnuts are an inspired combination with the dates.

1½ cups chopped dates
1 teaspoon baking soda
1 cup boiling water
½ cup granulated sugar
½ cup brown sugar
2 tablespoons (¼ stick) butter, softened
1 egg
2 teaspoons grated orange rind
 (optional)
1 teaspoon vanilla extract
1½ cups all-purpose flour
½ teaspoon salt

½ teaspoon baking powder
1¼ cups chopped black walnuts
WHIPPED CREAM MIXTURE
2½ cups heavy (whipping) cream
½ cup plus 2 tablespoons confectioners'
 sugar
2½ teaspoons light corn syrup (see note)
2½ teaspoons vanilla extract
2 teaspoons grated orange rind
 (optional)
Speck of salt

Preheat oven to 350° F. In a medium bowl, combine the dates, baking soda, and boiling water; set aside to cool. In a large mixer bowl, blend the sugars, butter, egg, rind, and vanilla. Add the flour, salt, baking powder, and 1 cup of walnuts. The mixture will be crumbly. Add the cooled date mixture to the flour mixture and mix just enough to blend. Pour into an oiled 12 x 7-inch cake pan and bake for 30 to 40 minutes. The cake should shrink slightly away from the sides of the pan when it is done. Let cool.

Prepare the whipped cream. In a large chilled mixer bowl, combine cream, confec-tioners' sugar, corn syrup, vanilla, rind, and salt, and beat until stiff peaks form.

Cut the cake into 8 large pieces. Cut each piece horizontally into 2 layers, then restack, cutting each piece into 12 cubes—you will have ¾ x 1-inch cubes. In a 3-quart bowl (approximately 8 inches in diameter, 5½ inches deep), alternate 4 layers of date-cake cubes with 4 layers of the whipping cream, beginning with the cake and ending with the cream. Sprinkle remaining chopped walnuts on top and refrigerate until ready to serve.

NOTE: The addition of the corn syrup stabi-lizes the whipped cream.

WHOOPIE PIES

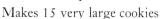

Makes 15 very large cookies

I know very well that Whoopie Pies aren't from eighteenth-century Europe.
But I do know that they are a favorite cookie in this part of the country, and all
the local Amish and Mennonite cookbooks have recipes for them.
Some people don't know about this cookie, and they ought to. It is like a giant, soft
Oreo gone berserk, if you will. And it is an absolutely marvelous cookie.
At first glance, the recipe appears long and complicated. The cookies are easy to
make, but there are some extra steps, and they are well worth it. These cookies
freeze well, and are a great picnic dessert.

4 cups all-purpose flour
1 teaspoon baking soda
1 teaspoon baking powder
1 teaspoon salt
1 tablespoon cream of tartar
1 cup unsweetened cocoa powder
½ cup (1 stick) butter, softened
½ cup lard, softened
2 cups sugar
2 teaspoons vanilla extract

2 eggs
1⅓ cups soured milk (see note)
FILLING
⅓ cup plus 3 tablespoons all-purpose flour
1½ cups milk
1½ cups (3 sticks) butter
¼ teaspoon salt
2 teaspoons vanilla extract
3¾ cups confectioners' sugar

Preheat oven to 375° F. Sift together the flour, baking soda, baking powder, salt, cream of tartar, and cocoa. Set aside. In a large mixer bowl, cream the butter, lard, sugar, and vanilla together until well blended, about 3 minutes. Add the eggs, 1 at a time, blending after each addition. Add the flour mixture to the sugar-butter mixture, alternating with the milk and beginning and ending with the flour. Blend well, but don't overmix. The mixture will look like cake batter and if it appears curdled, don't worry.

Cover cookie sheets with aluminum foil. Use ¼ cup of batter for each cookie, drop them onto the cookie sheets—one in each corner, and one in the middle. Make them as round as possible. At this point, each cookie will be about 2½ inches in diameter and they should be 3½ to 4 inches apart. Bake for 6 minutes and, if necessary, reverse the cookie sheets from front to back so they bake evenly —I have to do this in my oven. Continue baking 10 minutes longer. The only sure way to tell if they are done is to touch them with

your fingertip. If the top of the cookie springs back quickly, remove them from the oven; don't overbake.

Slide the foil off the sheet and allow the cookies to stand for 2 minutes. Remove them from the foil with a metal spatula to wax paper-covered racks to cool. If any of the cookies are irregular, trim them carefully into rounds with a pair of scissors while they are still warm. (Reuse foil.) Repeat with the remaining batter until you have 30 cookies.

Meanwhile, prepare the filling. Place the flour in a medium saucepan, and add the milk gradually, whisking smooth. Cook over moderate heat, cooking and whisking until the mixture becomes thick and bubbles up in the center. Simmer over low heat for 2 minutes. Remove from heat and set aside to cool.

Place the butter in a large mixer bowl and beat it until it is slightly softened. Add the salt, vanilla, and sugar gradually and beat for 2 minutes. Gradually, 1 large spoonful at a time, add the cooled milk mixture to the butter mixture. Then beat on high speed for 1 minute until the filling is smooth, light, and fluffy. If the filling seems too soft, refrigerate it until it firms up a bit.

Arrange the cookies in pairs, flat sides up. Place a generous ¼ cup of filling on 15 of the cookies, using all of the filling. Spread the filling to about ½ inch from the edge; it will be almost ½ inch thick. Top with another cookie, flat side down. Press the cookies to-gether so the filling comes to the edges.

Chill, then wrap each cookie individually in plastic wrap. Store in the refrigerator, but they taste better eaten at room temperature. They also freeze very well.

NOTE: If you do not have soured milk, add 1 tablespoon plus 1 teaspoon cider vinegar to 1⅓ cups regular milk and let stand ½ hour.

APPLE FRITTERS
◆
Serves 8–10

A dish frequently found on Amish and Mennonite tables, as well as at county fairs, apple fritters are prepared by mixing chopped apples into the batter, or by dipping thin apple slices in the batter, then deep-frying them.
If the apples are cut too thick, they remain unpleasantly raw. Marinating the apple slices first in a mixture of brown sugar and lemon juice and adding lemon rind to the batter give this fritter real panache. Summer Rambos, Yellow Delicious, or Granny Smiths are the ideal apples for this country delicacy.

8 medium-firm cooking apples
¼ cup brown sugar
¼ cup lemon juice
1 cup all-purpose flour
¼ cup granulated sugar
½ teaspoon ground cinnamon

¼ teaspoon salt
2 eggs, separated
Grated rind of 1 lemon
½ cup milk
Vegetable oil for deep frying
Confectioners' sugar

Core the apples, peel them, then slice them crosswise into scant ¼-inch slices. Combine the brown sugar and lemon juice in a 10-inch shallow dish, and add the apple slices, spooning the sauce over both sides of the fruit. Allow to stand 1 hour, turning the slices occasionally.

Preheat 2 to 3 inches of oil in an electric skillet to 375° F. Meanwhile, combine the flour, granulated sugar, cinnamon, and salt in a shallow bowl. In a small bowl, beat the egg yolks thoroughly and add the rind and milk; combine with the dry ingredients. In a mixer bowl, beat the egg whites until stiff and gently fold them into the flour mixture. The batter will be puffy and there should be some patches of white showing.

Dip the apple slices into the batter—it will not cooperatively adhere to the apple because of the marinade, but firmly push the slices into the batter until both sides are coated. With tongs, drop the apple into the hot oil and cook until the fritter is golden brown on one side—this takes about 2 minutes—then turn and fry the other side, about 1 minute. Drain on paper towels, and keep warm in the oven until all the fritters are prepared. Sprinkle very scantily with confectioners' sugar and serve hot.

KNEE PATCHES

Makes 4½ dozen

An old tradition on New Year's Day among the Swiss Amish and Mennonites
is to make Knee Patches. This confection has other names—Swiss Nothings or
Elephant Ears—but Knee Patches describes the way they are made. A simple
flour dough is rolled out into a circle, and then to further flatten it, the dough
is stretched over your kneecap (covered with a tea towel) until the round is
very, very thin. Then the dough is deep-fried and sprinkled with a mixture of
confectioners' sugar and cinnamon. This is quite fun to do, but admittedly, it
goes faster if there are three cooks doing it: one rolling, one stretching, one
frying. And in Amish kitchens, there are always that many around to help
make this delicious flaky pastry.

3 eggs
1 teaspoon vanilla extract
2 teaspoons salt
1 cup heavy (whipping) cream

4 cups unbleached all-purpose flour
2 quarts vegetable oil
¾ cup confectioners' sugar
½ teaspoon ground cinnamon

In a large mixer bowl, beat the eggs well.
Add the vanilla, salt, and cream; blend. Add
the flour and beat thoroughly. The dough will
be quite stiff. On a lightly floured surface (or
with a dough hook) knead the dough for 10
minutes.

Preheat oil in a fryer to 375° F. Pinch
off small pieces of dough about the size of a
large marble, and roll out as thinly as possible
—about 4½ inches in diameter. Seat yourself
(though I suppose that might be obvious),
cross your legs, cover your knee with a tea
towel, and stretch the dough over your kneecap until it is very thin. This works amazingly

well, as you will discover. Drop by twos in the
hot fat and cook until golden brown on both
sides, turning once, about 2 minutes on each
side. The patch will blister and puff. Remove
carefully, using 2 tablespoons and shaking
each piece over the kettle to remove the excess
fat. Drain on paper towels. Continue to make
remaining cookies.

When cookies are cool, combine the confectioners' sugar and cinnamon and sift lightly
over the top of each Knee Patch. Eat the same
day they are made—they don't keep particu-
larly well.

COCONUT CHOCOLATE CANDY

Makes 100 pieces

When I first ate this candy, I couldn't imagine that such a wonderful confection
could be duplicated so simply in a home kitchen. It very much resembles the
coconut candy bars we used to buy as special treats to eat during the movies on
Saturday afternoons. The candy keeps indefinitely in the refrigerator.

¾ cup (1½ sticks) butter
*1 14-ounce can sweetened condensed
    milk*
2 teaspoons vanilla extract
½ teaspoon salt

5⅔ cups confectioners' sugar (1½ boxes)
1 pound flaked coconut
1 pound pecans, finely ground
3 ounces paraffin (½ block)
1½ pounds semisweet chocolate morsels

In a large saucepan, melt the butter over low heat but do not allow to brown. Whisk in the condensed milk, vanilla, and salt. Then add the confectioners' sugar, coconut, and pecans. Mix quickly; you will have to use your hands. Coat a 9 x 13-inch baking pan with vegetable spray. Transfer the candy mixture to the pan and pat it in place firmly, using the palm of your hand to smooth the surface evenly. Cover and store in the coldest part of your refrigerator overnight.

In a double boiler set over hot (*not* boiling) water, melt the paraffin and chocolate chips. Cut the cold candy into 1-inch squares and, using a toothpick, dip the candy into the chocolate. Put on a cookie sheet lined with wax paper, then place in the refrigerator to harden. When the candy has set, transfer to storage containers and keep refrigerated until serving.

CRACKER JACK

Makes 6 quarts

A favorite at auctions and county fairs, Cracker Jack is also made at home as a
special but inexpensive treat. I especially like this recipe, for the caramel
poured over the popcorn isn't as sticky and heavily flavored as most.

6 quarts unseasoned popped popcorn
2 cups brown sugar
½ cup light corn syrup
1 cup (2 sticks) butter

1 teaspoon salt
¼ teaspoon cream of tartar
1 teaspoon baking soda

Preheat oven to 200° F. Divide the popcorn between 2 large bowls. Oil 2 lipped cookie sheets very well and set aside.

In a deep saucepan, combine the brown sugar, corn syrup, butter, salt, and cream of tartar. Insert a candy thermometer. Bring to a boil and cook the mixture over medium heat for about 5 minutes, stirring occasionally, until the thermometer registers 260° F. (hard ball stage). Remove from the heat and quickly stir in the baking soda. The mixture foams up.

Pour the syrup mixture over the popcorn, half into each bowl. Work quickly to coat all the popcorn with the caramel. Spread popcorn evenly on the cookie sheets and bake for 1 hour, stirring 3 times. Remove from the oven and spread popcorn on wax paper to cool, breaking up the larger pieces, if necessary. Store in airtight containers.

SHADES
of
AUTUMN

The days begin to shorten and a certain slant of diffused sunlight gives poignant notice that summer is over. In flower gardens the calendulas and zinnias have their last hurrah. Along the roadside, goldenrod nods in the rising wind and patches of leggy blue asters and purple thistles appear at the wood's edge ♦ Queen Anne's lace has turned into lacy golden cups, and tangled bittersweet, trailing along the fences, drops its leaves while the small, round, orange three-sided beads open, showing their red inner berries ♦ In the woods, the birds have daylong conversations among themselves; they chirp, caw, cluck, whistle, whirr, and mutter together as they rest before their flight south ♦ Later, green walnuts will fall and be gathered by the children so their mothers can begin shelling and picking out the nut meats for winter baking. Hedge apples will be brought into the house and placed in bowls for decoration, their knobby roundness giving off a sweet milky scent. Inedible buckeyes, treasured for their dark, shiny, smooth roundness, are collected by the children, and every farmboy carries one in his pocket all winter—for luck ♦ The last of the garden is harvested and stored for winter: apples, squash, pumpkins, and cabbages. Heavy frost loosens the maple trees' yellowing leaves, forming a golden carpet underneath ♦ High over the cornfields, a skein of wild geese etches a dramatic V against the sky. The nostalgic sound of their plaintive honking fades away as they fly out of sight.

Children play hide-go-seek in the field, in spite of encountering an occasional thistle.

PRESERVING THE HARVEST

Farm women spend the time right after school starts in the fall finishing up the last of their preserving for the winter. A glimpse into the cellar of an Amish housewife overwhelms one with its sheer numbers of jars on the shelves, and the work they represent. It is not unusual to find 600 quarts of canned fruits and vegetables, and 300 quarts of preserved meat and fowl. In the Elkhart-Goshen area, where the food is more German in its ethnic influence, homemade bologna is made in 50-pound batches and canned, too. It is a favorite at supper and in school lunch buckets.

One fall tradition that brings the Amish women together in each other's kitchens is sauerkraut making. Kraut is generally prepared in 50-pound amounts, packed in crocks with salt, and allowed to ferment and bubble for a week to ten days. It is frequently kept on the back porch, for it does get quite pungent. Once cured, it is packed into quart jars and set aside for winter use.

Canned fruits are used throughout the year in pies and cobblers, or served plain in their juice in bowls, accompanied by cookies or cake. Preserved tomatoes find their way into many sauces and soups, and homemade pickles are served as relishes to provide a sweet-and-sour counterpoint to rich meat dishes.

As you pass Amish farms, you often see specially built racks for holding rows and rows of empty upside-down glass fruit jars—outside the house, but close to the kitchen. This arrangement saves inside storage space. At canning time, the jars are brought inside, washed, sterilized, and filled, then returned to the rack as each jar's contents are used. The cycle of planting, harvesting, and preserving goes on and on, as timeless as the Amish themselves.

CROCKPOT APPLE BUTTER

BLUEBERRY JAM

SPICED CHERRY JAM

PRESERVED PEARS WITH LEMON

HOMEMADE SAUERKRAUT IN A CROCK

COUNTRY CHILI SAUCE

GOOSEBERRY RELISH

BREAD AND BUTTER PICKLES

VERY SPECIAL STRAWBERRY PRESERVES

HOMEMADE TOMATO SOUP

FRESH HOT TOMATO RELISH

TOMATO COCKTAIL

YELLOW TOMATO PRESERVES

◆

Preserving seasonal treats in your kitchen to enjoy all winter long or to give as gifts to very special people can be a very satisfying thing. If you have never canned or frozen food, or made jams before, it all might sound very complex, but after you have done it once, the mystery is gone. You do, however, need some special equipment.

You will need a large metal water-bath canner and a steam pressure canner for processing canned vegetables, fruits, and soups, plus canning jars, which are commonly called Mason (a brand name) jars. Don't use your leftover mayonnaise jars—you need the real thing. I use the two-piece metal cap, which is a lid and a screw-band combination. A jar lifter is a convenient thing to have to remove the processed jars from the hot-water bath. You will find these items in a hardware store.

Here are some general directions:

1. Canning equipment must be immaculate. Wash jars, lids, and screw bands in hot, soapy water. Discard any jars that are nicked or cracked.

2. Any jar that will be processed for less than 10 minutes *must* be sterilized for 10 minutes. Sterilize jars by covering them with water and boiling them hard for 10 minutes. Use the canner for this. Leave jars in the water until you are ready to use them. In another pan, sterilize the screw bands also for 10 minutes. The lids should be immersed in another pan of water, brought to a simmer, then removed from the heat. Avoid touching the tops of the jars and the lids with your hands; use tongs for removing them from the water.

3. Using a widemouthed funnel, fill the jars, leaving ¼ inch of headspace for jams and jellies, ½ inch for fruits and tomatoes, and 1 inch for low-acid vegetables. With a clean, damp cloth, wipe off the top lip of the jars before putting on the lid and screw band.

4. Return the water in the canner almost to the boiling point. Place the covered jars in it with the jar lifter; when all the jars are in, the water should cover them by 1 or 2 inches. Bring the water to a boil, then reduce heat to hold the water to a full boil. Begin timing the processing time at this point. Add more hot water if it boils away.

5. After processing, remove the jars from the hot-water bath and place them on towels in a draft-free place to cool. During this period, you will hear an occasional "pop"— that is the sound of the jars sealing.

6. When jars are cool, check the seal by pressing the center of the lid. If it is down and will not move, the jar is sealed. Label and date the jars, and store, without the bands, in a dark, cool place.

7. Jams and conserves should be processed for 10 minutes, or can be frozen. Jellies should be processed for 5 minutes. Paraffin is no longer recommended for sealing.

Home-canned foods will keep for many years. Some foods retain their color, flavor, texture, and food value longer than others, but whether the food is canned at home or in a factory, natural chemical changes are usually noticeable within a year. The cooler the storage space, the longer the canned food will keep its freshly cooked flavor and color.

One of the most comprehensive booklets about canning can be ordered from The Ball Corporation, Box 2005, Muncie, Indiana 47307-0005 for $2.50, which includes postage and handling. It will provide you with all the specific information you need about canning and freezing, and how to make jams, jellies, and preserves. Many excellent recipes are included.

It is not uncommon for Amish housewives to "put up" as many as 600 jars of fruits, vegetables, meats, and soups to feed their families in winter.

CROCKPOT APPLE BUTTER

Makes 4 pints

This is a simple version that starts with store-bought applesauce, cooked a long time in a crockpot. But it tastes just like the old-fashioned kind, baked down in a copper kettle over an open fire. Sweetened with honey, it has a smooth, smooth texture.

7 cups applesauce, preferably homemade, but a good-quality commercial kind (unsweetened) can be substituted
2 cups apple cider

1½ cups honey
1 teaspoon ground cinnamon
½ teaspoon ground cloves
½ teaspoon ground allspice

In a crockpot, mix all the ingredients. Cover and cook on low heat for 14 to 15 hours, or until the mixture is a deep brown. Pack while hot into 4 hot pint jars. Process in a hot-water bath for 10 minutes, counting the time after the jars have been immersed and the water comes again to a rolling boil.

BLUEBERRY JAM

Makes 3 cups

Blueberries marry well with other fruits, for they are a bit bland.
The addition of lemon to this jam gives it a little zip.

*1 quart blueberries, picked over and
washed*
½ cup cold water

4½ cups sugar
Grated rind and juice of 1 lemon

Combine all the ingredients in a large, heavy saucepan. Place over low heat and gradually bring the mixture to the boiling point, stirring all the while; this will take about 10 minutes. Cook rapidly for 2 to 3 minutes, skimming off the foam. If jam has not thickened enough to suit you (and this will vary from year to year, depending on the amount of water in the berries), cook a bit longer. I do not cook this jam to 220° F. on the candy thermometer, for I like it a bit runny. Pour into 3 hot half-pint jars. Let cool and freeze or process as for Spiced Cherry Jam, below.

SPICED CHERRY JAM

Makes 8 cups

This is a very pleasing jam, and a favorite thing to eat on Cornmeal Pancakes
(page 12) instead of the usual syrup. Of course, it is wonderful on hot
Baking Powder Biscuits (page 4) or toast, too. I prefer to freeze this jam;
the spicy flavor is more pronounced and the red color stays more
intense than if it is processed.

*4½ cups ground, or pitted, finely chopped
sour cherries (approximately 3
pounds or 2 quarts whole; see note)*
7 cups sugar
1 teaspoon almond extract
1 teaspoon ground cinnamon

*½ teaspoon (or more) red food coloring
(optional)*
¼ teaspoon ground allspice
¼ teaspoon ground cloves
1 6-ounce bottle pectin

Measure the prepared cherries into a large, heavy kettle. Add the sugar and stir well. Place over high heat and, stirring constantly, bring quickly to a full boil, with bubbles over the entire surface. Add the remaining ingredients except the pectin. Boil hard for 1 minute, stirring constantly. Remove from the heat and stir in the pectin. Skim off any foam. Ladle into 8 hot half-pint jars. Seal, then process for 4 minutes in a hot-water bath, counting the time from when the water comes again to a rolling boil after immersing the jars.
NOTE: The cherries can be chopped in a food processor after being pitted.

PRESERVED PEARS WITH LEMON

◆

Makes 6 cups

Preserved pears are not to be likened to pear jam; this dish consists of an equal amount
of fruit and heavy lemon-flavored syrup, with a hint of allspice and
cloves. Maybe we should call it a condiment. Some people call it pear honey.
My grandmother always served it in a tall cut-glass compote, and it was always
on the table whenever we had fried chicken and biscuits. The rich amber
pear preserves, with the added touch of lemon rind and raisins, were spooned on top
of the split buttered biscuits. It was all very messy, and very delightful.

6 cups sugar
3 cups water
⅓ cup powdered Fruit Fresh (see note)
¼ teaspoon ground allspice
12 whole cloves

6 large Bartlett pears (3–3½ pounds)
1 large lemon
½ cup seedless raisins
¼ cup orange juice
Speck of salt

Place 2 cups of the sugar and the water in a deep saucepan. Boil, uncovered, over medium-high heat for 5 minutes. Add the Fruit Fresh, allspice, and cloves. Stir and cook until the Fruit Fresh is dissolved; remove from the heat.

Wash the pears, cut into quarters, core, and peel with a potato parer. Cut into ½-inch slices and add immediately to the syrup. Bring again to a boil over high heat, lower heat to simmer, uncovered, for 15 minutes.

Slice the lemon thin, remove the seeds, and cut each slice into 6 wedges. Add to the pears, along with the rest of the sugar. Bring back up to a boil, and continue simmering over low heat, uncovered, for another 25 minutes. Add the raisins, orange juice, and salt, and cook 5 or 10 minutes longer, depending on how thin you want the syrup (see note). Cover and let stand in a cool place for 24

hours. Pears will keep indefinitely in the refrigerator.

To can, reheat the mixture and pour into 6 hot half-pint jars, leaving ¼ inch head space at the top. Adjust caps. Cover and process for 20 minutes in a hot-water bath, counting the time after the water comes again to a full boil. This mixture also freezes very well.

NOTE: Fruit Fresh is powdered ascorbic acid that is used to prevent fruits from darkening.

The longer you cook the preserves, the thicker they will be. The mixture will continue to thicken as it cools, and ideally the finished syrup will be the same texture as honey. The mixture can be thinned with hot water if you have cooked it down too much. Don't worry about the pears; they retain their shape. The texture of this preserve is a very personal thing, which is why there is so much leeway in the cooking time.

HOMEMADE SAUERKRAUT IN A CROCK

Makes 3½ quarts

Making sauerkraut is one of those jobs that can be a lot of fun if you have a lot of people helping you; a kraut day is still a tradition in many farm households. That first meal in the fall when the new kraut is served with pork elicits an "ahh" from everyone at the table. This is Midwest soul food, and the homemade variety is quite unlike what you find in the supermarkets.

For every 5 pounds of cabbage, use 3½ tablespoons of salt. You need widemouthed crocks because of how you will weight the cabbage down during its fermentation period. I give a new method for weighting down the cabbage as well as the old method. Crocks are available at hardwares, and old ones can be found in antiques shops.

15 pounds cabbage

10½ tablespoons coarse salt or brining salt (do not use iodized)

Remove all bruised and browning outer leaves from the cabbages. Quarter and remove the cores. Shred with a sharp knife, food processor, or slaw cutter. The cabbage should be sliced very thin.

Weigh about 5 pounds of the cabbage into a large bowl and mix in the 3½ tablespoons salt. Let stand for 10 minutes to wilt. Transfer to the crock and, using a potato masher, crush cabbage until juice forms and comes to the surface. Repeat with additional batches of cabbage until the crock is filled to about 5 inches from the top.

If enough brine has not formed from all that crushing to cover the kraut, add enough hot water to cover the cabbage completely. To weight down the cabbage, fill a large heavy-weight plastic food-storage bag with water, close it, and place it directly on the cabbage. (If you worry about 1 bag breaking, use 2.) The water-filled bag seals the surface and prevents the growth of mold. The amount of water in the bag can be adjusted to give just enough pressure to keep the cabbage covered with brine.

The traditional way to weight down the kraut is to spread a clean washable cloth directly on it. Tuck the edges down against the inside of the container. Place a dinner plate that just fits inside the crock so the cabbage is not exposed to the air. Place a weight—a large stone or brick, or a glass jar filled with water—on top. The brine should come to the cover but not over it.

The kraut will ferment better at room temperature (68 to 72° F.) and could be ready in 10 to 12 days. If you store it in a cooler place, the fermentation may take 2 to 3 weeks. The time varies considerably from batch to batch.

Check the kraut every few days; the gas bubbles that form indicate it is fermenting. Remove scum as it appears on the top of the cabbage, wash the cloth and plate, and put it back on again. As soon as the fermenting is completed (and I want to warn you, you will *smell* it; there's a lot of action going on in that crock and sometimes it even hisses), there will be no more bubbles rising to the top.

To can, heat the sauerkraut with its juices to a simmer (185 to 210° F.). *Do not boil.* Pack the hot kraut into 10 hot pint jars, and cover with the hot juice to ½ inch from the top of the jar. Process for 15 minutes for pints, 20 minutes for quarts, both counting from when water returns to a full boil. Cool and store.

COUNTRY CHILI SAUCE

Makes 6 pints

I make this chili sauce especially for Chili Sauce Salad Dressing (page 30).
It is also a great accompaniment to roast beef.

26 *large tomatoes*
2 *large green bell peppers*
2 *large onions*
1½ *cups cider vinegar*
1½ *cups sugar*
3 *tablespoons salt*

1 *tablespoon celery seed*
1 *tablespoon ground cinnamon*
1 *tablespoon ground cloves*
1 *teaspoon black pepper*
1 *teaspoon ground ginger*
1 *teaspoon ground allspice*

Peel, core, and chop the tomatoes, and place in a large, heavy saucepan. Wash, peel, and chop the peppers and onions and add to the tomatoes. Add the rest of the ingredients and mix well.

Bring to a boil and simmer over low heat, uncovered, for about 2 hours, or until mixture is as thick as you want. The amount of time will vary, depending on the amount of mois-ture in the tomatoes, which depends on the amount of rain the tomatoes received that particular summer. (It is this kind of unscientific stuff that drives cooks mad.) Stir frequently. Pour, boiling hot, into 6 hot pint jars, leaving ¼-inch head space. Process in a hot-water bath for 15 minutes, counting the time after the water comes again to a full boil.

GOOSEBERRY RELISH

Makes 4 pints

The cook who gave me this recipe insisted on calling it a relish. I probably would have called it a chutney, but the two are certainly first cousins. A bit sweet and a bit sour, it is delicious served with ham and biscuits or as an accompaniment to any curry.

2 *quarts gooseberries*
1½ *cups seedless raisins*
4 *medium onions, chopped*
   Slivered rind of 1 orange,
      plus the juice
3½ *cups brown sugar*
2 *teaspoons mustard seed*

1 *teaspoon ground allspice*
½ *teaspoon cayenne pepper*
¼ *teaspoon cloves*
¼ *teaspoon tumeric*
2 *tablespoons salt*
3½ *cups cider vinegar*

Wash and tail the gooseberries, but leave on the little brown seed on the opposite end— it adds texture. Combine all of the ingredients in a heavy kettle. Bring slowly to a boil. Lower heat and simmer and stir for about 1¼ hours, or until the desired thickness is reached. You can test this by placing a spoon-ful of the chutney on a saucer and chilling it briefly in the freezer and observing how runny it is after it is cool. Cook longer if necessary.

Pour boiling hot into hot pint jars, leaving 1 inch of head space. Adjust caps and process in a hot-water bath for 10 minutes, counting the time after the water returns to a full boil.

BREAD AND BUTTER PICKLES

Makes 10 pints

It is hard to find good commercial bread and butter pickles, so I make my own. These are a half-sweet, half-tart pickle, with lots of mustard seed and little onion rings to add texture. This recipe is quick to prepare, too. They are just the thing to eat with roast beef or ham sandwiches.

25 slender medium cucumbers (see note)
10 medium onions, as big around as the cucumbers
½ cup coarse salt
2 cups cider vinegar
2 cups sugar

1 cup water
2 teaspoons mustard seed
2 teaspoons celery seed
½ teaspoon turmeric
½ teaspoon ground cloves

Cut cucumbers and onions into thick slices. Place them in deep pans in layers, sprinkling each layer with the salt. Allow to stand 2 to 3 hours. Drain.

In another deep pan, mix the remaining ingredients and bring to a boil over high heat. Add the cucumber-onion mixture and bring to a boil; cook for 5 minutes over medium heat.

Transfer hot to 10 hot pint jars. Cover and process for 10 minutes in a hot-water bath, counting the time from when the water comes again to a boil after the jars have been totally immersed.

NOTE: If you can't find unwaxed cucumbers, substitute 30 Kirby cucumbers.

VERY SPECIAL STRAWBERRY PRESERVES

Makes 2 cups

Making preserves without commercial pectin yields a wonderfully fresh-tasting treat. Cooking them in small batches helps you control the temperature and the quality. Do not stir the jam too much—you want the berries to remain whole.

1½ pounds perfect strawberries
(1 rounded quart)

Pinch of salt
3 cups sugar

Wash and clean the berries, removing any hard and yellow ends. Place in a large, deep, heavy kettle, add 1 cup sugar, and stir gently to mix. Cook over low heat and bring to a boil, stirring now and then, until a syrup forms. This will take about 10 minutes. Gradually raise the heat to medium-high so the jam comes to a rolling boil and the sugar dissolves completely. Cook 5 minutes; skim off the foam and discard. Add the second cup of sugar

and boil another 5 minutes. Stir in the third cup, insert a candy thermometer, and cook until 220° F. is reached. Pour into a shallow heatproof 9 x 6-inch dish. Skim one more time; do not stir again after this.

Cover the dish with a tea towel and allow to stand overnight, unrefrigerated. The next morning, ladle the cold jam into 2 half-pint freezer jars, label, and freeze. Thaw and bring to room temperature before serving.

HOMEMADE TOMATO SOUP

◆

Makes 12 pints

Commercial canned tomato soups pale in comparison to this distinctively
flavored one. This is a wonderful dish to have for lunch or as an elegant first
course. Scented with cinnamon, cloves, and allspice, it is in a class of its own.
There are several ways to use this condensed soup base after it is canned. You
can add milk or water or, if you use commercial canned soups, a can of
mushroom soup is a nice addition.

1 peck tomatoes
(approximately 17 pounds)
2 medium onions
2 Hungarian hot peppers
3 small bunches celery
1 large bunch fresh parsley
½ cup coarse salt

1 cup brown sugar
1 cup all-purpose flour
1 teaspoon ground allspice
1 teaspoon ground cinnamon
1 teaspoon ground cloves
¼ teaspoon black pepper
½ cup (1 stick) butter

Core the tomatoes and chop them coarsely. Chop the onions, peppers, celery, and
parsley coarsely, and divide equally, along
with the tomatoes, between 2 very large, deep
kettles. Divide the salt between the 2 kettles,
too. Cover, bring to a boil, and simmer over
medium-low heat for 1 hour, or until all vegetables are very tender. Stir frequently. Put
mixture through a sieve or food mill. Transfer
the puree to a large kettle.

In a medium bowl, combine all remaining ingredients except butter. Add the seasonings gradually to the hot puree, beating in with
a whisk. Add the butter and whisk smooth.
Bring to a boil, then simmer over medium-

low heat for 3 minutes. Pour hot into 12 hot
pint jars, leaving ½ inch head space. Seal and
process in hot-water bath for 15 minutes,
counting the time from when the water reaches
a rolling boil after the jars have been totally
immersed.

To serve, add one 11-ounce can cream of
mushroom soup and 1 soup can of water to
every pint of tomato soup base. Heat and
serve. (Yield: 6–8 servings.) I seldom buy
commercial canned soups, preferring to make
my own, but once in a while I will make an
exception, and this is one of those times. You
can also prepare the soup base by adding 1½
cups milk to it, or even using 1½ cups water.

FRESH HOT TOMATO RELISH

◆

Makes 3 quarts

I have never seen a published recipe for this Hot Tomato Relish, and when my mother heard I was writing this cookbook, she said, "You surely will include the Manahan tomato relish, won't you?" "Of course I will!" Making this midwestern version of salsa was a fall tradition at our house, and we all helped. Grinding the horseradish caused us to weep copious tears, so we took turns at the old hand grinder. Today you can use a blender to prepare the horseradish, thank goodness, but you must use fresh horseradish root—the commercial stuff just won't work.
Do not can this relish; just store it in the refrigerator. It will keep its hotness until December, but generally it is eaten up long before then, for it is the perfect meat accompaniment.

1 peck tomatoes
  (approximately 17 pounds)
2 bunches celery, cleaned
8 onions, 2 inches in diameter, peeled
6 green bell peppers, seeded
½–¾ pound fresh horseradish

4 cups cider vinegar
1¼ cups sugar
½ cup coarse salt
2 tablespoons mustard seed
1 tablespoon black pepper

Peel, core, and slice the tomatoes into wedges. Remove the seeds and chop coarsely. Place the tomatoes in a sieve, and with a large spoon, stir tomatoes vigorously until juice is removed and tomatoes are pulpy. You will have to do this in several batches. Transfer the pulp to a large glass or ceramic bowl.

Using a food processor or blender (or metal hand grinder), process the celery, onions, and peppers to approximately a ⅜-inch dice. Add to the tomato pulp. Pare the horseradish and cut into ½-inch pieces—it is tough and fibrous. Fill the food processor bowl or blender about two-thirds full with water. Add the chopped horseradish and process until it is very fine. Drain well. Expect to cry a little. (If using a hand grinder, use the small-holed disk.) Drain well and add 1 cup of the ground horseradish to the tomato mixture, reserving any extra for another use. Add the remaining ingredients to the tomatoes and blend. Pack into 3 hot quart jars immediately. Cover tightly and refrigerate; this will keep several months.

NOTE: All the vegetables should be transferred, in small batches, to the sieve and the excess liquid forced out. Do not omit this step, or the relish will be watery and will spoil.

TOMATO COCKTAIL

Makes 5–6 quarts

Excess tomatoes? Use them up in this superb tomato juice. This is not only good chilled, but when heated makes a superb light first course. And you don't have to be too precise about the measurements, except for the tomatoes.

1 peck tomatoes
(approximately 17 pounds)
½ bunch celery
3 carrots
2 medium onions
2 medium green bell peppers

2 cooked beets (great for color)
Large bunch fresh parsley
Large bunch fresh spinach
¼ cup salt
1 teaspoon black pepper

Wash, core, and chop tomatoes very coarsely. Clean and coarsely chop the rest of the vegetables and combine in 2 large, deep kettles, dividing the ingredients equally between them. Cover and cook until the vegetables are completely softened—this will take about 45 minutes.

Put vegetables through a sieve or food mill. Pour the hot juice into 5 or 6 hot quart jars, leaving ½ inch headspace at the top. Seal and process for 15 minutes in a hot-water bath, counting the time from when the water returns to a full rolling boil after the jars have been immersed. (Pints require only 10 minutes.)

YELLOW TOMATO PRESERVES

Makes 9 cups

Yellow Tomato Preserves are a joy to behold, and a joy to eat.
A bit tangy, with a zip of citrus and a hint of spices, it is an unusual jam
and you'll be delighted with it.

2 pounds yellow tomatoes (4–5 large)
1 medium lemon
1 medium orange
1 1¾-ounce box powdered pectin
7 cups sugar

¼ teaspoon salt
1 teaspoon grated nutmeg
½ teaspoon ground cinnamon
¼ teaspoon ground allspice

Wash, core, peel, and slice the tomatoes —you should have 4 cups. Wash the lemon and orange, slice them thin, and chop them coarsely. Place the fruits in a large, deep kettle and stir in the pectin. Cook and stir over high heat until juices form and liquid boils. Add the sugar and salt and boil hard, uncovered, for approximately 10 minutes. Add the spices during the last few minutes of cooking.

Remove kettle from the heat and let the mixture cool a few minutes. Skim off foam with a metal spoon and discard. Pour the preserves into 9 hot half-pint jars, leaving ¼ inch headspace at the top. Seal and process for 10 minutes.

THE BAKE SALE

Both the Amish and Mennonites are noted for their baking skills. Local cookbooks bulge with recipes for pies, cakes, cookies, breads, and fruit desserts that are uncommonly good. Bake sales provide a way for these communities to earn money for special needs, such as equipment for the Amish schools or Mennonite youth projects. These irresistible bake sales draw customers like bees to honey.

Many of the cakes and cookies popular in this area contain fruit; this acts as a preservative so they remain fresh longer, a boon to the Amish and Mennonite farm wife who prepares large quantities of food to last a long time.

To the "English," a delightful aspect of the bake sale is finding an item remembered only from childhood, such as whole apple dumplings, German onion cake, or soft raisin-filled cookies with a dusting of white sugar on top. But these old-fashioned delicacies are getting hard to find even in this rural area, for some of the recipes are on their way to being lost or forgotten.

During a visit to Leah Yoder's kitchen, I asked her about Knee Patches (page 110), a type of delicate yet crispy deep-fried Swiss pastry. Leah told me she remembered her grandmother making Knee Patches when she was a little girl, but it had been such a long time she couldn't recall how it was done exactly. She did remember her grandmother sitting down and slapping the dough over her knee to make it very thin. When she mentioned Knee Patches to her grandmother, the older woman said, "You know, I don't think I even have a recipe for Knee Patches anymore. And it's been so many years since I've made them that I'm not sure if I can remember how I made up the dough." Later, in another community, I came across a recipe for Knee Patches and it gave me inordinate pleasure to send it to them.

Of course, the Amish want to eat new things just like everyone else. In a local restaurant noted for its Amish food, I saw a group of Amish girls eating croissants. Well, why not? However, a thick slice of good homemade Amish bread can hold its own with a croissant anytime.

CINNAMON BREAD

BUTTERMILK BREAD

CRESCENT SWEET ROLLS

GERMAN ONION CAKE

CARROT CAKE

OATMEAL CAKE

BANANA NUT CAKE

OLD-FASHIONED FILLED COOKIES

POTATO DOUGHNUTS

BIG WHITE SOFT SUGAR COOKIES

CINNAMON BREAD

◆

Makes 2 loaves

Toast this faintly sweet bread for breakfast. The top is a bit bumpy and golden brown; the inside has a thin spiral of cinnamon and brown sugar.

2 cups milk
2 tablespoons shortening, softened
  (see note)
1 cup warm water
1 package active dry yeast
¾ cup brown sugar
1 tablespoon salt

1 tablespoon vanilla extract
2 eggs, slightly beaten
2 cups quick oatmeal (not old-fashioned)
5½–6 cups unbleached all-purpose flour
2 teaspoons ground cinnamon
  Oil and butter for brushing

In a small saucepan, combine the milk and shortening; scald over medium heat. In a large, warm mixer bowl, combine the warm water and the yeast with a fork; set aside in a warm place to proof, until the mixture starts to bubble, about 10 minutes.

To the hot milk, add ¼ cup brown sugar, the salt, and the vanilla; mix. Add to the yeast-water mixture, then stir in the beaten eggs and oatmeal; blend. Add half the flour and mix well. Gradually work in the rest of the flour. Knead until smooth and elastic, about 5 minutes. Return to a large oiled bowl, and oil the top of the dough. Cover and let rise until doubled in bulk, about 1 hour, or a bit more.

After the dough has risen, punch down thoroughly and divide in half. On a floured board, roll out each half into a 13 x 8-inch rectangle, pressing out as many air bubbles as possible. Combine the remaining ½ cup brown sugar and the cinnamon, and sprinkle half of it on each rectangle (do not butter first). Roll tightly, beginning at a short edge. Pinch the edge of the dough to seal well; press in ends of roll. Place loaves, seam side down, in 2 well-greased 9 x 5 x 3-inch loaf pans. Brush lightly with oil. Cover and let rise in a warm place until doubled, 30 to 45 minutes.

Preheat oven to 400° F. Bake loaves for 10 minutes, lower heat to 350° F., and bake 25 to 30 minutes longer, or until loaves are a deep golden brown and make a hollow sound when tapped. Immediately spread the tops of the hot loaves with cold butter. Remove from pans and let cool. This bread freezes well.

NOTE: Half-lard and half-vegetable shortening works well in this recipe. If the dough rises too high and flops over the sides of the bread pans before baking, carefully cut off the excess raw dough with a pair of scissors.

BUTTERMILK BREAD

Makes 2 small loaves

Made with molasses and a bit of bacon fat, this flavorful loaf is fine-grained and golden inside, with a dark chewy crust. It stores and freezes well.

1 package active dry yeast
¼ cup warm water
2 tablespoons light molasses
2 cups buttermilk

2 tablespoons bacon fat
1½ teaspoons salt
5½–6½ cups all-purpose flour (see note)
2 tablespoons (¼ stick) butter, melted

Dissolve the yeast in warm water with 1 tablespoon of the molasses. Set aside in a warm place to proof for 5 minutes, until the mixture becomes frothy.

In a small saucepan, combine the buttermilk, bacon fat, remaining molasses, and salt; heat until lukewarm.

Place 3 cups of the flour in a large mixer bowl; beat in the buttermilk mixture until smooth, then mix in the yeast. Add most of the remaining flour (reserving 1 cup to use on the board while kneading), 1 cup at a time until the dough leaves the sides of the bowl. Turn out onto a lightly floured surface, using the reserved flour, and knead 10 to 12 minutes. Add flour as necessary to prevent dough from sticking. The finished dough should be smooth and elastic. Put the dough in a warm, buttered (or use vegetable shortening) bowl, turn once, and cover with a tea towel. Let the dough rise in a warm place until doubled in bulk, about 1 hour. (This can be done in an unheated oven, over a large, flat pan of hot water.)

Oil two 8 x 4-inch loaf pans. Punch dough down, divide in half, form into 2 loaves, and place loaves in pans, smooth side up. Cover and let rise in a warm place until doubled in bulk, about 1 hour.

Preheat oven to 425° F. Bake loaves for 10 minutes, lower heat to 350° F., and bake for another 25 to 30 minutes. If loaves begin to get too brown for your taste, cover lightly with a piece of foil. The finished bread should sound hollow when tapped with your knuckles. Remove loaves from the pans immediately. Brush tops of loaves with the melted butter. Let cool before slicing.

NOTE: It is nearly impossible to give a precise amount of flour in a bread recipe, as flours vary according to grade, moisture, and kneading techniques.

CRESCENT SWEET ROLLS

◆

Makes 4 dozen small rolls

These rolls are a Christmas tradition at our house. A most delicate, fine-textured sweet roll that uses 1 pound of butter, this breakfast treat is slightly flavored with mace and nutmeg. And the dough requires no kneading.

1 cup milk
1 package active dry yeast
4 cups sifted unbleached all-purpose
*   flour*
¼ cup granulated sugar
1 teaspoon salt
1 cup (2 sticks) cold butter
*   (no substitutes)*
3 eggs
1 teaspoon vanilla extract
FILLING
1 cup (2 sticks) butter, softened

1½ cups brown sugar, approximately
*   Grated nutmeg*
*   Ground mace*
GLAZE
2 cups confectioners' sugar
¼ cup milk
2 teaspoons vanilla extract
¼ teaspoon ground mace
*   Speck of salt*

In a small saucepan, scald the milk and allow it to cool to lukewarm. Measure ½ of it into a warmed cup and sprinkle in the yeast. Stir with a fork so it thoroughly dissolves.

Sift the dry ingredients into a large bowl. Cut in the butter with a pastry blender (or use a food processor) to make small crumbs. In a large mixer bowl, beat the eggs well. Add the remaining ½ cup of milk and the vanilla to the eggs; blend. Add the yeast mixture. Make a well in the flour mixture and pour in the yeast-milk mixture. Mix thoroughly by hand. The dough will be very soft. Form the dough into a ball, cover, and refrigerate overnight.

The next day, remove the dough from the refrigerator and punch down. Divide into 8 wedges, as you would a pie. One at a time, roll each wedge into a 12-inch round (keep the unused wedges in the refrigerator), and spread the round liberally with softened butter for the filling. Cut into 6 pie-shape wedges, and sprinkle each wedge with a generous teaspoon

of brown sugar, 2 shakes of nutmeg, and 1 shake of mace, keeping sugar well inside the edges. Roll up, starting at wide end of dough. Transfer to a greased baking sheet and form roll into a crescent with the tip of the dough underneath. Pat any seams closed, using a light touch—the dough is very tender. Repeat with remaining dough wedges. Cover with tea towels and let the rolls rise for 1 to 1½ hours.

Preheat the oven to 375° F. Bake for 6 to 9 minutes; rolls should be pale yellow, not browned. Meanwhile, combine the glaze ingredients, mixing well. When the rolls are done, remove from pan immediately and place on wax paper-covered racks. Glaze while still warm, using a teaspoon to glaze each roll liberally.

NOTE: These rolls freeze very well. They are delicious eaten at room temperature, but if you reheat them, do so very briefly in the microwave or the glaze will melt.

GERMAN ONION CAKE

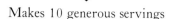

Makes 10 generous servings

This wonderful quick bread is topped with a mixture of sautéed onions, sour cream, and poppy seeds. Serve it hot, in wedges.

2 cups coarsely chopped onions (3 large)
2 tablespoons (¼ stick) butter
1 teaspoon salt
¼ teaspoon dried marjoram
¼ teaspoon black pepper
2 cups all-purpose flour
¼ cup cornstarch

4 teaspoons baking powder
5 tablespoons vegetable shortening
¾–1 cup milk
1 egg, well beaten
¾ cup sour cream
2 teaspoons poppy seeds
¼ teaspoon paprika

In a medium skillet, sauté the onions in butter over low heat until they just begin to brown, about 15 minutes. Season with ¼ teaspoon of the salt, the marjoram, and the pepper. Set aside to cool.

Preheat oven to 450° F. In a food processor bowl place flour, cornstarch, baking powder, and the remaining salt; mix. Add the shortening and process just until it is the texture of soft crumbs. Add the milk and mix quickly to form a soft dough.

Oil a 10-inch-round cake pan and lightly use your fingers to spread the dough out evenly. Spread the cooked onion over the top. Beat the egg and sour cream together. Spoon the mixture over the onion, and spread it out to the very edge of the pan. Sprinkle lightly with poppy seeds and paprika. Bake for 20 minutes. Let cool slightly, then cut into wedges.

CARROT CAKE

Serves 12–16

This wonderfully moist carrot cake appears at every Amish gathering, including weddings, and at lots of Mennonite functions, too. The frosted cake freezes very well.

2 cups all-purpose flour
2 teaspoons baking powder
1 teaspoon baking soda
1 teaspoon salt
1 teaspoon ground cinnamon
1¼ cups vegetable oil
2 cups granulated sugar
1 teaspoon vanilla extract
4 eggs
3 cups finely shredded carrots (¾ pound)

1 cup chopped pecans, medium fine
CREAM CHEESE FROSTING
1 8-ounce package cream cheese, softened
½ cup (1 stick) butter, softened (no substitutes)
1 pound confectioners' sugar
1 teaspoon vanilla extract
Speck of salt
½ cup coarsely chopped pecans

Preheat oven to 325° F. In a large mixer bowl, combine the flour and the next 4 ingredients. In another large mixer bowl, combine the oil, sugar, and vanilla and blend. Add the eggs, 1 at a time, and mix well. Quickly mix in the carrots and nuts. Pour this over the flour mixture, and combine gently. Pour batter into an oiled 9 x 13-inch cake pan, and bake for approximately 45 to 55 minutes, or until the top springs back when touched lightly with your finger, and it begins to shrink away from the sides of the pan. Let cool completely.

In a large mixer bowl, whip cream cheese and butter for frosting until well blended. Gradually add the confectioners' sugar, then the vanilla and salt. Beat well. Spread the cream cheese frosting on the cooled cake and sprinkle pecans over top.

NOTE: Because of the cream cheese in the frosting, the cake should be refrigerated, but the flavor will be better if you bring it to room temperature before serving.

OATMEAL CAKE

Makes 12 large servings

Oatmeal Cake is a popular Mennonite and Amish dessert. This cake is tender and moist, and the broiled frosting is like candy.

1 cup one-minute quick oatmeal, uncooked
1½ cups boiling water
1½ cups all-purpose flour
1½ teaspoon baking soda
½ teaspoon ground cinnamon
½ teaspoon grated nutmeg
½ teaspoon salt
½ cup (1 stick) butter, softened
1 teaspoon vanilla extract
1 cup brown sugar

1 cup granulated sugar
2 eggs
FROSTING
½ cup (1 stick) butter
1 cup brown sugar
1 5-ounce can evaporated milk
8 ounces flaked coconut
1 cup chopped nuts, either pecans or English walnuts
1 teaspoon vanilla extract
Speck of salt

Place the oats in a small bowl and pour the boiling water over them. Let stand 20 minutes.

Preheat oven to 350° F. Sift together the flour, baking soda, cinnamon, nutmeg, and salt on wax paper. Set aside. In a large mixer bowl, beat the butter until creamy. Add the vanilla and gradually add the sugars, beating until fluffy. Beat in the eggs, 1 at a time. Add the oatmeal mixture and blend. Add the flour mixture and blend again. Pour batter into an oiled 13 x 8-inch baking pan. Bake for 35 minutes, or until the top of the cake springs back when touched with your fingertip. While the cake is baking, prepare the frosting.

Melt the butter in a large saucepan. Add the brown sugar and cook until the mixture bubbles up. Add the milk, and bring again to a boil. Remove from the heat and add the rest of the ingredients. Spread the hot frosting on the hot cake as soon as the cake is done. Turn the oven up to broil and broil the cake about 6 inches from the heat for 2 minutes, or until the frosting bubbles all over the cake. Let cool before cutting.

BANANA NUT CAKE

Serves 16

The secret of this moist cake is in using old bananas. Black walnuts add a special touch. And the cake tastes even better after it mellows a bit, so make it a couple of days prior to serving, then frost it, cover tightly, and keep it at room temperature. It also freezes very well.

⅔ cup vegetable shortening
1⅔ cups granulated sugar
3 eggs, at room temperature
2¼ cups sifted cake flour
1¼ teaspoons baking powder
1¼ teaspoons baking soda
1¼ teaspoons salt
⅔ cup buttermilk, at room temperature

1¼ cups mashed bananas (see note)
⅔ cup finely chopped black walnuts
PENUCHE FROSTING
¾ cup (1½ sticks) butter
1½ cups brown sugar
¼ cup plus 2 tablespoons milk
½ teaspoon salt
1½ teaspoons vanilla extract
3–4 cups confectioners' sugar

Preheat oven to 350° F. In a large mixer bowl, cream the shortening and sugar until fluffy. Add the eggs, 1 at a time, and beat well after each addition. Sift the flour, baking powder, baking soda, and salt together, and add them to the butter mixture, alternating with the buttermilk. Then stir in the bananas and black walnuts. Pour into three 8-inch or two 9-inch oiled cake layer pans. Bake for 35 to 40 minutes, or until the top springs back when touched lightly with your finger. Allow to cool 10 minutes, then remove from pans and let cool completely before frosting.

In a small saucepan, melt the butter for the frosting. Stir in the brown sugar and bring the mixture to a boil over high heat. Reduce the heat, and simmer for 2 minutes, stirring constantly. Add the milk and bring again to a boil, stirring all the while. Remove from the heat and pour into a mixer bowl. Let cool. Add salt and vanilla, and gradually beat in the confectioners' sugar. Beat until the frosting is creamy and the right consistency for spreading. Spread between layers and frost top of cake.

NOTE: Bananas should be at least 7 days old for maximum flavor. Buy them ahead of time and ripen them until the skin is heavily flecked with brown—the browner the better.

OLD-FASHIONED FILLED COOKIES

◆

Makes 3 dozen cookies

Filled cookies, plump and soft, can be filled with either a raisin or date filling.
These are even better the day after they are baked.

3½ cups unbleached all-purpose flour
2 teaspoons baking powder
1 teaspoon salt
⅔ cup butter, softened (no substitutes)
¾ cup brown sugar
¾ cup granulated sugar
2 eggs
⅓ cup milk
1 teaspoon vanilla extract
RAISIN FILLING
1½–1¾ cups seedless raisins
1 cup brown sugar
1 cup water
1 teaspoon lemon juice

Speck of salt
1 tablespoon plus 1¼ teaspoons
* cornstarch*
2 tablespoons water
½ cup finely chopped pecans
DATE FILLING
1 cup brown sugar
2 tablespoons all-purpose flour
Speck of salt
1 cup water
1 cup chopped dates
2 teaspoons grated orange rind
½ teaspoon grated nutmeg
1 cup finely chopped pecans

Prepare the cookie dough first. Sift the flour, baking powder, and salt together; set aside. In a large mixer bowl, cream the butter and sugars thoroughly. Add the eggs, milk, and vanilla, and continue beating at high speed for 2 minutes. Lower speed, and gradually add the flour mixture; blend. Cover and refrigerate at least 3 hours or overnight, so dough will be stiff enough to roll.

To make the raisin filling, grind the raisins, using the conventional grinder attachment on your electric mixer or a hand grinder. Do not attempt to prepare the raisins in a food processor; the texture won't be right. You should have 1 cup of ground raisins. In a medium saucepan, combine the raisins, brown sugar, water, lemon juice, and salt. Bring to a boil over high heat, stir, then simmer over low heat for 3 minutes. In a small bowl, combine the cornstarch and water, and use to thicken the raisin mixture, cooking until the mixture bubbles up. Remove from heat. When cool, stir in the nuts.

To make the date filling, combine the brown sugar, flour, and salt in a medium saucepan. Gradually add the water, then add the dates, orange rind, and nutmeg. Bring to a boil over high heat, stir, and simmer over low heat, breaking up dates with a spoon, for 3 minutes. Remove from heat. When cool, add the nuts.

Preheat oven to 350° F. Roll out half of the dough until very thin, about ⅛ inch, on a lightly floured surface, keeping the other half in the refrigerator. Using a round 2¾-inch cookie cutter, cut thin rounds of dough. Transfer half the rounds to a lightly sprayed cookie sheet. Place a heaping teaspoon of filling on each cookie, then top with another round. Dip your fingertip in flour (this dough softens up quickly) and crimp the edges closed. (Rechill and reroll leftover scraps.) Bake cookies for *exactly* 8 minutes—cookies will be a pale yellow. Take from oven and allow cookies to stay on sheet until almost cool. Remove to a rack to finish cooling. Repeat with the remaining dough.
NOTE: Once baked, these freeze very well.

POTATO DOUGHNUTS

Makes 24 doughnuts

Doughnuts made with mashed potatoes stay fresh and moist for a long time.
These are nicely flavored with nutmeg, and have a lovely cakelike, fine texture.
They must be started one day in advance.

2 eggs
1 cup granulated sugar
2 medium potatoes, boiled and mashed
    to make 1 cup
5 tablespoons lard, melted
1 cup buttermilk
2 teaspoons vanilla extract

3½ cups unbleached all-purpose flour
2½ teaspoons baking powder
1½ teaspoons grated nutmeg
1 teaspoon baking soda
½ teaspoon salt
2 quarts vegetable oil
Confectioners' sugar

In a large mixer bowl, beat the eggs until frothy. Add the sugar and mix until well blended. Stir in the potatoes, lard, buttermilk, and vanilla. Sift the dry ingredients together and add to the potato mixture, mixing just until flour is completely moistened. Cover dough and refrigerate overnight.

Preheat oil in fryer to 370° F. On a heavily floured surface, roll out half the dough until ½ inch thick; refrigerate the other half. Using a heavily floured 2¾-inch doughnut cutter, cut out doughnuts with a twisting mo-

tion. Using a metal spatula, slide the doughnuts into hot fat and cook until golden brown on the underside, about 2 minutes. Turn carefully so you don't prick the doughnuts, and fry on the other side, about 1 minute. Remove from fat and drain on paper towels. Then fry doughnut holes, turning frequently with slotted spoon. Drain.

When doughnuts are cool, shake 4 at a time in confectioners' sugar, in a large paper sack. Sugar only as many as you plan to serve—they store better unsugared.

BIG WHITE SOFT SUGAR COOKIES

◆

Makes 3½ dozen cookies

Because the Amish women use wood-burning, heavy iron stoves in their kitchens, they are still able to make Big White Soft Sugar Cookies, just like our grandmothers made. I cannot tell you how many recipes I played around with before I developed this one. It comes very close to those cookies of our memories—white, soft, and cakelike, with just a touch of nutmeg. The secret is in the baking, and in using nonstick cookie sheets. The batter for these cookies must rest overnight, so plan accordingly.

1 cup buttermilk
1 teaspoon baking soda
1 cup vegetable oil
1½ cups sugar
2 eggs
1½ teaspoons salt

1½ teaspoons grated nutmeg
2 teaspoons vanilla extract
3 teaspoons baking powder
3 cups unbleached all-purpose flour
Sugar
Seedless raisins

In a measuring cup, mix the buttermilk and baking soda; set aside. In a large mixer bowl, combine the oil, sugar, and eggs; mix well. Add the buttermilk-soda mixture and blend. Then add the salt, nutmeg, vanilla, and baking powder and mix again. Blend in the flour (the batter will be very runny). Cover and refrigerate overnight.

The next day, preheat oven to 400° F. For the very best results, use ungreased nonstick baking sheets. Dark or shiny sheets conduct the heat differently, and the cookie will have crisp brown edges, which are just what you *don't* want. Use 1 heaping tablespoon of batter per cookie, and place on the sheets. Liberally sprinkle more sugar on top of each cookie and dot with 3 raisins. Keep batter refrigerated between bakings. Bake for just 5 minutes. The cookies should be just barely done—still almost white. If they are golden, you have left them in too long. Remove from oven, and allow the cookies to remain on the cookie sheet for 3 more minutes to continue baking. Carefully remove cookies with a metal spatula to a wax paper-covered rack to cool.

The cookies keep well in tightly covered containers or can be frozen. In either case, each cookie should be wrapped individually or between layers of wax paper. They are so tender, so moist, so cakelike that they cling together if this is not done.

THANKSGIVING

The Hoosier countryside in November is subdued in color. Bare trees make stark silhouettes against gray skies, and the frosts have blackened once-cheerful gardens and wildflowers along the roadsides. Bedraggled cornstalks rustle in muddy fields, and cold driving rains slant against the barns. The cows gather around the haystacks for protection from the wind, and geese cackle indignantly when they discover their ponds are covered with a skin of ice. But the market stands are bright punctuation marks on this somber landscape with their piles of enormous pumpkins, slate-blue Hubbard squash, colorful Indian corn, and bouquets of orange bittersweet. Jars of sorghum and apple butter and sacks of black walnuts disappear from the counters. Bushels of apples —Jonathans, Rome Beauties, Rambos, and if you are lucky, Northern Spys —are bought up by the city folk on their final forage into Amish country.

And then, unexpectedly, the rains stop, and there will be days of dazzling clarity. The sky is azure blue, the mornings sharp and clear with sunshine so bright it hurts your eyes. The farmers use this time to cut and haul in cords of wood for winter heat and to do maintenance on their outer buildings. The women begin preparing mincemeat and canning the sauerkraut that by now has finished curing in crocks and is stored on unheated back porches. Fall signals the time for certain foods: pot roasts, stews, spareribs and kraut, and pumpkin pies.

And it is time to think of the holidays. The Amish-Mennonite Thanksgiving menus are classic American menus: turkey, dressing, cranberries, winter squash, relishes, and pies. And oysters. The Amish and Mennonites serve oysters regularly, most frequently prepared in seasoned milk broth or as a scalloped dish, layered with crumbs and butter and inundated with cream. To find this affection for oysters in land-locked Indiana was at first puzzling, but in *Sauerkraut Yankees*, William Woys Weaver explains that in Lancaster, Pennsylvania, the Pennsylvania Dutch were just 100

APPLE SALAD

ROAST TURKEY WITH
SAGE DRESSING AND
GIBLET GRAVY

TURKEY STOCK

TURKEY SOUP

CREAMY MASHED
POTATOES

ROAST DUCKLING WITH
SAUERKRAUT AND APPLE
DRESSING

BAKED ONIONS WITH
SOUR CREAM

BRUSSELS SPROUTS WITH
DILL

STUFFED ACORN SQUASH

CUSTARD CORNBREAD

CRANBERRY SHERBET

EASY MINCEMEAT FOR PIE

miles from the sea, and the Delaware, Schuylkill, and Susquehanna rivers were once major waterways. Shellfish, including oysters, were packed live in barrels and sent upriver to Lancaster in a matter of hours. Dipped in batter and fried in hot butter, they were a popular breakfast dish. The enthusiasm for oysters is one of the culinary influences that these people have retained from their time spent in Pennsylvania, and it again points out how the history of a people can be traced through their cuisine.

APPLE SALAD
◆
Serves 10–12

This apple salad has a dressing that is made from thickened pineapple juice, with a tad of butter added for richness. The dressing can be made a day before serving. Resist the impulse to add marshmallows.

1 20-ounce can pineapple chunks
2 quarts chopped red-skinned tart
    apples such as Jonathan or
    MacIntosh, skins left on
2 cups green seedless grapes, halved
1¼ cups toasted pecans
1 cup chopped celery
½ cup chopped fresh parsley

DRESSING
¼ cup (½ stick) butter
¼ cup sugar
1 tablespoon lemon juice
2 tablespoons cornstarch
1 cup mayonnaise

Drain the pineapple, reserving the juice, and set chunks aside. Prepare the dressing. In a small saucepan, combine the pineapple juice, butter, sugar, and lemon juice and bring to a boil over medium heat. In a small bowl, combine the cornstarch and enough water to make a smooth mixture; add to the bubbling juice.

Reduce heat and cook until mixture is thick and smooth. Chill. Whisk in the mayonnaise. (This can be done a day in advance.)

Place the pineapple chunks and the rest of the salad ingredients in a large bowl. Toss well, then mix in the chilled dressing.

ROAST TURKEY WITH SAGE DRESSING AND GIBLET GRAVY

Serves 12

This is a well-seasoned crumbly dressing, and the currants add just a touch of sweetness. Start drying out your bread at least four days in advance. The dry dressing ingredients, as well as some of the vegetable ingredients, can be prepared several days ahead of time, so assembling the dressing can be done quickly on the day you are actually baking the turkey. Allow ¾ cup of dressing for each pound of turkey; extra dressing can be baked separately, but since the juices from the bird further moisten the dressing, you will need to add some additional liquid to the separate dressing. As soon as possible after serving the turkey, remove every bit of stuffing from the neck and body cavities and remove the meat from the bones. Cool the stuffing, meat, and any leftover gravy promptly. Allow 1 pound of uncooked turkey per person; that sounds like a lot, but a turkey has quite a bit of bone and you want some left over, of course. Do not wrap until cooled. And do save the carcass for soup. You can remove the giblets and the neck from the partially thawing turkey and prepare the gravy base the day before.

1 13-15 pound turkey, fresh or frozen
3 quarts dry ½-inch bread cubes (two 1-pound loaves)
¾ cup (1½ sticks) butter
1½ cups chopped celery
1 cup chopped onion
1 cup dried currants
¾ cup minced fresh parsley
4 teaspoons rubbed sage
¾ teaspoon dried thyme (optional)
¾ teaspoon grated nutmeg
1½ cups hot Homemade Chicken Broth (page 159), or Turkey Stock

1 egg, beaten
¼ cup (½ stick) butter, melted

GIBLET GRAVY
2 quarts plus 1 cup water
2 ribs celery, quartered
1 carrot, quartered
1 onion, quartered
1 bay leaf
4 whole cloves
¼ teaspoon salt
¼ teaspoon black pepper
7 tablespoons all-purpose flour

If using a frozen turkey, thaw the bird slowly, preferably in the refrigerator, allowing 24 hours thawing time for each 5 pounds of frozen bird. After thawing (or if you are using a fresh bird), remove the neck and giblets from the neck and/or body cavities; wash the inside and outside of the turkey and rinse the giblets in cold water; drain well. Set neck and giblets aside for the gravy.

Preheat the oven to 325° F. Prepare the dressing. In batches, pulse the bread cubes in a food processor until they are crumbled into small pieces and transfer them to the largest bowl you have. In a medium saucepan over

medium heat, melt the butter; add the celery and onion and sauté until the onion is transparent, about 6 to 7 minutes. After about 3 minutes, add the currants. Stir the butter mixture into the bread crumbs, then add the parsley, sage, thyme, nutmeg, and 1 cup of the hot broth. Combine well.

The turkey should be stuffed lightly, for the dressing will expand as it cooks. Fill the neck cavity, and fold the skin over the back and fasten with skewers; twist the wing tips under the back of the turkey to rest against the neck skin. Stuff the body cavity, then use skewers to close the cavity or tuck the ends of the legs under the band of skin at the tail, or simply tie the legs together with clean string.

To the remaining dressing, add the beaten egg and the remaining ½ cup of broth. Transfer to an oiled 2-quart casserole and bake at 325° F. for 1 hour covered, then 30 minutes uncovered.

Place the stuffed turkey on a rack, breast side up, in an open roasting pan. Brush the melted butter over the entire turkey. Place a meat thermometer in the fatty part of the thigh, being careful not to let the thermometer touch the bone. Roast until the meat thermometer reaches 185° F., or until the fleshy parts of the drumstick feel soft when pressed with your fingers (see chart below). During the roasting, brush the bird occasionally with the pan drippings. When the skin is a light golden brown, place a loose tent of aluminum foil over the legs and breast to prevent excess browning. When the turkey is two-thirds done, cut the cord or band of skin at the tail to release the legs and permit the heat to reach the heavy-meated part.

While the turkey is roasting (or the day before), prepare the stock for the gravy. Place 2 quarts of water, neck and giblets, celery,

carrot, onion, bay leaf, cloves, salt, and pepper in a deep kettle. Cover, bring to a boil, and simmer for 1 hour. Add the liver and cook 15 minutes longer. Strain the broth into a saucepan, reserving the giblets and liver. Cut the giblets and liver into very small pieces and return to the broth; refrigerate if you are preparing the stock in advance.

When the turkey is done, remove it from the pan to a carving board; pour off the drippings for the gravy. Skim the excess fat from the drippings, and add them to the strained giblet broth. Bring to a boil over medium heat. In a jar with a lid, combine the remaining 1 cup water and the flour; shake until smooth. Add slowly to the broth, and cook and whisk until the mixture is smooth and slightly thickened, about 5 minutes. Adjust seasonings. Transfer to a warmed gravy boat and serve hot with turkey and dressing. (Makes 6 cups gravy.)

Timetable for Roasting a Stuffed Turkey

8–12 pounds	3½–4½ hours
12–16 pounds	4½–5½ hours
16–20 pounds	5½–6½ hours
20–24 pounds	6½–7 hours

TURKEY STOCK

Makes 3 quarts

To me, one of the luxuries of having a whole roast turkey is knowing I'll have a carcass for soup stock. You will want to include all the scraps from the turkey— discarded skin, tiny bits of dressing clinging to the inside, and leftover dabs of gravy. If you are too busy to make stock right after Thanksgiving, you can freeze the whole bony mess and do it later.

1 turkey carcass
5 quarts water
1 medium onion, skin on, quartered
3 ribs celery, quartered

2 carrots, halved
2 bay leaves
8 whole cloves

In a large kettle, combine all the ingredients. Cover, bring to a boil over high heat, lower heat, and simmer for 3 hours. Stir the bones down into the stock now and then.

Strain, refrigerate overnight, then skim off fat. You will have enough stock for Turkey Soup and plenty left over to freeze.

TURKEY SOUP

◆

Makes 12 hearty servings

This is a very quick soup, quite perfect for the busy Thanksgiving weekend.
Of course, you can add any leftover vegetables from the holiday dinner or any
other fresh vegetables you prefer.

1 large onion
4 ribs celery
¼ cup vegetable oil
1 quart Turkey Stock (page 141)
1 15-ounce can navy beans
1 15-ounce can tomatoes, drained and
    chopped
1 10-ounce package frozen mixed
    vegetables

¼ cup quick-cooking pearled barley
1 bay leaf
¼ teaspoon black pepper
¼ teaspoon grated nutmeg
¾ teaspoon dried thyme (optional)
1 cup mashed potatoes
½ cup half-and-half, heated
2 tablespoons minced fresh parsley

Chop the onion and celery. Heat the oil in a large kettle, and cook onion and celery until the onion is transparent. Add the rest of the ingredients except the potatoes, half-and-half, and parsley. Cover, bring to a boil over high heat, and then lower heat to simmer for 10 to 12 minutes, or until the barley is tender. Add the potatoes, half-and-half, and parsley, and simmer 5 minutes longer.

CREAMY MASHED POTATOES

Serves 6–8

Sometimes there is just nothing quite so good as perfect mashed potatoes.
Serve the potatoes in a big bowl, make a deep well in the top of them with a spoon,
and add a chunk of soft butter. This will melt into a wonderful buttery lake.

6 medium potatoes
2 bay leaves (optional)
1⅓ cups half-and-half, or 1 12-ounce can
    evaporated milk
¼ cup (½ stick) butter

½ teaspoon salt
¼ teaspoon black pepper
¼ teaspoon grated nutmeg
Softened butter
Grated nutmeg

Peel the potatoes, cut in quarters, and place in a deep saucepan. Cover with hot water and add the bay leaves. Cover, bring to a boil, lower heat to medium, and cook for 15 to 18 minutes, or until the potatoes are fork-tender.

Drain well and return the potatoes to the saucepan. Add the half-and-half, butter, and seasonings, and cook over low heat, stirring continually, until heated through.

With an electric hand mixer or potato masher, beat the potatoes until they are light and fluffy. (You may need to add a bit more half-and-half.) Transfer to a 1½-quart bowl, garnish with additional butter, and sprinkle with a little nutmeg.

ROAST DUCKLING WITH SAUERKRAUT AND APPLE DRESSING

◆

Serves 6–8

Sauerkraut and duckling seem to be the perfect marriage. Brushing the roasting duck with a mixture of molasses and sauerkraut juice gives it a beautiful color and a crisp skin. Barbarie ducks, a recently developed breed that is leaner and has more breast meat, are available in most larger supermarkets. They are so moist, meaty, and lean that they are worth looking for.

2 tablespoons (¼ stick) butter
1 large onion, chopped
2 cups finely chopped apple, preferably
*   Yellow Delicious or Granny Smith*
5 tablespoons chicken broth or
*   white wine*
1 cup very well drained sauerkraut,
*   juice reserved*
½ cup chopped fresh parsley
¾ teaspoon dried thyme, or 2½ teaspoons
*   fresh thyme*

¼ teaspoon black pepper
¼ teaspoon celery seed
6 cups soft ½-inch bread cubes
1 egg
1 7-pound Barbarie duck, or 2
*   5-pound Pekin ducks*
BASTING LIQUID
½ cup molasses
⅛ teaspoon black pepper
⅛ teaspoon dried thyme, or ¾ teaspoon
*   fresh thyme*

In a large skillet, brown the butter over medium heat until deep gold, then add the onion and cook until it begins to brown, about 2 to 3 minutes. Add the apple and 3 tablespoons of the broth or wine, and cook, covered, on medium heat for 3 minutes, or until the apple is slightly cooked. Add the sauerkraut, parsley, thyme, pepper, and celery seed and stir to combine; remove from heat. Place the bread cubes in a large bowl. Pour the apple-kraut mixture over the cubes and toss lightly. In a small bowl, beat the egg, and add the remaining 2 tablespoons of broth or wine. Pour over the dressing and toss lightly again, just to combine. Set aside.

Preheat oven to 375° F. Remove the neck and giblets from the duck's body cavity; re-serve for soup stock. Rinse the duck under cold water and dry well with paper towels. Fill the duck with the dressing, packing loosely. (Any leftover dressing can be baked separately.) Fasten the opening with metal skewers and, using kitchen cord, truss the duck. With a fork, pierce duck all over—this allows the fat to drain off. Place the duck, breast up, on a rack in a shallow roasting pan.

In a small bowl, combine the basting liquid ingredients, and ¼ cup of reserved sauerkraut juice. Baste the duck with a brush and roast, allowing 20 minutes per pound, or approximately 2 hours and 20 minutes for a 7-pound duck. Baste every 20 minutes during the baking period. If the duck begins to over-brown, cover it lightly with a piece of foil.

BAKED ONIONS WITH SOUR CREAM

Serves 4

This simple onion dish is delicately sauced with sour cream, brown sugar,
a hint of lemon, and a bit of fresh parsley. The onions are baked
in their skins—what could be easier?

4 Bermuda or Vidalia onions,
3 inches in diameter
¼ cup (½ stick) butter, at room
temperature
¼ cup sour cream, at room temperature

1 tablespoon brown sugar
1 tablespoon lemon juice
1 tablespoon finely minced fresh parsley
¼ teaspoon salt
¼ teaspoon black pepper

Preheat oven to 375° F. Place the unpeeled onions in a foil-lined shallow pan. Bake, uncovered, for 1½ hours. Warm a heatproof shallow serving dish. When onions are tender, remove from oven. Spear each with a fork, snip or cut off both ends, and remove skin. Place the peeled onions in the warmed dish. Immediately add the butter and sour cream so they will melt from the heat of the onions. Then add the rest of the ingredients and toss lightly to mix.

BRUSSELS SPROUTS WITH DILL

Serves 10

In the garden these miniature cabbages grow on long stalks and are
almost too pretty to pick. The liberal addition of chopped fresh dill and
pimiento makes this an attractive and tasty dish.

1½–2 pounds cleaned Brussels sprouts,
or 3 10-ounce packages frozen
¾ cup water
¼ cup (½ stick) butter
1 teaspoon instant chicken bouillon
powder (optional)

1 teaspoon sugar
½ teaspoon salt
¼ teaspoon black pepper
¼ cup minced fresh dill
1 1-ounce can chopped pimientos

In a medium saucepan, combine all but the dill and pimiento. Bring to a boil, then simmer, covered, for 12 to 15 minutes (only 5 minutes if you are using frozen sprouts); there should be very little liquid remaining in the pan at the end of the cooking time. Add the dill and pimientos. Toss lightly and serve immediately.

STUFFED ACORN SQUASH

◆

Serves 4

For very special occasions, like Thanksgiving, even the busy rural cook might prepare stuffed acorn squash.

2 medium acorn squash
1 slice heavy-textured brown bread
2 teaspoons butter, melted or softened
1 medium onion
½ cup chopped fresh parsley

¼ cup (½ stick) butter
¼ cup sour cream
   Salt and pepper
   Sugar

Preheat oven to 350° F. Cut squash in half lengthwise. Scrape out the seeds with a spoon and place cut side down in a foil-lined shallow baking pan. Pour hot water into pan halfway up the side. Bake for 1½ hours or until the squash is tender. Set aside to cool slightly.

Meanwhile, whirl bread in a food processor or blender until you have fine crumbs; add the melted butter and combine quickly. Set aside. Process onion and parsley until evenly chopped. Using a tablespoon, carefully scoop out squash meat, reserving shells. Place squash in a food processor bowl with the onion and parsley. Add butter, sour cream, salt, pepper, and sugar to taste. Process until smooth. Adjust seasonings. Return mixture to the shells and sprinkle with the buttered crumbs. Place shells in a shallow, oiled baking pan and bake for 15 to 20 minutes more. (If squash has been prepared in advance and chilled, bake 25 to 30 minutes.)

CUSTARD CORNBREAD

◆

Serves 8

In this most unusual cornbread recipe, milk is poured over the top of the batter just before baking and not mixed in. The finished product has a thin custard layer on top. Eat this with lots of butter and a fork.

2 tablespoons (¼ stick) butter
1⅓ cups yellow cornmeal
⅓ cup all-purpose flour
¼ cup plus 1 teaspoon sugar
1½ teaspoons salt
1 tsp baking powder

2 eggs
2 cups milk
1 cup buttermilk
   Paprika
   Butter

Set oven at 400° F. Place butter in a heavy 9-inch skillet and heat it in the warming oven. Do not allow the butter to brown. (You can use a 9-inch-square baking pan, but I prefer the skillet.) Meanwhile, sift the cornmeal, flour, sugar, and salt together into a large bowl. Add the eggs, and break them up with a fork. Then stir in 1 cup of the milk and the buttermilk and mix with a spoon. Pour into the skillet over the butter; do not mix. Pour the last cup of milk over the top of the batter. Do *not* stir in. Sprinkle paprika over the top. Bake for 30 to 35 minutes, until golden. Cut into wedges, and serve warm with butter.

CRANBERRY SHERBET

Makes 3 quarts

Pureed cranberries are combined with sugar and orange and lemon juices, then beaten egg whites are added. This wonderful dessert can seldom be bought in ice-cream shops these days. It is worth the few extra minutes it takes to prepare, and can be made up to a week in advance.

1 pound cranberries (4 cups)
2 quarts plus 1 cup water
6 cups sugar
½ cup lemon juice

½ cup orange juice
2 teaspoons unflavored gelatin
2 tablespoons cold water
4 egg whites

In a large saucepan, combine the cranberries, 1 cup of the water, and 2 cups of the sugar. Bring to a boil and cook just until the sugar is dissolved and the berries pop open. You can help them along by mashing them a bit with a spoon as they cook. Cool slightly, then puree in a food processor or force through a sieve. Add the orange and lemon juices to the puree.

Meanwhile, boil the remaining 2 quarts of water and the remaining 4 cups of sugar for 20 minutes in a large, deep saucepan over medium heat. Dissolve the gelatin in the cold water, mixing well with a fork. Add a little of the hot sugar syrup to the gelatin mixture, then stir back into the remaining hot syrup. Add the cranberry mixture and blend. Pour into refrigerator trays or two 13 x 8-inch flat pans and freeze until mushy, about 30 minutes.

Pour into a large bowl, breaking the mixture up slightly. In a medium bowl, beat the egg whites until stiff. Fold about 4 cups of the cranberry slush into the whites until combined. Then add this to the remaining cranberry slush. Pour back into pans and freeze about 30 minutes longer, until the mixture is frozen about 1 inch in from the edges of the tray. Stir the sherbet again, then freeze until firm. When completely frozen, soften slightly, pack in plastic containers, and store in the freezer until serving.

EASY MINCEMEAT FOR PIE

◆

Makes 5 quarts

Homemade mincemeat is so much better than the watery commercial variety,
but frequently the recipes are for such large amounts that the cook moans
with despair at the thought of making her own. Here is a sensibly sized recipe, and it is a
triumphant combination of beef, apples, cider, and spices. It can be made
in advance and frozen. It is also marvelous served warm over ice cream,
as an upside-down cake topping, or used in a trifle. One quart
is enough for a nine-inch pie.

3½–3¾ *pounds beef shank, 2-inch*
    crosscut, trimmed
 ½ *pound ground suet (have butcher do*
    this)
2½ *quarts chopped cooking apples,*
    such as Cortland, McIntosh, or
    Northern Spy
 2 *pounds seedless golden raisins*
 1 *10- or 16-ounce box dried currants*
 ¼ *pound citron, diced*
 2 *tablespoons diced candied orange peel*
 3 *cups apple cider*

 2 *cups sugar*
 2 *cups light corn syrup*
 ¾ *cup cider vinegar*
    Grated rind and juice of 1 lemon
 4 *teaspoons ground cinnamon*
 2 *teaspoons salt*
 2 *teaspoons grated nutmeg*
 2 *teaspoons ground allspice*
 2 *teaspoons ground ginger*
1½ *teaspoons ground cloves*
 2 *1-pound cans pitted sour cherries,*
    drained

In a large kettle or pressure cooker, cook meat until tender (see note). While meat is still warm, grind coarsely or use a food processor to shred it. (A food processor can also be used for chopping the apples.) In a large, deep pot, combine all ingredients except the cherries. Simmer, uncovered, until mixture is juicy but not runny, about 1½ to 2 hours. Add the cherries for the last 15 minutes of cooking. Let cool. Mincemeat not used within 3 days can be frozen for up to 6 months.

NOTE: The shank is a very flavorful cut, but requires long cooking. A pressure cooker is ideal for this, and should be used according to directions. An alternative method is to preheat the oven to 325° F., place the shanks in a large roaster, and add enough warm water to completely cover the meat. Bake for 3 hours, or until the meat is tender, making sure there is always plenty of liquid in the pan.

THE QUILTING BEE

The role of the Amish woman is defined quite simply: She is to care for the house and raise the children. She also cooks, sews, gardens, looks after the chickens, and helps with the milking. She does have voting rights in the church meetings, and can nominate men for ministerial roles. She sometimes owns the farm jointly with her husband and will share a checking account with him. Divorce is not something she or her spouse think about.

An Amish housewife receives recognition and status for her accomplishments as a home-maker; her skills have a direct bearing on her family's quality of life. I found the women to be hard working, well organized, and effi-cient, and to my delight, all were list makers, a trait we identify with "English" career women.

Because she is a member of an extended family, living with three genera-tions on the same farm, the Amish wife is surrounded daily by other women. Her neighboring relatives and friends often come together to assist one another in the preparation of large meals, to preserve foods, to quilt,

and sometimes just to talk. In some commu-nities, this gathering of women is laughingly called *glucken*, which means "setting hens." After visiting in Amish homes, it is my obser-vation that these women do not suffer the feel-ings of isolation and loneliness that the "English" women do, and they certainly have no questions or conflicts about what their role is in their marriages or communities.

The Amish woman's handmade rugs, quilts, embroidered pillowcases and towels, the bright flowers in her garden, and the col-lection of inexpensive but cheerful dishes ac-quired at auctions in her glass-fronted kitchen cupboards all bring warmth and charm (though that word would never be used or even thought of in relation to herself and her sur-roundings) to her family's daily life.

An activity all the women enjoy is quilt mak-ing. The craft has survived because it is both func-tional and decorative in an acceptable way, and the techniques and patterns are passed from generation to generation.

CHICKEN AND ONIONS

CARROT AND RAISIN SALAD

TUNA AND CREAM CHEESE
SANDWICHES

PENNSYLVANIA DUTCH
SANDWICHES

ORANGE BEETS WITH SPICE

HOT CABBAGE SALAD

LARGE PEARL TAPIOCA
PUDDING

LEMON GRAHAM NUT
PUDDING

SHOO-FLY COOKIES

BLACK WALNUT LAYER
CAKE

AMISH HALF-A-POUND
CAKE

When a girl marries, she is expected to have completed several quilts for use in her new house. Her mother may give her additional quilts as a wedding gift. Quilts, though a reflection of the stitcher's skill as a seamstress, are also a reflection of her appreciation of beauty. When a woman gives a quilt as a gift, it is a visible and permitted expression of affection in a society that is publicly undemonstrative by custom and choice.

For a quilting bee, the hostess will invite fifteen women to work on one quilt for the day. If her house is large enough, she may ask twice as many women and get two quilts completed. A quilting frame is set up, and the unfinished quilt is put in and stretched. The women gather around the frame, and the stitching and conversation begin. They work from nine until four, exchanging news about their children, gardens, and relatives.

At an Amish quilting bee, a meal is served at noon and provides a much needed break. The hostess offers the hot main dishes, which are called "the warms," and her friends bring in the rest—"the colds." Since only women attend these gatherings, lighter foods are served than if the men were present. But noodles are always on the menu.

Mennonite women, too, are noted quilters, though their quilting parties are apt to take place monthly in their churches, where they spend the day working, taking a noon break for a potluck or brown-bag lunch.

Many of the quilts produced at these quilting bees are auctioned at the Michiana Relief Sale in September, although sometimes the quilts are made as gifts. When a Mennonite minister leaves for another church assignment, for instance, the group will give him a quilt consisting of stitched blocks from each family in the congregation.

The quilting bee, a quaint idea to most of us, is alive and flourishing in Indiana. And I also noted that, as the women congregate and talk around the quilting frame, the conversation is frequently about food.

CHICKEN AND ONIONS

Serves 4–5

This sautéed chicken, cooked slowly with onions, is good either hot or at room temperature. For a one-dish meal, add potato and carrot chunks to the skillet, cooking them the full hour along with the chicken.

1 large onion
½ cup vegetable oil
1 3-pound broiler, or 3 pounds
* chicken pieces*

Salt and pepper
Paprika
Chopped fresh parsley

Peel the onion and slice ¼ inch thick. Heat the oil in a heavy skillet, and sauté the onion slices on one side until golden, about 3 minutes. Turn the onions and place chicken on top of them. Season the chicken with salt, pepper, and paprika to taste. Cover, reduce heat to low, and cook slowly for about 1 hour. After 30 minutes, turn the chicken so onion is on top. Add more paprika and continue to cook for an additional 30 minutes, or until chicken is tender. Sprinkle parsley over top.

CARROT AND RAISIN SALAD

◆

Serves 6

An old favorite, pleasantly updated with grated orange rind
and chopped pecans.

3 cups grated carrots
   (approximately 5 large)
1 cup chopped celery
⅔ cup seedless dark raisins
½ cup coarsely chopped pecans

2 tablespoons chopped fresh parsley
¾ cup plus 2 tablespoons mayonnaise
1 tablespoon sugar
1 teaspoon grated orange rind
½ teaspoon salt

In a large bowl, combine all the ingredients in the order given, and toss lightly with a fork. If desired, serve on individual plates atop a bed of bibb lettuce leaves.

TUNA AND CREAM CHEESE SANDWICHES

◆

Makes 8 thin sandwiches

When the women meet for an all-day quilting bee, you will frequently find a
platter of assorted sandwiches on the table, and this one is a favorite.

1 8-ounce package cream cheese,
   softened
2 tablespoons lemon juice
½ cup mayonnaise
1 7-ounce can water-packed tuna, well
   drained

½ cup finely chopped ripe black olives
½ cup chopped toasted pecans
¼ teaspoon black pepper
   Softened butter
16 thin slices white bread

In a medium mixer bowl, combine the cream cheese, lemon juice, and mayonnaise, and blend well. Then quickly mix in the remaining ingredients. Spread on buttered bread.

PENNSYLVANIA DUTCH SANDWICHES

Makes 6 sandwiches

This unusual combination for a sandwich makes a hit every time they are served. They taste best if prepared one day ahead.

8 ounces Swiss cheese, julienned
8 ounces boiled ham, julienned
1 cup mayonnaise
1 8-ounce can sauerkraut, well drained

Scant teaspoon caraway seed
(optional)
Softened butter
12 slices dark rye bread

In a medium bowl, combine everything but the bread and butter. Chill overnight.

Spread butter on one side of each bread slice. Top with cheese-ham mixture and another buttered slice of bread.

NOTE: Party rye slices can be used instead of conventional rye bread.

ORANGE BEETS WITH SPICE

Serves 4–6

Beets are a popular vegetable among the Amish and Mennonites, and one of their favorite ways to prepare them is in an orange sauce.

2 pounds fresh young small beets
2 teaspoons cornstarch
¼ teaspoon salt
¼ teaspoon ground allspice
⅛ teaspoon black pepper

1 tablespoon grated orange rind
¼ cup brown sugar
⅔ cup orange juice
2 tablespoons (¼ stick) butter
Minced chives

Cut off the beet tops if necessary, and wash the beets well. Simmer, covered, in enough water to cover for 45 minutes to 1 hour or until tender. Cooking time will depend on the size and age of the beets. Drain and cover with cold water; trim off the tops and roots and slip off the skins. Slice ¼ inch thick and set aside.

In a medium saucepan, combine the cornstarch, salt, allspice, pepper, orange rind, and brown sugar. Gradually add the orange juice and stir until smooth. Add the butter. Cook and stir over medium heat until the mixture thickens, about 3 minutes. Add the beets and heat through. Place in individual serving dishes and sprinkle with chives.

HOT CABBAGE SALAD

Serves 4

Part of the fun of researching this cookbook was happening upon
recipes still in use today that the Amish and Mennonites brought with them from Europe.
And some of these identical recipes are still popular in the parts of Europe
from which they came. A perfect example of this is an Alsatian dish,
éminclé de choux verts aux lardons chauds, which translated means
"hot cabbage and bacon salad."

3 slices bacon
¼ cup chopped onion
6 cups coarsely shredded cabbage
    (approximately a 1½ pound head,
    see note)
2 tablespoons water
¼ teaspoon salt

¼ teaspoon sugar
⅛ teaspoon black pepper
1 tablespoon cider vinegar, or a bit more
    to taste
1 tablespoon finely snipped fresh or
    frozen dill (optional)

With scissors, cut the bacon into small pieces and sauté in a large skillet over medium-high heat until about three-quarters done, about 2 minutes. Add the onion and continue cooking another minute, until the onion browns a bit. Then add the cabbage, water, salt, sugar, and pepper. Sauté and toss about 2 or 3 minutes, but do not allow the cabbage to become overcooked—you want it to be slightly wilted, but still crisp. Add the vinegar and the dill, then toss again. Serve immediately.

NOTE: Use an old-fashioned slaw cutter or the slicing disk of the food processor to prepare cabbage. The shredding disk will make the texture too fine.

LARGE PEARL TAPIOCA PUDDING

Serves 8–12

This is another unique pudding and a very old recipe. Cooking the large pearl
tapioca slowly for hours in a brown-sugar sauce gives this dessert an intense
flavor. The addition of English walnuts provides a satisfying crunch.
Frequently this pudding was cooked in the oven or in a double boiler, but I get
ideal results, requiring no watching, with a crockpot.

1 cup large pearl tapioca
4 cups water
3 cups brown sugar
    Speck of salt

1½ teaspoons vanilla extract
1 cup chopped English walnuts
    Whipped Cream Topping (page 176)

Place the tapioca and water in a crockpot. Soak overnight.

Do not drain tapioca. Add brown sugar and salt and cook for 12 hours on low. Stir once in awhile. The tapioca becomes clear and the texture is gelatinous at the end of the cooking period. Let cool. Add vanilla, a bit more salt if needed, and the walnuts. Transfer to a shallow serving bowl and spread top liberally with Whipped Cream Topping.

NOTE: Large pearl tapioca requires long, slow cooking to become transparent. And each pearl has a tiny bit of starch in the middle of it that sometimes never completely cooks up which, though edible, looks unpleasant. The crockpot is absolutely perfect for cooking these big pearls—and that little starchy bead completely disappears.

LEMON GRAHAM NUT PUDDING

Serves 4–6

With homemade graham nuts a cottage industry in this part of the country, recipes for using it abound in local cookbooks. This is a tart lemony pudding with a delicate cakelike layer, plus the surprise of graham nuts rising to the top of the dish.

¼ cup (½ stick) butter, softened
1 teaspoon grated lemon rind
1 cup sugar
2 eggs, separated
3 tablespoons lemon juice
2 tablespoons all-purpose flour
¼ cup Homemade Graham Nuts (page 3), or Grape Nuts® cereal
1 cup milk
Half-and-half (optional)

Preheat oven to 325° F. In a large mixer bowl, cream the butter and lemon rind. Add the sugar gradually and blend well. Beat the egg yolks and stir in thoroughly. Add lemon juice, flour, graham nuts, and milk; mix well. Beat the egg whites and add approximately 1 cup of the flour mixture to the whites; fold in gently. Then fold the flour-whites mixture into the sugar mixture. Pour the batter into an oiled 5-cup casserole 3 inches deep. Place casserole in a pan of hot water and bake for 1¼ hours. The pudding will be golden brown. Let cool. Serve with half-and-half, if desired.

SHOO-FLY COOKIES

Makes 40 cookies

Shoo-fly pies are not made here as commonly as in Pennsylvania. However, this cookie recipe is a wonderful substitute. It is like a tender gingerbread in a pastry crust, with a thin, subtle layer of molasses pudding on the bottom.

Pastry for a 2-crust, 9-inch pie
(page 170)
¼ cup molasses (see note)
¼ cup light corn syrup
Pinch of salt
1 teaspoon baking soda
1 cup boiling water

CRUMB TOPPING
¾ cup (1½ sticks) butter (¼ of that can
be lard), at room temperature
1 cup brown sugar
1½ cups all-purpose flour
1 teaspoon ground cinnamon
½ teaspoon grated nutmeg

Line a 2-quart rectangular glass baking dish with pastry, crimping the dough well at the top and over the sides—you do not want it to slip during baking. With a food processor or mixer, combine the crumb ingredients; reserve.

Preheat the oven to 325° F. In a medium bowl, combine the molasses, corn syrup, salt, baking soda, and boiling water. Pour ½ cup of the liquid into the pie shell and sprinkle with one-third of the crumb mixture. Repeat twice, ending with crumbs. Bake for 35 to 40 minutes. Watch carefully in the beginning, and if crust begins to slip down, pat it back up with a knife. The top will be golden. Let cool and cut into 1½-inch squares.

NOTE: If you really like molasses, use less corn syrup and increase the molasses.

BLACK WALNUT LAYER CAKE

Serves 12–16

Black walnuts are a bit hard to find, but when you do, use some of them in this cake. The cake is finely textured and the black walnut flavor makes it very special. Serve it at room temperature, so the cake will be properly soft.

2¼ cups sugar
Rind of 1 lemon
¾ cup (1½ sticks) butter, softened
2 teaspoons vanilla extract
3 cups sifted cake flour
3¾ teaspoons baking powder

½ teaspoon salt
1 cup plus 2 tablespoons buttermilk,
at room temperature
6 egg whites, at room temperature
1½ cups chopped black walnuts
Penuche Frosting (page 134), doubled

Preheat oven to 350° F. With a food processor, process ¼ cup of the sugar and the lemon rind until the lemon is grated. (Or grate by hand, and include the ¼ cup sugar with the remaining sugar when creaming it with the butter.) In a large mixer bowl, beat the sugar-lemon-peel mixture, the butter, the remaining 2 cups sugar, and the vanilla for 3 minutes, or until the mixture is light and fluffy.

On a piece of wax paper, sift the cake flour, baking powder, and salt together 3 times. Add flour mixture to the butter mixture, alternating with the buttermilk and beginning and ending with the flour mixture. Beat the egg whites until very stiff. Fold them and the walnuts into the cake batter. Pour into 3 oiled 8-inch round cake pans. Bake for 30 minutes, or until the top of the cake springs back when lightly touched with your finger. Remove to a wire rack and allow the cake layers to stand in their pans for 10 minutes. Tip out and immediately cover with a terrycloth towel—the steam will keep the cake moist. When cake is completely cooled, fill and frost with a double recipe of Penuche Frosting.

AMISH HALF-A-POUND CAKE

Serves 10–12

As I was leaving one Amish kitchen, a very shy young housewife who had not
said a word during my whole visit, but had watched and listened intently
during all the interviews, came up to me and pressed this recipe into my hand.
"This is a real funny cake recipe," she said. "You start baking it in a cold
oven. I thought maybe you'd like to see it." Then she blushed at her own
aggressiveness and hurried into the other room.
We think of pound cake as one pound of sugar, one pound of butter,
one pound of eggs, and so on, and this cake's ingredients comprise just about half
those measurements. And after baking, the cake is just about half as dense
as a conventional pound cake. It is a very moist, finely textured cake, with a
subtle hint of mace. I was very pleased she gave me the recipe;
it is an excellent cake.

2 cups sifted all-purpose flour
1½ cups sugar
4 eggs, at room temperature
2 teaspoons vanilla extract
2 teaspoons baking powder

½ teaspoon salt
1 cup (2 sticks) butter, partially softened
½ cup milk
¼ teaspoon ground mace, rounded

In a large mixer bowl, combine all the ingredients at once, beating them together on medium speed for 20 minutes. Pour the batter into a well-greased 10-inch tube pan and place in a cold oven. Set the oven temperature to 350° F. and bake for just 1 hour. Remove the cake from the oven, immediately invert onto a wire rack, and tip it out. If cake sticks in the pan, carefully loosen the cake from the sides of the pan with a thin, sharp knife and give the cake pan a good whack on the countertop to shake the cake loose. Cool completely before serving.

WINTER'S REST

In Indiana, winter means snow. At first the flakes descend gently, and then the winds rise, whirling the snow into frenzied gusts. Drifting to the top of the window sashes and covering up the sheds, the snow chokes off the lanes to the roads ♦ Overnight, the entire countryside becomes a fairyland scene of soft whiteness that mantles the houses and the gaunt bareness of the trees. In the morning, farmers walk to their barns in the dark, carrying kerosene lanterns and, from a distance, resemble giant bobbing fireflies ♦ By noon, the sun appears with dazzling brightness, casting pastel shadows on the snowy fields. Horse-drawn sleighs are brought out for visits to the neighbors' homes, and on frozen ponds, young people skate and sled. Children make angels-in-the-snow ♦ In the dooryard, mourning doves and chickadees scavenge about for cracked corn and crumbs. Juncos chase one another with glad little cries, and squirrels watch from nearby wild sumac trees. In the barnyard, the horses, their winter coats thick and plushy, nicker companionably to each other as they burrow their noses in piles of hay ♦ Inside the house, the family life centers around the kitchen and the stove. The homey fragrance of popcorn scents the air, and the checkerboard is brought out. Outside the kitchen window, the mercury slips lower in the thermometer ♦ In the nearby woods, the solitude is broken only by the raucous cry of the blue jays and the freezing crack of trees in the middle of the night.

When farm chores are done, men play checkers at the general store.

THE SOUP POT

Soup is a part of every typical Amish-Mennonite meal in winter, and the soup pot is on the back of the range or wood stove most of the time. As in European kitchens, leftover scraps of food, bones from roasts, bits of broth, and cooking liquids end up in the ever-simmering, ever-ready soup. The children and working men come in out of the cold for a bowl whenever they choose. It is a flavorful and varied sustenance.

The noon meal in winter includes a thick soup, meat, noodles, perhaps two cooked vegetables, hot breads, a plate of cheese, and even two desserts. The pace is more leisurely in this season, and the men will pull a rocking chair close to the stove and take time to rest a bit. This is a good opportunity for them to read the *Budget*, a ninety-seven-year-old weekly newspaper that serves the Amish and Mennonite communities throughout the Americas, including the Mennonite missions abroad. Leafing through the *Budget*, one can read of the weather, crops that have been planted and harvested, who

has visited whom, of accidents and sickness, of births and deaths in communities between Canada and Florida.

The advertisements seem to be from another era, offering custom-made buggies, blue granite canners, vegetable cutting machines, walking plows, and root beer extract in bulk. In communities not served by phone, radio, or television, this newspaper is a vital link among families and friends.

I left my snowy boots on the porch at Ruth Peachy's house on a winter afternoon and entered her warm kitchen. Three women were there: One was making a roux in an enormous deep soup pot, another was chopping onions, and Ruth was stirring up a batch of cornbread. She gave me a cup of coffee, and I took my usual seat by the table, got out my legal pad, and prepared to take down the recipes that were given to me from memory.

"We're real busy today," said Ruth. "One of the neighbor men passed away, and we're fixing food to take in to the family for a meal after the funeral—

HOMEMADE CHICKEN
BROTH

COUNTRY POTATO SOUP

AMISH BEAN SOUP

NINE BEAN SOUP

BROWN STOCK
(BEEF BROTH)

CHICKEN CORN SOUP

DUTCH PEA SOUP

SAUERKRAUT SOUP

CLEAR CHICKEN SOUP
WITH CRACKERBALL
DUMPLINGS

there's about a hundred people coming. Since it is so cold, we thought soup would go good, so we're taking a couple of kinds—sauerkraut and pea—over there to them. And cornbread —we call things like that 'go-withs.' "

There is one particular soup that the Amish are noted for, and that is their bean soup. It is served after Sunday services and is made by the family who hosts church that day. A more tasty version has a ham bone with lots of meat still on it among its ingredients, but a "thin" cook (a term used to indicate a person who is a bit stingy with more costly ingredients) prepares the soup without bone or meat. Sometimes pieces of bread are added to further thicken it.

Ruth was also making Big White Soft Sugar Cookies (page 137) that day, which she calls winter cookies. Like many Amish cooks, she prefers to make them in the winter, for the iron wood stove heats up the kitchen too much in the summer. But she maintains, as my grandmother did, that the wood stove bakes them better than a kerosene stove does. The cookies stay softer, and that is the way they should be—almost like flat white cakes.

When I left Ruth's house, I passed the Amish cemetery, with its simple, flat unidentified headstones. A long, slow-moving cortege of horse-drawn black buggies appeared in single file, their somber silhouettes stark against the snow.

HOMEMADE CHICKEN BROTH

◆

Makes 8–9 cups

I wish that I could suggest a shortcut to good chicken broth or beef stock—
I can't. To get the deep, true flavor of the recipes that call for stock,
it is best to make them from scratch. Fortunately,
the recipes make large quantities that can be frozen, so you
don't have to do it too often.

1 4–5 pound roasting chicken
2 medium onions, quartered
2 large carrots, halved
2 ribs celery, halved
1 green bell pepper, halved
½ cup fresh parsley sprigs

6 whole cloves
2 bay leaves
1 teaspoon salt
½ teaspoon white pepper
3–3½ quarts water

Place the chicken, including the neck and the giblets (but not the liver), in a large stockpot. Add the rest of the ingredients. The water should cover the chicken completely. Cover and bring to a boil over high heat; then skim off froth as it forms on top. Reduce heat and simmer for 2 hours.

Remove the chicken from the pot, allow to cool a bit, then remove the meat and skin, reserving the meat for another use (soup, salad, or sandwich filling). Return the bones and skin to the pot. Simmer the broth, covered, for 2 hours more.

Strain the broth through a sieve into a bowl, pressing the vegetables and bones with a rubber spatula to extract any liquid. Chill broth overnight in the refrigerator and skim off the fat. Freeze any stock that will not be used within 2 to 3 days in 1-quart containers.

COUNTRY POTATO SOUP

◆

Serves 4–6

Potato soup is a classic farm dish, and is made in many different ways: without meat, or with bacon, ham, or sausage. This one is rich and creamy, and flavored with bacon. I find it an immensely comforting soup.

8 slices lean bacon
¼ cup chopped celery
½ cup chopped onion
2 medium potatoes, peeled and cut in
    1-inch cubes (about 3 cups)
2½ cups water
1 bay leaf
½ teaspoon salt

¼ teaspoon grated nutmeg, rounded
¼ teaspoon dried marjoram, rounded
    (optional)
¼ teaspoon celery salt
¼ teaspoon black pepper
1 cup milk
1 tablespoon Worcestershire sauce
2 tablespoons finely minced fresh parsley

Chop the bacon coarsely. In a deep soup kettle, sauté the bacon, celery, and onion over medium heat until the onion is golden, about 5 minutes. Add the potatoes, water, and seasonings; bring to a boil over high heat. Reduce heat and simmer, covered, for 15 minutes or until potatoes are tender. Mash potatoes slightly—about one-quarter of the cubes should still be whole. Remove the bay leaf. Add the milk, Worcestershire sauce, and parsley, and bring again to a boil. Serve hot.

Obituary cards line a glass-fronted cupboard where a cheerful collection of china accumulated mostly from auctions is stored.

Amish cemeteries are usually just a fenced-off corner of a field. The nameless markers are usually carved from wood, although those in the community cemetery shared by both the Amish and Mennonites, BELOW, *are of stone.*

AMISH BEAN SOUP

Serves 6

In every Amish and Mennonite restaurant, you will find bean soup on the menu, though in their homes it is eaten mostly in the winter. It is the perfect way to finish off a baked ham, as meat, bone, and even the drippings go in the soup. If a potato is not used for thickening, Rivels (page 43) are sometimes added. At some tables, a cruet of vinegar is passed to sprinkle on the soup. Cornbread is the perfect accompaniment.

1 pound navy beans
3 quarts water
1 teaspoon salt
Pinch of baking soda
½ cup shredded carrot
1 cup chopped celery
2 medium onions, chopped
2 bay leaves

1½ pounds ham meat
Ham bone
Leftover ham drippings
1 cup mashed boiled potato
½ teaspoon black pepper
½ teaspoon dried thyme (optional)
2 tablespoons Worcestershire sauce
¼ cup chopped fresh parsley

In a large soup kettle, combine the beans, water, salt, and baking soda. Bring to a boil, cover, and simmer for 5 minutes. Remove from the heat, skim off foam, re-cover, and let stand for 2 hours. (The beans can also be soaked overnight if you prefer.)

Add the remaining ingredients except the parsley and simmer, covered, for about 1½ to 2 hours. Watch beans, for the cooking time will vary and the beans should not get mushy. Remove the ham bone and dice any overly large pieces of meat and return to the soup. Add the parsley just before serving. This soup freezes very well.

NINE BEAN SOUP

Makes 8 generous servings

This mix recipe took the Midwest by storm a couple of years ago, and it is easy to see why. The resulting soup is robust, flavorsome, and has many variations. A packet of the dried beans with the recipe attached is a fine hostess gift.

1 package soup beans (see note)
2 quarts water
2 teaspoons salt (omit if using ham)
1 ham bone and scraps, or 1 turkey leg,
*   or 1½ pounds chuck roast*
1 28-ounce can tomatoes, coarsely
*   chopped*

1 large onion
1 teaspoon chili powder, or 2 teaspoons
*   mixed dried herbs (thyme, savory,*
*   sage, oregano)*
2 tablespoons lemon juice
Brown sugar to taste
¼ pound pasta (any kind)
cup

In a very large soup kettle, soak 1 package of bean mix in the water with the salt overnight. Next day, add the meat and bring to a boil over high heat. Reduce heat and simmer, covered, for 2 hours. Add the tomatoes and onion, chili powder or herbs, and the remaining ingredients. Cook 1 hour longer. If the soup gets too thick, add more broth or water. Remove meat, chop it into bite-size pieces, and return to soup. This soup freezes very well.

NOTE: To make the soup bean mix, assemble 1 pound each of dried white navy beans, white lima beans, black beans, kidney beans, pinto beans, green peas, lentils, garbanzos, and barley. You'll also need 9 small, dried hot chilies. In a very large—and I do mean large—bowl, mix the legumes. Divide mixture equally among 9 bags; this is approximately 2 cups mixture per bag. Add 1 chili to each bag and close tightly. Store in refrigerator until ready to use. (If kept for several months, the bean mixture will become stale and possibly wormy unless refrigerated.)

BROWN STOCK (BEEF BROTH)

◆

Makes 2½–3 quarts

No cookbook worth its salt would omit a recipe for Brown Stock—though in this part of the country it is called Beef Broth. It has many uses, including that of the base for Onion Rivel Soup (page 43). I like to simmer the stock gently overnight in the oven, which is a very easy method, or you can cook it on top of the stove.

5 pounds beef soup bones, cut in
    6-inch lengths
6 carrots, scrubbed and halved
3 large onions, skin left on, quartered
6 ribs celery, including the leaves
1 turnip, scrubbed and quartered

3 bay leaves
12 whole cloves
12 peppercorns
    Large handful parsley sprigs
5 quarts water

Preheat oven to 400° F. Place the bones in an oiled 12 x 17-inch baking pan, and bake for 30 minutes. Add the carrots and onions and bake another 30 minutes, turning the vegetables and bones at least once during the last cooking period. When the bones are deeply browned (and this may take a few minutes longer), transfer them, along with the browned vegetables, to a large, ovenproof stockpot. Reduce the oven temperature to 140° F. if you are using the oven method to simmer the stock. Pour the fat out of the pan, deglaze with a little water, and add this to the stockpot.

Add the remaining ingredients, cover, and place the pot in the oven for 12 hours. Alternatively, you can simmer stock on top of the stove for at least 12 hours.

Remove the bones and vegetables with a slotted spoon, then pour the stock through a fine sieve. If you want a clearer broth, line the sieve with dampened cheesecloth. (I must admit, I generally skip this step.) Refrigerate for several hours, or until the fat rises to the top and forms a hard layer. Discard the fat, use the broth as needed, or freeze.

ABOVE: *Auctions also provide the Amish and the "English" young boys with an opportunity to enjoy a brief though somewhat cautious encounter.*

ABOVE: *The Saturday night washtub is stored on the outside wall of a shed.* OPPOSITE: *Bulk garden seeds are dipped out with wooden scoops at Yoder's Shipshewana Hardware.*

CHICKEN CORN SOUP

Makes approximately 6 servings

This is a thick, subtly flavored soup. Carrot and parsley give it added color.

6 tablespoons (¾ stick) butter, or
    rendered chicken fat
¼ cup finely chopped onion
1 cup finely chopped celery
6 tablespoons all-purpose flour
2 cups Homemade Chicken Broth
    (page 159)
1 1-pound can cream-style corn

¾ cup milk
¾ cup half-and-half
2 tablespoons shredded carrot
1 tablespoon finely minced fresh parsley
¼ teaspoon grated nutmeg, rounded
⅛ teaspoon black pepper
1½ cups very coarsely shredded cooked
    chicken

In a large saucepan, cook the butter, onion, and celery over medium heat for 3 minutes. Stir in the flour, and cook 5 to 6 minutes longer, or until the mixture is golden. Add the broth, and whisk until smooth, raising the heat a bit. Add the remaining ingredients except chicken, and then lower heat and simmer for 3 minutes. Add chicken just before serving—allow soup to stand a few minutes to heat the chicken pieces.

DUTCH PEA SOUP

Serves 6–8

Dutch Pea Soup can be made with either yellow or green peas. Each has its own distinctive flavor. Serve with cornbread and maple syrup.
The peas must be soaked overnight.

1 cup dried yellow or green peas
6 cups water
½ pound bacon or ham pieces
½ teaspoon salt
12 peppercorns

Speck of baking soda
1½ cups chopped celery
½ cup chopped onion
1 teaspoon dried savory (optional)
½ cup chopped fresh parsley

Soak peas in the water overnight in a large kettle. The next day, add the meat, salt, and peppercorns. Cover and bring to a boil over high heat. Add the baking soda. Skim off foam; you may have to do this twice. Lower heat, and simmer for 1½ hours. Add celery, onion, and savory and cook 30 minutes longer. Remove meat pieces and chop finely, if necessary. Return to soup and add parsley. The soup freezes very well.

SAUERKRAUT SOUP

Makes 6 large servings or 10–12 appetizer servings

Swiss Mennonite in origin, this is Indiana's answer to New England clam chowder—creamy smooth, tangy, and studded with bits of sausage and sauerkraut. It is one of the most unusual recipes in this book.

1 pound smoked sausage (Kielbasa) in a
large link, casing left on
6 tablespoons chopped onion
¼ cup all-purpose flour
½ teaspoon dried thyme, rounded
½ teaspoon black pepper

3 cups milk
1 cup half-and-half
1 8-ounce can sauerkraut, with juice
1½ tablespoons lemon juice (optional)
2 tablespoons finely chopped fresh
parsley

Chop the sausage coarsely by hand or in a food processor. Transfer the chopped sausage and onion to a deep pan, and sauté over medium heat until the sausage is lightly browned, about 8 minutes. On a small plate or wax paper, combine the flour, thyme, and pepper. Add to the sausage and brown all together until the mixture bubbles up, about 5 minutes. Add the milk and half-and-half all at once, and cook, stirring until the mixture again bubbles up, about 5 minutes. Add the sauerkraut and its juice and bring to a boil; the mixture will continue to thicken. Taste for tartness, and add lemon juice if desired. I prefer it quite tart, but for people unaccustomed to this soup, it may be sour enough without the lemon juice. Add parsley, and serve at once.

CLEAR CHICKEN SOUP WITH CRACKERBALL DUMPLINGS

Serves 4–6

Crackerball Dumplings are sort of a farmer's matzoh ball, made with saltine cracker crumbs instead of matzoh meal. Simmer them in clear chicken broth and serve as a first course with fresh thyme scattered over the top.

1 egg
2 tablespoons (¼ stick) butter, melted
6 tablespoons fine soda cracker crumbs
1 tablespoon milk
1 teaspoon finely minced fresh parsley
½ teaspoon finely minced onion

¼ teaspoon celery salt
Dash of black pepper
2 quarts clear Homemade Chicken
Broth (page 159)
Minced fresh thyme (optional)

In a small bowl, beat the egg slightly. Stir in the melted butter. Add the remaining ingredients and mix. Shape into walnut-size balls. Allow to stand 30 minutes to "swell."

Bring the broth to a simmer in a large saucepan. Drop the balls into the broth and cook over medium-low heat, covered, for 10 minutes. Do not lift the lid. Ladle the soup into bowls, allowing 2 or 3 crackerballs per serving. Sprinkle thyme over the tops of the soup. Serve immediately.

PIES, PIES, PIES

If there is one thing that distinguishes the Amish and Mennonite cuisine, it is their justifiably famous pies. It is not unusual to find forty different kinds on a restaurant menu; in fact, it is expected. The array is truly mind-boggling. Pastry making is a skill the girls learn early from their mothers, and one which they take for granted. When I inquired about pastry recipes, they looked puzzled. "Everyone knows how to make pie crust," they said. "There's no recipe for it—you just take lard and flour and add some water." Sure.

Because the Amish and Mennonites still raise their own berries, they are able to make pies most of us only have heard of—gooseberry, currant, and elderberry. Their cream and custard pies are great delicacies and at Amish gatherings, they are served at the noon meals, for frequently there is no way to refrigerate them. The shoo-fly pie, omnipresent in Pennsylvania, is not common here, but might be available in some restaurants because the tourists request it, thinking it is indigenous to this area.

I have encountered some unusual pies in communities where old recipes have survived —Bob Andy Pie and Collage Pie, for instance. Oatmeal Pie is sort of a poor man's pecan pie, and is very good. But the outstanding one, I think, is the Brown Sugar Pie. The recipe that appears here is my Dunkard great-grandmother's, and is one of those folk recipes that is seldom written down. I think it alone is worth the price of this book.

NOTE: Do not use foil pans for any syrup or custard pies—the foil does not conduct the heat properly, and the texture won't be right. Some cooks bake a foil-pan pie on a cookie sheet and position it on the lowest rack in the oven, and get fair results. Still, when you have taken the time and spent the money on good ingredients to make a decent pie, use the proper pan to get the proper results.

HOT WATER PIE CRUST

PAT-IN-PAN PIE CRUST

GOOSEBERRY PIE

AMISH BROWN SUGAR PIE

BUTTERMILK PIE

BOB ANDY PIE

AMISH APPLE PIE

COLLAGE PIE

CURRANT PIE

OATMEAL PIE

VELVET CUSTARD PIE

BROWNED BUTTERSCOTCH PIE

WHIPPED CREAM TOPPING

SOUR CREAM RAISIN PIE

MERINGUE TOPPING

PUMPKIN PIE WITH PRALINE

RAISIN PIE (FUNERAL PIE)

LEMON SPONGE PIE

HOT WATER PIE CRUST

◆

Makes pastry for two 8-inch pies with top crusts or two 9- or 10-inch pies without top crusts

When you mention a hot water pie crust, people look askance, for traditional pie crust recipes always emphasize cold ingredients and ice-cold water. And we're talking about *boiling* water here. But this makes a tender, flaky crust. At one stage, it looks like unappetizing putty, but don't worry about that. I make it in huge amounts, cut it into wedges, and freeze it for nearly instant pies. This is an old, old recipe, and it's been years since I have seen it published.

1 cup lard, very soft
1 teaspoon salt

½ cup boiling water
3 cups all-purpose flour

Place the lard and salt in a large bowl and beat a bit with a tablespoon until the lard is completely softened. You can also do this with an electric hand beater. Pour boiling water over the lard and blend again. Let this mixture cool to room temperature, but stir often so water and lard won't separate (though it is not the end of the world, or the crust, if it does). Stir in the flour, and form the mixture into a ball. If you use your hands, do it quickly. Chill for several hours or overnight, then let the cold dough sit out at room temperature for about 30 minutes before rolling out.

If you are preparing a shell to fill later or if your recipe requires a prebaked crust, preheat the oven to 425° F. Roll out a portion of the dough to ⅛-inch thickness. Transfer the crust to a pie pan and pat it in snugly. Form a decorative edging along the rim and trim off the edges. Prick the surface of the pastry all over with a fork. Bake for 15 minutes or until golden. Check it often and if necessary prick more to release air bubbles. If the crust begins to slip down the sides of the pan, pat it up with the back of a fork.

VARIATION: For large amounts to freeze, use the proportions that follow below. Wrap each wedge in plastic wrap, bag it, and freeze. Any unused portion can be refrozen. To make 9 crusts, use 6 cups (3 pounds) lard; 2 tablespoons salt; 3 cups boiling water; 18 cups all-purpose flour (about 5 pounds). For 12 crusts, use 8 cups (4 pounds) lard; 8 teaspoons salt; 1 quart boiling water; 24 cups all-purpose flour (about 7 pounds).

PAT-IN-PAN PIE CRUST

◆

Makes pastry for a single-crust 8- or 9-inch pie

I have always felt no pie crust recipe could ever replace my mother's Hot Water Pie Crust. Then I kept finding this one in book after book, so I finally tried it, and it is a winner. Quick, crisp but tender, it needs no rolling out. I highly recommend this pie crust, especially if you think you can't make a good pie. *This recipe can only be used for one-crust pies*—you can't double the recipe and roll out a top crust. The mixture is just too tender to transfer from the pastry board or cloth to the pie.

1½ cups plus 3 tablespoons
all-purpose flour
1½ teaspoons sugar

½ teaspoon salt
½ cup vegetable oil
3 tablespoons cold milk

Place the flour, sugar, and salt in the pie pan and mix with your fingers until blended. In a measuring cup, combine the oil and milk and beat with a fork until creamy. Pour all at once over the flour mixture. Mix with a fork until the flour mixture is completely moistened. Pat the dough with your fingers, first up the sides of the plate, then across the bottom. Flute the edges.

Shell is now ready to be filled. If you are preparing a shell to fill later, or your recipe requires a prebaked crust, preheat the oven to 425° F. Prick the surface of the pastry with a fork and bake 15 minutes, checking often, and pricking more if needed.

VARIATION: For a 10-inch shell, use 2 cups all-purpose flour; 2 teaspoons sugar; 1 teaspoon salt; ⅔ cup vegetable oil; 3 tablespoons milk.

GOOSEBERRY PIE

Serves 6

Gooseberry Pie is tricky. The fruit is so firm that frequently it doesn't cook in the pie, and you end up eating sour, hard berries. By cooking a few of the berries first, the breakdown of the fruit is hastened during baking. Part of the pleasure of this pie is stemming the raw fruit; it is rather like playing with jade beads. Just remove the top stem—the little brown seed on the bottom is part of the delight of the fruit.

Pastry for a 9-inch 2-crust pie
(page 170)
1 quart gooseberries, stemmed and
washed
1½ cups granulated sugar
¼ cup brown sugar

2 tablespoons minute tapioca
Speck of salt
¼ teaspoon grated nutmeg
Drop of red food coloring (optional)
2 tablespoons (¼ stick) butter
Granulated sugar

Preheat the oven to 350° F. Line pie pan with half the pastry. In a deep saucepan, crush 1 cup of the berries with a potato masher (or use a food processor to coarsely chop—not puree—the fruit). Add the sugars, tapioca, salt, nutmeg, and food coloring, if used. Cook over medium heat until bubbly, about 3 to 5 minutes. Reduce heat slightly and cook 2 minutes more. Add the rest of the berries and combine. Pour into the pie shell; dot with butter. Cover with the top crust, cut slits for steam, and sprinkle with sugar. Bake for 1 hour, or until juice bubbles up in center of pie. Let cool.

AMISH BROWN SUGAR PIE

Serves 6

Sugar milk pies were called *miliche flitche*, or "poor man's pie," because
of the simplicity of their ingredients. But I think the man who is served this pie is
to be envied! People beg for this recipe, for it is what they remember eating
as a child, but can never find in cookbooks. These are the kinds of recipes that
I fear will be lost, and why this cookbook came into being. Don't be afraid to mix
the pie right in the shell; your grandmother did it that way to save time, and
it is still a good way to do it today.

*1 unbaked 8-inch pie shell
    (page 170)
1 cup brown sugar
3 tablespoons all-purpose flour*

*Speck of salt
1 12-ounce can evaporated milk
2½ tablespoons butter
Ground cinnamon*

Preheat oven to 350° F. In the pie shell, place the brown sugar, flour, and salt. Mix with your fingers. Pour the evaporated milk over the flour and sugar, but do not stir or mix this in. Dot with butter, and drift cinnamon liberally over all. Bake for 50 minutes, or until the filling just bubbles up in the middle.

The filling will never completely set, but that's the way it's supposed to be. This pie is better eaten at room temperature. If you refrigerate leftovers (it is highly unlikely there will be leftovers), reheat them in the oven before serving.

NOTE: Recipe can be doubled and prepared in a 10-inch pie shell. For that size, bake 1 hour and 20 minutes. (Yield: 12 servings.)

BUTTERMILK PIE

Serves 6

Buttermilk Pie sounds strange, but this one has a marvelously subtle,
unidentifiable flavor and a quivery irresistible texture. "What *am* I eating?" is
the question everyone asks when they first taste this pie. "Something very
special" is the obvious answer.

*1 unbaked 9-inch pie shell
    (page 170)
½ cup (1 stick) butter, softened
1½ cups sugar
3 tablespoons all-purpose flour
3 eggs, well beaten*

*1 cup buttermilk
1 teaspoon lemon juice
1 teaspoon vanilla extract
Speck of salt
Grated nutmeg*

Preheat oven to 350° F. Set out pie shell. Place the softened butter in a large mixer bowl. Add the sugar and cream well. Add flour, eggs, buttermilk, lemon juice, vanilla, and salt; mix. Pour into the unbaked pie shell. Sprinkle nutmeg lightly over the top. Bake for 1 hour or until the top is golden brown.

BOB ANDY PIE

Serves 8–10

Bob Andy Pie is a regional recipe, unlike any I have found elsewhere. It is a bit like a spicy brown chess pie. This one is very thick, rich, and gently quivery. No one has been able to explain the name.

1 unbaked 9-inch pie shell
(page 170)
1 cup granulated sugar
1 cup brown sugar
2 tablespoons all-purpose flour
½ teaspoon ground cinnamon

¼ teaspoon ground cloves
¼ teaspoon salt
3 eggs
2 cups milk
1 tablespoon butter, melted
1 teaspoon vanilla extract

Preheat oven to 350° F. Set out pie shell. In a large mixer bowl, combine the next 6 ingredients. In another mixer bowl, beat the eggs well. Add the remaining ingredients. Blend liquid mixture into flour mixture, then pour into the unbaked shell. Bake for 45 minutes. The filling will still be shaky when you remove it from the oven. The pie puffs up, but levels off as it cools. Serve at room temperature.

AMISH APPLE PIE

Serves 10–12

Most apple pies are good; this one is exceptional. It is thick and rich, and it serves ten or twelve people.

STREUSEL
⅓ cup granulated sugar
¼ cup brown sugar
½ cup plus 2 tablespoons all-purpose flour
1 teaspoon ground cinnamon
1 teaspoon grated nutmeg
Speck of salt

½ cup (1 stick) butter, cold
½ cup coarsely chopped English walnuts

4 large apples, McIntosh or Granny Smith (4 cups)

1 unbaked 10-inch pie shell (page 170)
1 cup granulated sugar
3 tablespoons all-purpose flour
½ teaspoon ground cinnamon
1 egg
1 cup heavy (whipping) cream
1 teaspoon vanilla extract

In a food processor bowl, mix the first 6 streusel ingredients. Add the butter and process until the mixture is crumbly; it should still have a dry look to it—don't overprocess. Add the nuts, then set aside.

Preheat oven to 350° F. Peel, core, and thinly slice the apples; there should be 4 cups. Place the apples in the pie shell. In a small bowl, mix the sugar, flour, and cinnamon. Beat the egg in a medium bowl, and add the cream and vanilla. Add the sugar mixture to the egg mixture and blend. Pour over the apples. Bake for 1 hour in the lower one-third of the oven. After 20 minutes, sprinkle streusel over the top and continue baking approximately 40 minutes longer, or until the top puffs and is golden brown.

COLLAGE PIE

Makes 2 pies, 16 servings

No one knows why this version of Shoo-Fly Pie is called Collage Pie. And in
some cookbooks, it is called College Pie. No matter; it is a lovely molasses
custard pie, with a fine, thin cake layer on top.

2 unbaked 9-inch pie shells
  (page 170)

SYRUP

1 egg
1 cup brown sugar
1 tablespoon all-purpose flour
¼ teaspoon salt
1 teaspoon vanilla extract
½ cup molasses
2 cups water

½ cup buttermilk
½ teaspoon baking soda
¼ cup lard
1 cup granulated sugar
1 egg
2 teaspoons vanilla extract
1 teaspoon ground cinnamon (optional)
¼ teaspoon salt
1 cup all-purpose flour

Preheat oven to 350° F. Set out pie shells. Prepare syrup first. In a medium bowl, beat the egg until frothy. In a small bowl, mix the brown sugar, flour, and salt; blend into the egg. Add the vanilla, molasses, and water. Set aside.

In a measuring cup, mix the buttermilk and baking soda. In a mixer bowl, beat the lard until it is softened; beat in the granulated sugar, egg, vanilla, cinnamon, and salt. Then add half the flour, all of the buttermilk mixture, and then the rest of the flour. Blend. Pour half the syrup into one shell, the remaining half into the other shell. Pour the batter in a spiral pattern over the syrup. It will not cover, but that is all right—it will come together evenly during the baking. Bake for 40 minutes. Let cool completely before cutting.

CURRANT PIE

Serves 6

Fresh currants are rare these days. If you are lucky enough
to find a source, make this deep-red, tart, and altogether wonderful pie.
Eat it a bit warm, à la mode.

Pastry for a 9-inch 2-crust pie
  (page 170)
3 cups fresh red currants
2 cups sugar
¼ cup minute tapioca

1 teaspoon almond extract
Speck of salt
3 tablespoons butter
Sugar

Preheat oven to 350° F. Line pie pan with half the pastry. In a large bowl, combine all remaining ingredients but the butter. Fill pie shell and dot with butter. Roll out remaining pastry, place on top of filling, and cut slits in top so steam can escape. Sprinkle more sugar on top crust, and bake for 45 minutes, or until juices bubble up through the slits.

OATMEAL PIE

Serves 8–10

Oatmeal Pie is a classic dessert among the Amish and Mennonites in northern Indiana. It is likened to a budget version of pecan pie, which isn't fair; it is certainly good enough to stand on its own. This version has a rich delicate bottom custard and a top rather like a chewy oatmeal cookie. I like to add a bit of orange to this, but that is not traditional.

1 prebaked 9-inch pie shell
   (page 170)
4 eggs
1 cup sugar
2 tablespoons all-purpose flour
1 teaspoon ground cinnamon
1/4 teaspoon salt

1 cup light corn syrup
2 tablespoons (1/4 stick) butter, melted
1 teaspoon grated orange rind (optional)
1 teaspoon vanilla extract
1 cup one-minute quick oatmeal,
   uncooked

Preheat the oven to 350° F. Set out pie shell. In a large bowl, beat the eggs until frothy. Combine the sugar, flour, cinnamon, and salt in a small bowl. Add to the eggs and blend. Add the corn syrup, melted butter, orange rind, and vanilla and blend again. Mix in the oatmeal, and pour into the baked pie crust. Bake for 45 minutes. Let cool completely and serve at room temperature.

VELVET CUSTARD PIE

Serves 6–8

To me, this is the perfect custard pie—delicate in flavor, smooth in texture, not overly sweet, and with no bubbles or a trace of weepiness in the finished product.

1 unbaked 9-inch pie shell
   (page 170)
2 1/2 cups milk
4 eggs

3/4 cup sugar
1 1/4 teaspoon vanilla extract
1/4 teaspoon salt
Grated nutmeg

Preheat oven to 350° F. Set out pie shell. In a small saucepan, scald the milk over high heat; set aside. In a large mixer bowl, thoroughly beat the eggs, sugar, vanilla, and salt together. Add 1 cup of the hot milk to the egg mixture, beating it in slowly. Add the rest of the milk and continue to beat slowly. Pour the custard into the shell, and sprinkle with nutmeg. Bake on the lowest oven shelf for 40 minutes or until it is pale gold. Remove to rack, and cool completely before cutting and serving.

BROWNED BUTTERSCOTCH PIE

Serves 6–8

By cooking brown sugar and water together first, an authentic butterscotch base
for an old-fashioned-style butterscotch pie is assured. It is not a stiff
butterscotch custard, but gently runny.

*1 prebaked 9-inch pie shell
(page 170)
1¼ cups brown sugar
⅓ cup water
2 eggs
⅓ cup all-purpose flour*

*2 cups milk, scalded
½ teaspoon salt
¼ cup (½ stick) butter
1 tablespoon vanilla extract
Whipped Cream Topping*

Set out pie shell. In a large, heavy sauce-pan, combine ½ cup of the brown sugar and the water, bring to a boil over medium heat, and continue cooking for about 3½ minutes, or until mixture is thick and bubbly. Set aside.

In a large mixing bowl, beat the eggs until frothy. Add the flour and blend until smooth. Add the remaining ¾ cup brown sugar and blend. Then slowly add the scalded milk, stirring all the time. Over low heat,

reheat the sugar-water mixture until liquified again. Then pour the milk-egg mixture into it, stirring with a rubber spatula all the time. Cook over medium-low heat until mixture bubbles up and is very thick, 3 to 5 minutes. Add salt, butter, and vanilla. Let cool for 15 minutes, then pour into baked shell. Chill in refrigerator. Frost the pie with the Whipped Cream Topping. This is very rich.

WHIPPED CREAM TOPPING

Makes 1½ cups or enough to liberally cover 1 pie

The addition of corn syrup to the cream helps stabilize it and the cream does
not go flat, but stays nice and perky for a couple of days, though most pies
don't last that long. Sometimes, cooks complain that their cream doesn't whip.
An older cream (check the date on the container) whips better than newer
cream, and the bowl and beater should be well chilled before using.

*1 cup very cold heavy (whipping) cream
¼ cup confectioners' sugar
1 teaspoon vanilla extract*

*1 teaspoon light corn syrup
Speck of salt*

In a cold mixer bowl, combine all the ingredients and whip until the cream is stiff and forms well-defined peaks. Don't walk

away and leave this while it is beating, though, for the mixture can turn into butter in a matter of seconds.

SOUR CREAM RAISIN PIE

Serves 6

Raisin Pie is a specialty of this area, but this is a light version, with the raisins suspended in a sour cream custard that is silky and a bit soft.

*1 prebaked 9-inch pie shell
   (page 170)
1 12-ounce can evaporated milk
1 tablespoon cider vinegar
1 cup seedless golden raisins
1 cup sugar*

*2 tablespoons cornstarch
¼ teaspoon salt
3 egg yolks
   Meringue Topping or Whipped Cream
   Topping*

Set out pie shell. In a small bowl, combine the evaporated milk and vinegar; set aside for 1 hour to sour.

Put the raisins in a small saucepan and cover with water. Simmer, uncovered, until most of the water has evaporated, about 3 to 5 minutes, leaving about 3 to 4 tablespoons of liquid. In the top of a double boiler, mix the sugar, cornstarch, and salt. Slightly beat the yolks and add them to the sugar mixture. Then stir in the soured milk. Place over hot water.

Drain the raisins, and add the juice to the mixture. Stirring with a rubber spatula, cook until thickened completely (it will bubble up in the center), about 10 minutes. Add the raisins, remove from the heat, and allow the mixture to cool slightly. While it is still warm, pour the filling into the baked crust.
NOTE: If using meringue, top the pie while the filling is warm and brown slightly in the oven. If using Whipped Cream Topping, chill beforehand.

MERINGUE TOPPING

Makes 2½ cups or enough to liberally cover 1 pie

To keep the meringue from "weeping," never add more than 2 tablespoons of sugar for each egg white; also, the oven temperature for browning the meringue should not be above 325° F. The addition of cornstarch gives the whites stability.

*3 egg whites, at room temperature
¼ teaspoon salt
¼ teaspoon cream of tartar*

*6 tablespoons sugar
1½ teaspoons cornstarch*

Preheat oven to 325° F. In a large mixer bowl, beat together the egg whites, salt, and cream of tartar until soft peaks form. Gradually add the sugar, 1 tablespoon at a time. Continue beating until stiff peaks form; sprinkle in the cornstarch just before the beating is completed. The peaks should not topple over when the beater is raised, however the meringue should appear moist, not dry.

Spread the meringue on lukewarm filling in the pie shell (this helps keep it from shrinking away from the filling as it cools), clear over the edge of the crust. Swoop the meringue into attractive peaks. Bake for 15 to 18 minutes, or until the peaks are golden brown. Cool the pie gradually (there should be no warmth left in the meringue at all), and then refrigerate.

PUMPKIN PIE WITH PRALINE

◆

Serves 10–12

Cooking the pumpkin in butter before mixing it with the rest of the
ingredients gives this pie an unusual richness. To dress up the pie, place this
praline mixture on the bottom of the shell and bake the shell a bit before
adding the filling. But the pie is marvelous, either way.

PRALINE (OPTIONAL)

2 tablespoons (¼ stick) butter, softened
⅓ cup brown sugar
⅓ cup chopped pecans

2 unbaked 8-inch pie shells, or one
  unbaked 10-inch pie shell
  (page 170)
2 tablespoons (¼ stick) butter
1 29-ounce can pumpkin puree
½ cup granulated sugar
½ cup brown sugar

1 tablespoon all-purpose flour
1 tablespoon bitters (optional)
1 teaspoon ground cinnamon
½ teaspoon ground ginger
½ teaspoon salt
¼ teaspoon grated nutmeg
¼ teaspoon ground cloves
1 egg, beaten
1 12-ounce can evaporated milk
¼ cup milk
1 cup water

Prepare the praline filling, if desired.
Preheat oven to 450° F. In a small bowl,
cream together the butter and brown sugar.
Blend in pecans. Press firmly into the bottom
of the unbaked pie shells. Bake for 10 minutes, watching carefully so crusts do not puff
up or slip down. Prick puffs with a fork if
you see this happening, and pat the slipping
crusts back up in place with the back of a fork.
(This may not happen, but if it does, that is
what you should do.) Let cool before filling.
  Preheat oven to 400° F. Melt the butter
in a large skillet; add the pumpkin puree.
Simmer for 10 minutes, stirring now and then
with a wooden spoon. In a large mixer bowl,
mix together the next 9 ingredients. Add the
egg, and mix again. Add the hot pumpkin
gradually, then blend in the milks and water.
Pour into pie shells and bake for 1 hour. Let
cool completely before cutting.
NOTE: The filling can be made a day in advance and refrigerated. If you've used the praline, you may have extra pumpkin filling; bake
it in individual custard cups.

RAISIN PIE (FUNERAL PIE)

Serves 8

The Amish traditionally serve this raisin pie at the well-attended meals held after funerals, so it is frequently called Funeral Pie. This is a thick juicy pie, nicely spiced.

Pastry for a 9-inch 2-crust pie
(page 170)
2 cups seedless raisins
2 cups water
½ cup brown sugar
½ cup granulated sugar
3 tablespoons cornstarch

1 teaspoon ground cinnamon
½ teaspoon ground allspice
Speck of salt
1 tablespoon cider vinegar
2 tablespoons (¼ stick) butter
1 teaspoon grated orange rind (optional)

Preheat oven to 400° F. Roll out the pie crusts and line pie pan with half. In a medium saucepan, simmer the raisins and ⅔ cup of the water over medium heat for 5 minutes. In a small bowl, combine the next 6 ingredients. Gradually stir in the remaining 1⅓ cups water. Add to the raisins, stirring until the mixture bubbles up. Add the vinegar, butter, and orange rind and continue cooking until the butter melts. Cool mixture until it is almost lukewarm.

Pour the cooled raisin mixture into the unbaked shell. Top with the second crust, cut slits in the top to allow steam to escape, and bake for 25 minutes, or until the top crust is golden brown and the pie is bubbling up in the middle. Allow to cool completely before cutting.

LEMON SPONGE PIE

Serves 6

A golden brown cakelike layer tops this pie and a delicate lemon custard remains on the bottom. This is a very old recipe and seldom made anymore. Pity.

1 unbaked 9-inch pie shell
(page 170)
2 eggs, separated
1 cup sugar
3 tablespoons all-purpose flour

2 tablespoons (¼ stick) butter, melted
Grated rind and juice of 1 lemon
¼ teaspoon salt
1 cup milk

Preheat oven to 425° F. Set out pie shell. Beat the egg yolks until smooth; beat the whites until stiff. In a large mixer bowl, combine sugar, flour, melted butter, egg yolks, and grated rind. Then add lemon juice, salt, and milk; blend. Fold in the egg whites, then pour into shell. Bake for 10 minutes, then reduce oven to 350° F. and bake for 20 minutes longer. Let cool completely before cutting and serving.

THE BLIZZARD PANTRY

When it is below zero and the wind is howling around the corners of the house, going out in a buggy—covered or open —is not anyone's favorite jaunt. The farmer's wife has anticipated this sort of weather, and with her basement of canned goods and her root cellar full of potatoes, onions, squash, carrots, and apples, she can prepare sumptuous meals anytime. And the various desserts these women devise from flour, sugar, butter, milk, eggs, and spices is astonishing.

Butchering takes place during the first cold snap, and if it is cold enough, the meat will be left outside in a protected place to freeze, then packed away in insulated containers that also remain outside. However, if there is a risk of warmer weather returning, the meat is taken into town and stored at the frozen locker plant. Some of the more progressive Amish have generators that run off bottled gas, which enable them to have freezers and refrigerators. Whole smoked hams and bacon are also staples during the winter months.

A housewife will try to shop only once a week, and the whole family goes to town for these excursions. In addition to the expected items, the grocery stores sell homemade graham nuts, large and small pearl tapioca in bulk, homemade sausage and bologna, noodles, head cheese, souse, and uncommonly large sacks of flour and sugar. In Amish communities, most of the women still do their own baking, including the bread.

The local hardwares are another favorite place for the Amish to shop, and these stores are filled with items used by a people who live simply, but who have special needs. Kerosene lanterns, five-gallon ice-cream makers (which, alas, have to be cranked by

ROAST LOIN OF PORK WITH
POTATOES AND ONIONS

COLE SLAW WITH
MAYONNAISE DRESSING

TOMATO PUDDING

TOMATO DUMPLINGS

ESCALLOPED CORN

MILE-HIGH ANGEL
FOOD CAKE

CINNAMON PUDDING

BAKED RICE PUDDING
WITH CLEAR LEMON SAUCE

hand), old-fashioned cast-iron skillets affectionately called spiders, huge crockery mixing bowls, and heavy iron cookware line the shelves. Also sold here are the round, shiny tin lunch buckets children carry to school.

The fabric shops are a quilter's paradise, with thousands of bolts of cloth in every shade and hue crammed into floor-to-ceiling shelves.

I met Amanda Bontrager, an Amish mother of seven children, coming out of the grocery, pushing an overflowing grocery cart to her buggy. She grinned. "A farmer's wife just doesn't run out of staples like flour and sugar when she lives so far from the grocery. She learns pretty quick to make good lists and plan ahead."

The winter sky had become that particular shade of ominous blue-gray, which means snow is on the way. As she unhitched the horse, and prepared to start for home, she said to me, "You remember those pictures you and your photographer friend took of the jars of food in my canning room last summer? Tonight we're going to eat some of it."

ROAST LOIN OF PORK WITH POTATOES AND ONIONS

Serves 8

To come into the house on a snowy night to this fine meal is a real treat. Some cooks prepare it in a Dutch oven on top of the stove, but I have given the oven method. The rich juices of the meat season the potatoes wonderfully. This is another dish that originates in Alsace-Lorraine.

1 4–5 pound loin of pork, bone in
Salt and pepper
Grated nutmeg
3 medium onions

8 small potatoes
2–4 cups Homemade Chicken Broth,
approximately (page 159)
2 tablespoons chopped fresh parsley

Preheat oven to 375° F. Season the roast with salt, pepper, and nutmeg. Place in a large roasting pan and cook, uncovered, for 45 to 55 minutes, until lightly browned.

Meanwhile, slice the onions thinly (there will be about 1½ cups) and peel and thinly slice the potatoes. Remove the roast from the pan and pour off all fat. Layer the potatoes and onion in the roasting pan (reserve a few onion slices for the top of the roast), and season with more salt, pepper, and a very small amount of nutmeg. Add enough broth to almost cover the potatoes. Place the pork on the potatoes and arrange onion slices on top. Reduce oven temperature to 325° F., cover, and continue roasting for 1½ to 2 hours longer, or until a meat thermometer registers 170° F. Check now and then to make sure the liquid has not cooked away; if it gets low, add more broth. The potatoes should be served moist, but not soupy. Sprinkle chopped parsley over the roast just before serving.

COLE SLAW WITH MAYONNAISE DRESSING

Serves 4–6

This mayonnaise-based cole slaw has extra zip because of the mustard seed, and it is unusually attractive. This is the best cole slaw of its type that I have found.

1 small head green cabbage
    (about 2 pounds)
1 small red onion
¼ green bell pepper
½ cup parsley sprigs
1 medium carrot

¾ cup mayonnaise
¾ cup sugar
1 teaspoon celery seed
1 teaspoon mustard seed
½ teaspoon salt
¼ teaspoon black pepper

In the bowl of a food processor, using the steel knife blade, place pieces of cabbage and pulse until they reach the desired fineness. I like the pieces to be the size of my little fingernail. Transfer to a large bowl. Chop the onion, pepper, and parsley and add to the cabbage. Shred the carrot and add to the mixture. In a small bowl, combine the remaining ingredients, pour over the cabbage, and toss. Refrigerate at least 2 hours before serving.

TOMATO PUDDING

Serves 4–6

A vegetable side dish that's as good as dessert, Tomato Pudding is a midwestern specialty. Slightly sweet and rich, it puffs as it bakes, but the end product is a bit caramelized. Like many country dishes, the ingredients are always on hand, and it is quickly prepared.

1 quart bread cubes, in 1-inch cubes,
    without crusts
½ cup plus 2 tablespoons (1¼ sticks)
    butter, melted
2 cups tomato puree
½ cup water

½ cup brown sugar
1 bay leaf
1 tablespoon orange juice
1 tablespoon lemon juice
½ teaspoon salt
⅛ teaspoon black pepper

Preheat oven to 375° F. Place the bread cubes in an oiled, flat 1-quart glass baking dish. Pour the butter over the cubes and set aside. In a medium saucepan, combine the rest of the ingredients and simmer, covered, for 5 minutes. Remove the bay leaf and pour the mixture over the buttered bread cubes. Do not stir. Bake in a pan of hot water for 1 hour; the top of the pudding will be puffed and dark brown. Serve immediately.

TOMATO DUMPLINGS

Serves 4–6

What a wonderful recipe this is! Puffy light dumplings are simmered
on top of well-seasoned stewed tomatoes. It is an almost-forgotten vegetable
side dish. This is country cooking at its very best.

¼ cup (½ stick) butter
½ cup finely chopped onion
¼ cup finely chopped green bell pepper
¼ cup finely chopped celery
1 bay leaf
1 28-ounce can whole tomatoes, coarsely
    chopped, with juice
2 teaspoons brown sugar
½ teaspoon salt
½ teaspoon dried basil or 1 tablespoon
    fresh (optional)

¼ teaspoon black pepper
DUMPLINGS
    1 cup all-purpose flour
    1½ teaspoons baking powder
    ½ teaspoon salt
    1 tablespoon butter, cold
    1 egg, beaten
    6 tablespoons milk
    1 heaping tablespoon finely minced fresh
      parsley

In a medium saucepan, melt the butter and sauté the onion, pepper, celery, and bay leaf until the onion becomes transparent, about 5 minutes. Add the tomatoes and seasonings, bring to a boil, and simmer, uncovered, for 3 minutes.

In a medium bowl, combine the first 3 ingredients for the dumplings. Cut in the cold butter with a pastry blender or 2 knives until the mixture resembles coarse oatmeal. Add the egg, milk, and parsley. Blend lightly; don't overmix. Drop by tablespoonfuls (approximately 6) on top of the simmering tomatoes. Cover tightly, and cook over medium-low heat for 20 minutes. Do not lift the cover during the cooking period. Serve in bowls, topped with butter.

ESCALLOPED CORN

◆

Serves 6

This smooth and sweet corn pudding is something like a flan.

¼ cup (½ stick) butter
2 eggs
2 tablespoons sugar
2 tablespoons all-purpose flour

1 1-pound can cream-style corn
1 cup milk
Salt and pepper
Paprika

Set oven to 350° F. Place the butter in a 1-quart (10 x 6-inch) glass baking dish and place in preheated oven to melt. In the meantime, prepare the corn batter. In a medium bowl, beat the eggs. Add the sugar and flour and blend. Add the corn and milk, and combine thoroughly. Pour over the melted butter, but do not mix in. Sprinkle with salt, pepper, and paprika. Bake for 45 minutes; the pudding will be golden brown and slightly puffy.

MILE-HIGH ANGEL FOOD CAKE

Serves 12

The local bakeries and roadside stands sell the most perfect angel food cakes. When you see angel food cakes, you are also going to find homemade noodles—all the yolks left over from the cakes go into the noodles. Or would it be the other way round?

1½ cups egg whites (11–14 whites)
1⅛ cups sifted cake flour
1¾ cups sugar
¾ teaspoon salt

1½ teaspoons cream of tartar
1 teaspoon vanilla extract
1 teaspoon almond extract

Preheat oven to 375° F. Let the egg whites come to room temperature in a large mixer bowl. Be sure there is not a speck of yolk in the whites or they won't beat up. Sift the flour and ¾ cup of the sugar together 5 times.

Add the salt to the egg whites and beat until foamy on medium speed. Sprinkle in the cream of tartar and extracts. (The cream of tartar will stabilize the foam and keep it white.) Continue beating until the whites are stiff and stand in peaks, about 3 minutes, but don't overbeat until dry. Gradually increase the mixer speed to medium-high and sprinkle in 1 cup of sugar, 1 tablespoon at a time. Beat only until the sugar is blended, about 1½ minutes. Turn mixer to low and sprinkle in the

sifted flour-sugar mixture evenly and quickly. Beat only enough to blend, about 1½ minutes, scraping the bowl to help speed the process. Pour batter into an ungreased 10-inch tube pan and draw a thin spatula or knife around the pan in a circular motion 3 times.

Bake for 30 to 35 minutes, or until the cake is golden brown. Turn off the oven and leave cake in oven for 5 minutes more. Remove and set the pan upside down to cool and set the cake. If the pan does not have special feet attached to its sides for this purpose, place it over an inverted funnel or bottle. Cake should hang about 1½ hours, until it is thoroughly set. Serve unfrosted or with a fresh fruit sauce. This cake freezes well.

CINNAMON PUDDING

◆

Serves 12

A rich brown-sugar sauce is poured over the top of this quickly prepared cinnamon-flavored batter. The cake rises to the top during baking, and coarsely chopped pecans add texture. This pudding reheats well in a microwave oven.

SAUCE
2 cups brown sugar
1½ cups water
2 tablespoons (¼ stick) butter
⅛ teaspoon salt
1 teaspoon vanilla extract

2 cups all-purpose flour
1 cup granulated sugar

2 teaspoons baking powder
2 teaspoons ground cinnamon
½ teaspoon salt
1 cup milk
2 tablespoons (¼ stick) butter, melted
1 teaspoon vanilla extract
1 cup very coarsely chopped pecans

Preheat oven to 350° F. Prepare sauce first. In a medium saucepan, combine the first 4 ingredients. Bring to a boil over medium heat and cook, uncovered, for 5 minutes. Remove from heat, stir in the vanilla, and set aside while you prepare the batter.

In a mixer bowl, combine the flour, sugar, baking powder, cinnamon, and salt. Combine the milk, melted butter, and vanilla in a small bowl, and add all at once to the flour mixture; blend quickly. Spread in an oiled 9 x 13-inch cake pan, then pour the reserved sauce over the top. Do not mix in. Scatter the pecans over the liquid. Bake for 40 to 45 minutes, or until the center bubbles up. Serve warm with cream or ice cream.

BAKED RICE PUDDING WITH CLEAR LEMON SAUCE

Serves 6

Rice pudding, that soothing comfort food, is even more delicious laced with either currants or golden raisins. The Clear Lemon Sauce is optional, for this pudding is very satisfying all by itself.

2 cups scalded milk
⅓ cup long-grain white rice
½ cup dried currants or golden seedless raisins
3 eggs
2 cups half-and-half
½ cup sugar
2 teaspoons vanilla extract
Speck of salt

Grated nutmeg
CLEAR LEMON SAUCE (Optional)
1 cup sugar
2 tablespoons cornstarch
Speck of salt
2 cups boiling water
¼ cup (½ stick) butter
Grated rind and juice of 1 lemon
½ teaspoon grated nutmeg

In a heavy medium saucepan, combine the scalded milk and the rice and bring to a boil. Reduce heat and cook, covered, over low heat about 20 minutes, until the rice is tender. Stir once during the cooking period and be careful not to let the mixture boil.

Preheat oven to 350° F. Transfer the rice to an oiled 2-quart soufflé dish and sprinkle the currants or raisins over the top. In a medium bowl, beat the eggs well. Add the half-and-half, sugar, vanilla, and salt and blend. Pour over the rice and fruit. Drift nutmeg over the top. Bake the pudding in a shallow pan of hot water for 1 hour.

Combine the sugar, cornstarch, and salt in a small saucepan. Gradually stir in the boiling water. Bring to a boil over high heat and boil, uncovered, for 3 minutes. Add the butter, lemon rind and juice, and nutmeg; cook 2 minutes longer. Serve warm over rice pudding. (Yield: 2 cups sauce.)
NOTE: If doubling the pudding recipe, use a 9 x 13-inch glass baking dish. The sauce is also good on gingerbread.

THE HOLIDAYS

The Amish and Mennonite menus for Christmas and New Year's are typically midwestern American. Since Christmas is a visiting day and there will be guests, the Amish meal is a large one and would include seasonal specialties such as roast beef, escalloped oysters, cranberries in some form, and pumpkin pies for dessert.

The Mennonite menu would be similar, and in some families, desserts might be mincemeat pie or steamed pudding, another link to the days when these people lived in Pennsylvania, next to settlements of British families where they were exposed to those holiday food customs.

The Amish do not celebrate Christmas with a tree, nor are gifts exchanged in some districts. When gifts *are* given, they are practical in nature, possibly clothes, and sometimes money. The Mennonites do have all the usual trappings of the holidays: trees, lights, decorations, and gaily wrapped presents.

In the little northern Indiana towns, the Mennonite youths go caroling on Christmas Eve, and some of the carols are sung in German, just as their great-great-grandparents sang them back in Europe in the 1800s.

New Year's is another day for families and friends to congregate and enjoy one another's company. Traditionally, cabbage or sauerkraut is served at these gatherings and pork is the favorite accompaniment.

Dropping in at Martha Troyer's house on one New Year's Day afternoon, I found the house full of people. Men were gathered by the coal stove, the older children were playing Chinese checkers, and the women were sitting in the kitchen, just chatting. Many small toddlers in dark dresses, long black stockings, and little black high-top shoes ran about happily.

Later, as I walked out into the gathering dusk, a line of buggies was driving up the lane—young men coming to call. In eternal procession, as though they were drawn with a black pen on the gray sky, a symbol of Amish country life as unchanged as the Amish themselves passed me by.

MULLED CIDER

ROAST PRIME RIB OF BEEF

ESCALLOPED OYSTERS

HONEY CARROTS WITH
SWEET PICKLE

ONION PATTIES

ONION PIE

GERMAN CABBAGE ROLLS

POTATO PANCAKES

AMISH SWEET-AND-SOUR
RED CABBAGE

PUMPKIN-BLACK WALNUT
BISCUITS

AMISH CHRISTMAS CAKE

SAND TARTS

STEAMED CHRISTMAS
PUDDING WITH TWO
SAUCES

CHOCOLATE LAYER CAKE
WITH DATE FILLING

CRANBERRY CAKE WITH
BUTTER SAUCE

MULLED CIDER

Serves 18

Our farm had a large orchard, which was planted by my grandmother. She took extra pride in the special varieties of fruit trees she grew, and her cider was much sought after by connoisseurs of that drink. To this day no one knows her secret blend of apples, but it is speculated that Northern Spys may have given her brew its distinction. Molasses gives it a wonderful richness and color, and the cider is equally good served cold.

⅓ cup molasses
1 cup water
2 tablespoons lemon juice

16 whole cloves
1/16 teaspoon cinnamon oil (see note)
½ gallon freshly pressed apple cider

In a small saucepan, combine the molasses, water, lemon juice, cloves, and cinnamon oil. Bring to a boil over high heat, lower heat, and simmer, uncovered, for 4 to 5 minutes. Meanwhile, in a large deep kettle, heat the cider over low heat. Pour the molasses mixture into the cider and blend. Transfer to a heat-proof punch bowl and ladle out into 4-ounce punch cups.

NOTE: Cinnamon oil is a highly concentrated flavoring and is available at pharmacies or specialty food shops. Do not use ground cinnamon in this drink; it won't dissolve.

ROAST PRIME RIB OF BEEF

Serves 10–12

This is roast beef cooked to perfection, rare all the way through.

1 4–5 pound prime rib of beef,
  rolled and tied
1 tablespoon powdered mustard
1½ teaspoons salt
½ teaspoon paprika

¼ teaspoon ground allspice
¼ teaspoon black pepper
1 small onion
2 garlic cloves
  Parsley sprigs

Preheat oven to 200° F. With a long sharp knife, make several deep slits in the beef to form pockets of different depths. In a small bowl, combine the mustard, salt, paprika, allspice, and pepper. Cut the onion and garlic into slivers. Stuff the pockets with pieces of onion, garlic, bits of parsley, and some of the spice mixture. Rub any leftover spices over the outside of the roast. Roast meat, allowing 1 hour per pound. You will have perfect rare roast beef. Slice thin and serve with pan juices.

ESCALLOPED OYSTERS

Serves 4

Oysters are one luxury that the Amish permit themselves and are a special
holiday dish. This Escalloped Oysters recipe will have a better flavor and
texture if it is made the night before. Since it is baked in a pan of hot water,
be sure to allow sufficient cooking time.

1 pint oysters, drained
2 cups coarse soda cracker crumbs
  (no substitutes)
  Salt and pepper
  Powdered mustard

½ cup (1 stick) butter (no substitutes),
  in thin slices
1½ teaspoons Worcestershire sauce
¾ cup half-and-half
  Paprika

The night before serving, prepare the
oysters. In an oiled deep 1-quart glass casserole, alternate layers of oysters and crushed
crackers. The bottom and top layer should be
crackers. Top each layer of oysters with a little
salt, pepper, and a light sprinkling of mustard. Top the mustard with pieces of butter.
Combine the Worcestershire and half-and-
half. With a fork, make holes evenly around
the casserole, down into the crackers, and pour
the cream in. Pat the holes closed with a fork.
Sprinkle the top with paprika. Refrigerate
overnight.

Next day, bring casserole to room temperature; this will take 1 hour. Preheat oven
to 325° F. Bake, uncovered, in a shallow pan
of hot water for 1½ hours, or until the top is
a deep golden brown.

NOTE: For large family dinners, use 6
12-ounce cans oysters, drained; 6 cups cracker
crumbs; scant 1 cup (2 sticks) butter; 1 tablespoon Worcestershire sauce; 2 cups half-and-
half; paprika. Use a deep 3-quart glass casserole (10 inches diameter, 3½ inches deep).
Bring the casserole to room temperature and
bake uncovered for 2½ hours. (Yield: 16–20
servings, if serving lots of other side dishes.)

HONEY CARROTS WITH SWEET PICKLE

Serves 4

These carrots are a company dish—the green sweet pickles add
an attractive and unusual touch.

1 pound carrots
3 tablespoons butter
¼ cup honey
¼ cup orange juice
½ teaspoon grated orange rind

½ teaspoon salt
½ teaspoon ground ginger
¼ teaspoon black pepper
3 tablespoons finely chopped sweet pickle
  (not relish)

Peel the carrots and slice ¼-inch thick.
Melt the butter in a large skillet; add all the
ingredients but the sweet pickles. Cover and
cook over low heat for 20 minutes, stirring

occasionally. Uncover, raise heat to high, and
cook about 3 minutes to reduce the sauce to a
glaze. Stir in the pickles just before serving.

ONION PATTIES

Makes 15–20 patties

These resemble a delightfully crisp, thin fritter, but locally they are called patties.
This is an absolutely marvelous vegetable side dish; don't overlook it.

¾ cup unbleached all-purpose flour
1 tablespoon yellow cornmeal
1 tablespoon sugar
2 teaspoons baking powder
2 teaspoons rubbed sage
1 teaspoon salt

2 tablespoons finely minced fresh parsley
3 shakes Tabasco
¾ cup milk
2½ cups finely chopped onion
Vegetable oil for frying

In a large mixer bowl, combine the first 6 ingredients. Then add the parsley, Tabasco, and milk; blend. Add the onion and mix thoroughly.

Heat the oil, 1 inch deep, in an electric fry pan or skillet from 360 to 380° F. Drop the batter by teaspoonfuls into the hot fat, flattening them slightly as you do so. Fry until the patties are golden brown on the bottom, about 2 minutes, then turn and fry the other side for another 2 minutes. When the second side is browned, remove the patties to paper towels. Drain, and keep them warm in a very low oven while you fry the rest of the batter. These keep quite well, and can be made an hour in advance of serving.

ONION PIE

Serves 8

This is a Mennonite dish, sometimes called *tzvivelle* pie. Rich but delicate, and subtly seasoned, it is a perfect lunch dish and an ideal accompaniment to char-broiled steak.

3 tablespoons butter
2 cups sliced onions
    (approximately 1 pound)
½ teaspoon minced garlic
1 unbaked 10-inch pie shell
    (page 170)
6 eggs, beaten

1 cup half-and-half
½ teaspoon salt
½ teaspoon Tabasco
¼ teaspoon white pepper
¼ teaspoon grated nutmeg, rounded
¼ teaspoon powdered mustard
    Paprika

In a large skillet, place the butter, onions, and garlic. Sauté over medium-low heat until the onions are soft, golden, and just beginning to brown; don't rush this—it takes about 20 minutes. (This can be done in advance and refrigerated until needed.)

Preheat the oven to 350° F. Spread the onion mixture in the bottom of the pie shell.

Combine the beaten eggs and the half-and-half. Add seasonings except paprika and blend. Pour the egg mixture over the onions and sprinkle with paprika. Place the pie on the lowest rack of the oven and bake for 40 to 50 minutes. The top will be puffed and brown and still a bit shaky; that's all right.

GERMAN CABBAGE ROLLS

Makes 16 rolls, or 8 servings

Northern Indiana's German heritage gave us some great classic dishes.
These well-seasoned cabbage rolls are cooked in a robust tomato sauce topped
with crushed gingersnaps. Serve with Potato Pancakes.

SAUCE

1 28-ounce can tomatoes
1 8-ounce can tomato sauce
1 cup water
1 small onion, chopped
¼ cup chopped fresh parsley
3 tablespoons lemon juice
2–3 tablespoons brown sugar
1 bay leaf
½ teaspoon celery salt
½ teaspoon ground allspice
¼ teaspoon black pepper

1 large head green cabbage
    (approximately 4 pounds)
2 pounds lean ground beef,
    or 1 pound beef and 1 pound pork
1 cup cooked white rice
1 large onion, finely chopped
½ cup finely minced fresh parsley
2 teaspoons rubbed sage
1½ teaspoons salt
½ teaspoon black pepper
8 gingersnaps, crushed

Prepare sauce. In a medium saucepan, combine ingredients, bring to a boil over high heat, turn heat to low, and simmer, uncovered, for 30 minutes.

Meanwhile, drop the uncored cabbage into a very deep kettle two-thirds full of boiling water. The cabbage floats, so turn it about in the water now and then. Cover and cook over medium heat for 2 to 3 minutes. Remove the cabbage to the sink (it holds lots of water) and separate the leaves from the head at the core end. You will need 16 large leaves, and will have to re-immerse the head to get this many softened leaves. Cut off the tough white section at the base of the leaf and set aside.

Preheat oven to 350° F. In a deep bowl, combine the meat and the next 6 ingredients. Place 1 large spoonful of the meat mixture on each cabbage leaf; fold the sides of the leaf to the center and fold over the top and bottom, envelope-fashion. Lay the rolls in a single layer in an oiled 10 x 15-inch baking pan, with the seam side down.

Pour the tomato sauce over the rolls, then sprinkle the crushed gingersnaps over all. Cover and bake for 30 minutes; uncover and bake 30 minutes longer. The rolls will be nicely browned and the sauce a bit thickened. Serve with some of the sauce ladled over the rolls.

POTATO PANCAKES

Makes 18–20 pancakes

Potato pancakes can be a time-consuming dish to prepare if the potatoes are grated by hand. However with the food processor or blender, they can be made in a jiffy.

¼ cup milk
2 eggs
1 medium onion, quartered
3 tablespoons all-purpose flour
2 tablespoons chopped fresh parsley
½ teaspoon salt
½ teaspoon black pepper

½ teaspoon baking powder
Dash of Worcestershire sauce
Dash of grated nutmeg
2 large potatoes (approximately 1 pound), peeled
Vegetable oil for frying

If using a food processor, place all the ingredients except the potatoes in the bowl. Process, using the steel blade, until well blended. Remove blade and put on grating blade. Grate potatoes on top of egg mixture. Transfer all to a mixing bowl, and replace with steel blade. Return mixture to processor bowl and process briefly to further chop the potatoes.

If using a blender, chop the potatoes coarsely. Place all ingredients in blender, adding potatoes after the onion. Process until potatoes are chopped finely—do not overblend, for you don't want the potatoes pureed.

Heat an electric skillet to 360° F. (or use a regular skillet over medium heat). Heat 1 tablespoon of oil for each batch of pancakes. Drop the batter by tablespoons into the hot oil, and flatten out to a pattie approximately 3 inches in diameter. Fry about 2 minutes, until nicely browned, then flip over and fry another 2 minutes on the other side. Keep pancakes warm in the oven while frying the rest.

AMISH SWEET-AND-SOUR RED CABBAGE

Serves 4–6

If sauerkraut was not served at the New Year's table, this might be the very delicious substitute. The addition of bacon to the traditional sweet-and-sour red cabbage gives it smoky undertones. This can be made in advance and reheated.

¼ pound bacon, diced
½ cup chopped onion
2 medium tart apples, peeled and coarsely chopped
5 cups shredded red cabbage (2 pounds)

¼ cup plus 2 tablespoons cider vinegar
¼ cup plus 2 tablespoons brown sugar
½ teaspoon ground allspice
½ teaspoon salt
¼ teaspoon black pepper

In a heavy saucepan, cook the bacon, onion, and apples over medium-low heat until onions are limp, about 3 minutes. Add the cabbage. Cook about 10 minutes, uncovered, over medium heat until the cabbage wilts, stirring now and then. Add the remaining ingredients. Reduce heat to low, cover, and cook for 20 minutes. The cabbage should be moist, but not juicy. If liquid accumulates, remove lid at the end of the cooking period to cook off some liquid.

PUMPKIN–BLACK WALNUT BISCUITS

◆

Makes 12 biscuits

A batch of these intriguingly flavored biscuits is a nice addition to any meal.
This particular biscuit has a tendency to overbrown on the bottom, so use a
light-colored metal baking sheet instead of a nonstick sheet. Serve the biscuits
hot with butter, and if you must have jelly with them, choose a delicate apple
jelly so the subtle pumpkin flavor is not masked.

2 cups unbleached all-purpose flour
2 tablespoons sugar
1 tablespoon baking powder
1 teaspoon baking soda
¼ teaspoon salt
¼ teaspoon ground cinnamon
¼ teaspoon grated nutmeg

¼ teaspoon ground allspice
½ cup (1 stick) butter, cold
⅓ cup finely chopped black walnuts
⅔ cup canned or mashed cooked pumpkin
½ cup buttermilk, or a bit more if needed
   Sugar

Preheat oven to 450° F. Sift together the flour, sugar, baking powder and soda, salt, and spices into a large bowl. Cut in the butter (or use food processor) until the mixture resembles coarse crumbs. Add the nuts. In a small bowl, whisk together the pumpkin and buttermilk. Add it to the flour mixture and stir to combine. The dough will be quite stiff and not all the flour will be incorporated.

Turn the dough out onto a lightly floured cloth and knead gently a few times to work in the rest of the flour. Roll out the dough to a ½-inch thickness and cut with a 2-inch-round cutter. Transfer the biscuits to a lightly oiled shiny baking sheet, and sprinkle tops with sugar. Bake for 10 minutes—do not let them get too brown. Serve immediately with butter.

AMISH CHRISTMAS CAKE

Makes 24 medium slices

When I was first given this recipe, I nearly threw it away, thinking, "This looks pretty ho-hum." Am I glad I didn't, for it is a fooler. It is much easier to make than a fruitcake; it doesn't have that heavy fruit density, but has the flavor and nonperishable qualities. And it is a snap to prepare, another boon during the busy holidays. Very moist, with a nice texture, it is quite perfect just as it is, but it could be "dressed up" by serving a hot brandy sauce poured over individual slices.

1 cup chopped pecans
1 cup (2 sticks) butter
2 cups sugar
2 cups seedless raisins
2 cups water
1 teaspoon ground cinnamon

1 teaspoon grated nutmeg
1 teaspoon ground cloves
1 tablespoon grated lemon rind
1 tablespoon grated orange rind
3½ cups sifted all-purpose flour
1 teaspoon baking soda

Preheat oven to 350° F. In a large, deep kettle, combine the first 8 ingredients. Simmer, uncovered, over moderate heat, for 4 minutes, then let cool to room temperature. Add the lemon and orange rinds, and transfer to a large mixer bowl.

Sift together the flour and baking soda and, using slow speed, gradually beat it into the raisin mixture. Pour the batter into an oiled and floured 10-inch tube pan. Bake for 1 hour, or until the top of the cake is medium brown and springs back up when touched with your finger. Let cool in the pan for 10 to 15 minutes, then tip out onto a wire rack to finish cooling. This cake freezes well and will keep, tightly wrapped in foil, for 2 weeks in the refrigerator.

SAND TARTS

Makes 180 cookies

Sand Tarts are crisp little sugar cookies, traditionally served only at Christmas. But they are also ideal as a tea cookie or as an accompaniment to ice cream or sherbet all year long. The dough should be made one day and rolled out the next.

½ pound (2 sticks) butter (no substitutes), softened
2 cups sugar
1 teaspoon salt
2 teaspoons vanilla extract
3 eggs, separated

3 cups all-purpose flour
TOPPING
¼ cup sugar
¾ teaspoon ground cinnamon
1 egg, beaten
4 cups whole pecans, approximately

In a large mixer bowl, beat the butter to further soften. Add the sugar and beat until creamy. Add the salt and vanilla. Beat the egg yolks thoroughly and add to the butter-sugar mixture. Beat the egg whites until dry, stiff peaks form. Using a rubber spatula, fold whites into the butter-sugar mixture rather thoroughly, but stop while some white patches are still visible. Add 1½ cups of the flour and fold in. Then add the remaining 1½ cups flour, blending lightly but thoroughly. Chill overnight.

The next day, preheat oven to 350° F. Divide the dough into quarters. Roll out one-quarter at a time, keeping the rest of the dough refrigerated. Roll dough until very thin, less than ⅛ inch, and use a 2-inch scalloped cookie cutter to form cookies. Place on an ungreased cookie sheet.

In a small bowl, combine the sugar and cinnamon for the topping. Brush some beaten egg on each cookie (you don't have to paint the whole cookie) and sprinkle on some of the sugar mixture. Top with a whole pecan. Bake for 9 to 10 minutes, watching carefully so cookies don't get too brown; 45 seconds can make a difference. Cool on wire racks. Packed in tins, they keep indefinitely.

STEAMED CHRISTMAS PUDDING WITH TWO SAUCES

Serves 12

This traditional suet pudding, or steamed pudding, reflects England's influence
on midwestern America's cuisine. Insist on kidney suet for this recipe—
it is a better-quality fat, and since it melts during the steaming, it creates a deep rich
flavor and smoothness of texture that you can't duplicate any other way. This
pudding is served always with a thin sauce: choose either lemon or chocolate—
or both. I have broken this recipe down into steps so you can prepare
it over several days. It isn't nearly as complicated as it looks. I have simply
held your hand through this, since it is seldom prepared anymore,
and I do want you to try it.

STEP 1

COMBINE THE BASE INGREDIENTS.

1 cup ground kidney suet
(have butcher do this for you)

1 cup ground raisins
1 cup finely chopped pecans

Regrind the suet a second time at home. Use a conventional grinder for this, as well as for the raisins; the food processor doesn't produce the right texture. Place ingredients in a bowl and store in refrigerator until you are ready to proceed with recipe. (These 3 ingredients can be prepared several days in advance.)

STEP 2

PREPARE AND STEAM THE PUDDING.

2⅓ cups unbleached all-purpose flour
½ cup brown sugar
1 teaspoon baking powder
½ teaspoon baking soda
½ teaspoon salt
1 teaspoon grated nutmeg

½ teaspoon ground cinnamon
½ teaspoon ground ginger
¼ teaspoon ground cloves
1 cup milk
½ cup dark corn syrup
1 teaspoon vanilla extract

In a large bowl, combine the dry ingredients. Add the suet, raisins, and nuts from step 1. Mix well, using your hands if necessary, so everything is evenly combined. Combine the milk, corn syrup, and vanilla in a small bowl. Pour this over the dry ingredients and blend again. Grease a 6-cup pudding mold or bowl (mine is 5 inches tall, 6 inches wide) and pour in the mixture. Top with foil—do not use a metal lid.

There are two ways to steam this pudding. I prefer the pressure-cooker method, since it is much quicker. Place the mold on a rack in a pressure cooker. Add 5 cups water. Bring to a boil with the lid on the cooker, but with the vent cock off. Steam for 20 minutes without the vent cock. The steam coming out of the lid opening should be gentle, not violent. After 20 minutes, put the vent cock on. Continue cooking for 1 hour longer at 10 pounds pressure. Remove from heat, and allow pressure to return to the down position. Remove pudding immediately from the steamer. Wrap the hot pudding in foil and cover with a heavy terry-cloth towel. Allow to cool completely, then remove the towel. The pudding can be stored up to 1 week in the refrigerator or frozen indefinitely.

The alternative steaming method is to place the mold or bowl in a deep saucepan with 1 inch of boiling water, cover, and steam for 5 to 6 hours. Keep replenishing the water, and watch carefully to make sure the pan doesn't boil dry. When done, wrap the pudding as above and store until ready to serve. (The pudding can be made up to 1 week in advance and refrigerated.)

STEP 3

PREPARE THE SAUCE.

LEMON SAUCE

- *1 cup granulated sugar*
- *1 cup brown sugar*
- *2 tablespoons all-purpose flour*
- *½ teaspoon grated nutmeg*
- *Speck of salt*
- *2 cups boiling water*
- *¼ cup lemon juice*
- *Grated rind of 1 lemon*
- *¼ cup (½ stick) butter*
- *Sweetened whipped cream*

In a medium saucepan, combine the first 5 ingredients. Add the boiling water, blend with a whisk, and then add the rest of the ingredients. Simmer, uncovered, for 10 minutes. Serve hot over the pudding with sweetened whipped cream.

CHOCOLATE SAUCE

- *2 cups granulated sugar*
- *¼ cup cornstarch*
- *5 tablespoons cocoa powder*
- *Speck of salt*
- *1 quart boiling water*
- *½ cup (1 stick) butter*
- *4 teaspoons vanilla extract*

In a medium saucepan, combine the first 4 ingredients. Add the boiling water, blend with a whisk, and then add the rest of the ingredients. Bring to a boil, then remove from heat. Serve hot.

◆

When ready to serve, bring the pudding to room temperature. Leaving on the foil, place the pudding in the steamer basket of a vegetable cooker set over boiling water. Steam for 2 hours. Or you can put the pudding back in its cooking container, place the container in 1 inch of boiling water, cover, and simmer for 2 hours.

When pudding has steamed, remove from heat and let cool slightly. Serve warm, cut in small wedges, passing either or both sauces separately.

CHOCOLATE LAYER CAKE WITH DATE FILLING

Serves 12

My mother made this cake, and it also appears in many rural community cookbooks. The date filling makes it special, and the frosting is unusually good. Because the cake has a custard filling, it needs to be kept refrigerated.

4 ounces unsweetened chocolate
2½ cups sifted cake flour
2 teaspoons baking powder
¾ teaspoon salt
½ cup (1 stick) butter, softened
2 cups granulated sugar
2 eggs
2 teaspoons vanilla extract
2 cups buttermilk, at room temperature

DATE FILLING
1 cup milk
½ cup chopped dates
1 egg
¼ cup sugar

1 tablespoon all-purpose flour
Speck of salt
½ cup plus 2 tablespoons chopped black walnuts or pecans
1 teaspoon vanilla extract

FUDGE FROSTING
1 pound confectioners' sugar
⅓ cup plus 2 tablespoons cocoa powder
¼ cup (½ stick) butter, softened
1 egg white
1 teaspoon vanilla extract
¼ teaspoon salt
5 tablespoons evaporated milk

Preheat oven to 350° F. Melt the chocolate in the top of a double boiler over barely simmering water (or in the microwave). Sift the flour, baking powder, and salt together. In a large mixer bowl, cream the butter and sugar until the mixture is fluffy. Add the eggs, 1 at a time, beating well after each addition. Blend in the melted chocolate and vanilla. Add the dry ingredients to the chocolate mixture, alternating with the buttermilk and beginning and ending with the flour. Do not overbeat.

Pour the batter into three 8-inch buttered cake layer pans. Bake for 25 to 30 minutes, or until the cake has shrunk away a bit from the sides of the pans and the tops spring back when touched with your finger. Allow to stand in pans for 10 minutes, then turn out onto a rack to cool. While the cakes are cooling, prepare the filling and frosting.

To make the filling, heat the milk and dates in the top of a double boiler over hot water until the milk is scalded. Beat the egg, then add the sugar, flour, and salt; beat again. Add ½ cup of the hot milk mixture to the egg mixture, then stir back into the pan and cook for 3 minutes, until thick, stirring with a rubber spatula. Let cool. Add the nuts and vanilla. Refrigerate for 1½ hours before filling the cake.

To make the frosting, combine all the ingredients in a large mixer bowl. Beat on high speed for 1 minute, or until the frosting is light and creamy.

To assemble, place 1 cake layer on a large plate and cover to within ¼ inch of the edge with half the chilled filling. Top with another cake layer and the remaining filling mixture. Finish with the last cake layer. Frost the sides and top of the cake with the fudge frosting, forming swirls on the top with a knife. Refrigerate, but bring to room temperature before serving.

CRANBERRY CAKE WITH BUTTER SAUCE

◆

Serves 8

Truly an attic recipe, Cranberry Cake is a most delicate dessert, studded with fruit.
It is served with a sheer butter sauce poured over the top.
Serve it at least once during the holidays.

2 cups all-purpose flour
1 cup granulated sugar
2½ teaspoons baking powder
½ teaspoon salt
1 egg
3 tablespoons butter, melted
⅔ cup milk
1 teaspoon vanilla extract

2 cups whole cranberries
BUTTER SAUCE
1 cup (2 sticks) butter
2 cups brown sugar
1½ cups half-and-half
1½ teaspoons ground cinnamon
Speck of salt

Preheat oven to 350° F. In a large mixer bowl, combine the dry ingredients for the cake. In a small mixer bowl, beat the egg and add the melted butter, milk, and vanilla. Pour this mixture over the dry ingredients and beat on medium speed for 2 minutes. Stir in the cranberries by hand. Pour into an oiled 9-inch-round cake pan and bake for 40 minutes, until the top of the cake springs back when lightly touched with your finger.

Meanwhile, prepare the butter sauce. In the top of a double boiler, melt the butter over low heat. Add the brown sugar, half-and-half, cinnamon, and salt. Cook over hot water for about 5 minutes, whisking smooth. To serve, cut the cake in wedges and serve warm with the sauce ladled over the cake.
NOTE: The sauce will curdle on reheating, so do not make it ahead of time.

AUTHOR'S NOTE

◆

Though all of the Amish women very generously shared their kitchens and recipes with me, just a portion of them were willing to have their names listed among all the others—Mennonites and "English"—who provided assistance, recipes, or interviews for this book. To all of those individuals whose experiences and recipes appear on these pages and whose privacy I have agreed to protect, I wish to acknowledge their help. This book would not have been possible without them.

Hazel Adams, Clarence Baker, Suetta Bechtel of The Oil Lamp Restaurant, New Paris, Amos Bontrager, Susie Bontrager, Edna Borkholder, Esther Collyer, Yvonne Diamond, Barbara Ehrhardt, Magdalene Eicher, First Mennonite Church of Berne, Fisher's Antiques of Shipshewana, Fort Wayne Public Library, Ada Marie Frank, Esther Grabill, Gayle Grabill, Gordon Grabill, Sally Gray, Greenfield Herb Garden of Shipshewana, Suzanne Hall, Lois Hamilton, Rebecca Harrer Antiques of Shipshewana, The Herald Press, Scottsdale, PA, Holley Hobbs, Ardith Holley, Kay Johnson, Gwen Kaag, Jo Keyes, Dr. T. R. King, Barbara Lambright, Lena Lehman of Goshen College, Mary Ann Lengacher, Mabel's Patchwork Quilts of Millersburg, Nancy Weatherwax Manahan, Nellie Manahan, Laura McCaffrey, Ann McDonald, Esther Miller, Fern and Ralph Miller, R and F Noodles of Shipshewana, Lou Jane Miller, Mary Miller, Ruth and Paul Miller of Green Meadows, Shipshewana, Esther Mishler of The Buggy Wheel Restaurant, Shipshewana, Nancy's Fancies of Warsaw, David Pottinger, June Reed, Amanda Schmucker, Katie Schmucker, Rita Schobert, Lydia Schwartz of Shipshewana Auction, Gladys Shultz, Mary Ann Sidell, Eleanor Wade, Faye Walters, Ethel White, Beulah Wilson, Emma Witmer, Woodlawn Amish Mennonite Church, The Daniel M. Yoder Family, Fern Yoder, Dr. S. L. Yoder of Goshen College, Yoder's Department Store of Shipshewana, Yoder's Little Amish Country Store of LaGrange, Yoder's Shipshewana Hardware.

SELECTED BIBLIOGRAPHY

AMISH SOCIETY, *by John A. Hostetler.* Johns Hopkins University Press, Baltimore, Maryland. Third Edition, 1980.

THE AMISH: AN ILLUSTRATED ESSAY. Applied Arts Publishers, Lebanon, Pennsylvania. 1983.

QUILTS FROM THE INDIANA AMISH: A REGIONAL COLLECTION, *by David Pottinger.* E. P. Dutton, New York. 1983.

SAUERKRAUT YANKEES, *by William Woys Weaver.* University of Pennsylvania Press, Philadelphia, Pennsylvania. 1983.

AMISH COOKING. Harold Press, Scottsdale, Pennsylvania.

AMISH COOKING. Pathway Publishing, Aylmer, Ontario.

AMISH-COUNTRY COOKBOOK: FAVORITE RECIPES GATHERED BY DAS ESSENHAUS. Bethel Publishing, Elkhart, Indiana.

ART OF PENNSYLVANIA DUTCH COOKING, *by Edna Eby Heller.* Doubleday, New York.

CORNUCOPIA—A COOKBOOK. Holdeman Mennonite Church, Wakarusa, Indiana.

DAILY BREAD. North Main Street Mennonite Church, Napanee, and Bourbon Mennonite Church Chapel, Bourbon, Indiana.

DUNKARD-DUTCH COOKBOOK. Applied Arts Publishers, Lebanon, Pennsylvania.

FAVORITE RECIPES. Mennonite Board of Missions Voluntary Service, Elkhart, Indiana.

HOMEMAKER'S COOKBOOK. Goshen College Mennonite Church, Goshen, Indiana.

LEAH'S COUNTRY KITCHEN, *by Leah I. Schwartz.* Berne, Indiana.

MELTING POT OF MENNONITE COOKERY, *compiled by Edna Kaufman.* Bethel College Women's Association, North Newton, Kansas.

MENNONITE COMMUNITY COOKBOOK, *by Emma Showalter.* The Mennonite Community Association, Scottsdale, Pennsylvania. 1957 edition.

NEW PARIS INDIANA SESQUICENTENNIAL COOKBOOK. General Publishing & Binding, Iowa Falls, Iowa.

OUR FAVORITE RECIPES. Women's Fellowship of the Clinton Frame Mennonite Church, Goshen, Indiana.

OUR SWISS PANTRY. Women's Missionary Society of the First Mennonite Church, Berne, Indiana.

PEEK INTO OUR PANTRY. Women's Study Club of the Eighth Street Mennonite Church, Goshen, Indiana.

WISLER COUNTRY COOKING. Fairview Mennonite Church, Elkhart County, Indiana. General Publishing & Binding, Iowa Falls, Iowa.

INDEX